# DOWN'S SYNDROME: AN INTRODUCTION FOR PARENTS

*By the same author:*

(with Patricia Sloper)
Helping Your Handicapped Baby

*HUMAN HORIZONS SERIES*

# DOWN'S SYNDROME: AN INTRODUCTION FOR PARENTS

Cliff Cunningham

A CONDOR BOOK
SOUVENIR PRESS (E&A) LTD

First published 1982 by
Souvenir Press (Educational & Academic) Ltd,
43 Great Russell Street, London WC1B 3PA
and simultaneously in Canada

Reprinted 1983
Reprinted 1984
Reprinted 1986
Revised Edition 1988
Reprinted 1990
Reprinted 1992
Reprinted 1997



ISBN 0 285 65046 7

Printed in Great Britain by
The Guernsey Press Co., Ltd, Guernsey, Channel Islands.

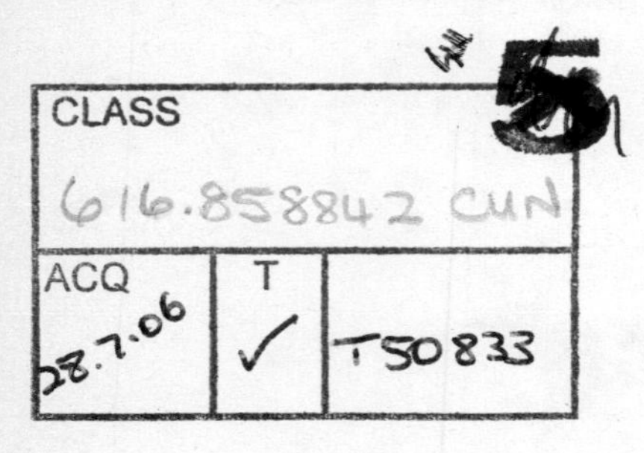

TO YOU—BECAUSE YOU ARE INVOLVED

# CONTENTS


Acknowledgements to the First Edition 11
Preface to the Second Edition 12
Dear Parent 13

INTRODUCTION: 'I USED TO THINK OF HER AS A STRANGER' 15

1: 'WILL WE COPE?' WHAT ARE THEY LIKE?' 19
Will we cope? 19
'What are they like?' 20

2: FEELINGS AND REACTIONS 26
Coming to terms with the handicap 26
First reactions and feelings 29
Shock and disbelief 29
Instinctive reactions 30
Feelings of grief 33
Feelings of inadequacy 34
Feelings of uncertainty 35
Feelings of anger and hostility 38
Feelings of embarrassment 39
Changes over time 39
Summary of the main points 41

3: WHAT EFFECTS WILL IT HAVE ON THE FAMILY? 43
'How will I tell the other children?' 46
'Telling the relatives?' 49
Reactions of grandparents 51
Does the presence of a child with Down's syndrome disrupt the marriage? 54
Possible conflicts between partners 57
Do families with a child with Down's syndrome suffer more ill-health than other families? 60

Does the presence of the child restrict social activities? 61
Do mothers find they can go out to work? 66
Summary of points in this chapter 67

4: WHAT CAUSES DOWN'S SYNDROME? 70
1. What produces the condition in the baby? 70
Where are the chromosomes found? What are they? 71
How do chromosomes work? 72
A normal set of chromosomes (the Karyotype) 76
How does the extra chromosome get into the cell? 78
Down's syndrome: Trisomy 21 78
Are there different types of Down's syndrome? 82
Standard Trisomy 21 82
Mosaic Trisomy 21 82
Translocation Trisomy 21 84
2. What are the chances of having another baby with Down's syndrome? 86
Is Down's syndrome inherited? 86
Is there a tendency for some families to have Down's syndrome babies? 88
What is the risk of having another baby with Down's syndrome? 88
3. Why did it happen to us? What causes it? 89
Is the likelihood of having a baby with Down's syndrome different for different races, social and economic levels, countries and geographic areas? 90
Is it true that older mothers are more likely to have a baby with Down's syndrome? 91
Why should older mothers have more Down's syndrome babies? 91
Is Down's syndrome related to the father's age? 92
Why do so many young mothers have Down's syndrome babies? Are more younger mothers having Down's syndrome babies? 93
4. How common is Down's syndrome? 93
How common are conceptions of Trisomy 21? 94
How common are births of babies with Down's syndrome? 94
How many adults and children are there with Down's syndrome? What is the *prevalence* of the condition? 95

Facts in this chapter 97
Genetic counselling 98

5: CHARACTERISTICS OF DOWN'S SYNDROME 100
Physical and medical characteristics 102
Do the baby's looks tell you how handicapped he or she will be? 106
Does the 'floppiness' in the new baby tell you how handicapped he or she will be? 106
Physical and medical characteristics in childhood and adulthood 107
The skull and face 108
Upper airway obstruction 109
Hearing 110
Growth 111
Posture 114
The skeleton 115
Atlanto-axial dislocation 116
The skin 117
Facial plastic surgery 119
The digestive system 120
The heart 122
Circulation 124
Leukaemia 125
Vision 125
Sensitivity and arousal 126
Sensory co-ordination 126
Speed of responding 128
Ageing, epilepsy and deterioration 130
'Biochemical' differences 131
Vitamin and mineral therapy 132
5-hydroxytryptophan therapy 133
Cell therapy 134
Thyroid treatment 134
Conclusions on medical treatments 135
The lungs and respiratory system 136
The reproductive system 138

6: PERSONALITY AND TEMPERAMENT 142
Influences on personality and temperament 143
Information from older studies 144

Recent studies 145
The baby 146
The young child 147
Older children and adults 158
Management 160
Facts in this chapter 163

7: MENTAL, MOTOR AND SOCIAL DEVELOPMENT 165
1. Changes in thinking and treatment 165
2. Terminology and testing 170
Mental ability tests 173
Behavioural assessments 180
Parental and professional collaboration 182
Mental age: expectations and protectiveness 183
3. Development in Down's syndrome 184
'What are the benefits of early intervention and stimulation?' 187
'What about the drop-off in the IQ scores? Is there a deterioration in the children's mental abilities?' 190
Developmental stages 199
'If they do develop more slowly, does their mental growth continue for longer?' 201
'Is there a difference between their social and mental abilities?' 202
Some conclusions 203
4. Early developmental attainments 204
Choosing a pre-school facility 209
Later developmental attainments 216
Comments 217
'What if there are no early intervention programmes available to us?' 219
'How much do parents need to do?' 221
To conclude 222

Concluding Remarks 224

APPENDIX: Prenatal tests for some handicapping conditions 227
Children learn what they live 229
Resources 230
Index 238

# ACKNOWLEDGEMENTS TO THE FIRST EDITION

This book has two sources of influence. One is my contact with parents and colleagues over many years; the other is the work of many people who have spent part of their lives studying and writing about Down's syndrome.

At a more personal level I must thank Dana Brynelsen for her supportive comments on drafts; Margaret Flynn for her help on the section dealing with brothers and sisters; Robert Craven for his help with the illustrations; David Griffiths for his help with the photographs; June Hayes-Light and David Hall and the students of Pengwern Hall for letting me use their photographs, and of course the parents who lent me photographs and who read and commented upon the draft. Special thanks are extended to Dian Donnai and the Department of Medical Genetics at St. Mary's Hospital, Manchester, for help with the chapter on chromosomes.

My most grateful thanks are extended to Miss Ellen Cullen for the typing and lay-out of the book and her endless patience with the redrafts.

Finally, I must thank my wife Marta, who as ever has combined honest criticism with patience and support. My children will be glad to know 'the chapters' are finished and once again they can dominate my time and play elephants outside the study.

I have been supported over the last eight years by research grants from the Social Science Research Council and the Department of Health and Social Security.

Cliff Cunningham
September 1981

# PREFACE TO THE SECOND EDITION

It is an indication of the amount of activity related to Down's syndrome that I have needed to update this book only five years after the first edition. I am indebted to all the parents and professionals who have written to me over those five years and given me ideas for changes and additions and the encouragement to revise the book. I am again grateful to Dr Dian Donnai and also to Dr Richard Newton of the Royal Manchester Children's Hospital for help on the medical aspects. I am indebted to Dr Jennifer Dennis of the Park Hospital for Children, Oxford, and Dr David Southall of the Cardiothoracic Institute, London, for allowing me to describe their work on preliminary upper airway obstruction and to Dr Joyce Ludlow for generously allowing me to incorporate her work in Chapter 7. I of course take all responsibility for errors.

I must thank my colleagues who, at various times, have been members of the Manchester Down's Syndrome Cohort Research team: Tricia Sloper, Meg Aumonier, Jiri Berger, Sheila Glenn, Liz Byrne, Anne Rangecroft, Christina Knussen, and Chris Lennings, and also the associated students who have made a large contribution: Margret Arnlsdottir, Gyda Haroldsdottir, Vicki Gibbs and Stephanie Lorenz. The Manchester Down's Syndrome Cohort programme is funded by the DHSS.

Cliff Cunningham
July 1987

NOTE TO THE 1997 REPRINT

Thank you again to all the parents who sent in photographs for the new picture selection, and to the Down's Syndrome Association, Belinda Whiting and Stephen Leighton for kindly giving me permission to reproduce photographs from their collections.

Dear Parent

I ask you to read this page before you read the book. I make this request because of a problem which I cannot resolve.

If a baby is born and appears quite normal, we parents are not given a detailed catalogue of information about the risks of what might go wrong in the future. We are not told about the chances that a heart condition, hearing problem, visual defect, personality disorder and so on might appear. We are not given lists of statistics about the risk of delinquency, drug abuse or success at school or work. We go home and dream our dreams for a happy future. If we were given such a list, we would need to learn to live with the information and control our imaginings of what might happen.

But if you have a baby born with a condition like Down's syndrome, which is recognisable from birth or shortly after, then many facts and figures are available. Much of this information is about possible medical and developmental problems and about how they can be helped. But the majority of children with Down's syndrome do not have many of these problems. Therefore you will not need all of the information. Unfortunately, my problem is that I do not know which information you will need.

If you are a parent of a baby with Down's syndrome, you will have to decide just how much information you want and how much you can cope with at a time. You will also need to keep it in perspective. One of our parents of a six-year-old boy summed this up better than I can:

> You just have to get as many answers to the questions that go around in your head as you can . . . you need to do this as soon as you can so that you can get over a lot of the

> worrying and puzzling . . . you find when you get some of the information you can see just how silly the worrying was . . . but mind you, you can have too much . . . if you keep thinking about the future and all the things that can happen you'd go mad . . . best thing to do, is get all that over with as quick as you can, then love him and do what you have to to help . . . just take things from day to day as they come up . . . you know, once I got over all the shock and worrying and just helped him and that, things changed. I got to know him and I can truthfully say I've had a lot of joy these last years.

Whether we are parents, professionals or members of the general public, the danger we all face is that our knowledge of a handicap will cloud our vision of the baby, child or person as he or she really is. We need to be constantly alert to this danger and must make efforts to stop focusing solely on the handicap. I often feel parents learn to do this better than we professionals. But for most parents who have just learnt that their baby has Down's syndrome it is not an easy process. Fortunately, according to the large majority of parents whom I have known in my work, as they begin to get over their grief and shock, they also begin to see the baby rather than the condition. They begin to learn to live with, and in most cases, to enjoy their new member of the family.

I sincerely hope you will find this book—with all its limitations—of some help in this process.

Cliff Cunningham

PS If like me, you are inclined to skip through the introductions to books, please don't miss p. 17 on the use of the book.

*Introduction*

# 'I USED TO THINK OF HER AS A STRANGER'

> As I learnt more about Down's syndrome I felt I understood her better and somehow it helped me get closer to her . . . you know for quite a time I used to think of her as a stranger . . . like you think of someone from a different country . . . not one of us.

The words of this mother of a three-year-old girl with Down's syndrome succinctly highlight one of the more subtle reasons why parents need information about this condition. As we increase our knowledge and understanding about the condition we seem to get closer to the baby or child. This point was also forced upon me by a father of a ten-day-old boy with Down's syndrome. I was on my first visit to the home and had been answering questions such as 'How was it caused?', 'What effect did it have on the child's physical and mental development?', 'What chances were there of any more babies being affected?', 'Were the other children in the family likely to be affected?', 'Would relatives have more risk of having a Down's child?', 'What will he be like when he's grown up?', 'What will he do?', 'What can we do to help?', 'What help can we expect?', 'Where do we get help from?' and so on, when the father said: 'I wish you had come yesterday. My brother and his family were here and kept asking what was wrong with the baby and I couldn't tell him. I felt a right fool. He's my son and I didn't even know anything about him.'

These two parents are part of a group of nearly 200 families who have young children with Down's syndrome and who are involved in our research about how to help the development of the children. The research began nearly ten years ago. My research colleagues and I regularly visit the homes of families—at least every six weeks—for the first two years of the child's life. From the age of two we visit every six months. During the regular home visits we have become convinced of the parents' need for comprehensive information about Down's syndrome. And, as the above quotes indicate, this need for information is far more complex than the simple need to know what to do or where to go.

The parents, and many friends and relatives of the families we work with, have told us that they want accurate, up-to-date, truthful and unbiased information about Down's syndrome. They complain about the difficulty in getting information and about the widespread myths surrounding the condition. How often have I heard the mother of an energetic, highly exploratory toddler with Down's syndrome say, 'I thought they were all gentle and passive', or a 21-year-old mother say, 'But aren't they only born to older women?' Other parents in the project have urged that we write down the information we give them in response to these questions. They want it for future reference, and also in order to explain to relatives, friends and professionals more about Down's syndrome.

Feelings about having a child with Down's syndrome are just as important as facts. And parents have made it quite clear to me that information about how other parents felt and coped with their feelings when the baby was born was of great help to them.

I am fortunate. I do not truly know what it is like to have a child with Down's syndrome. The experience and knowledge I have gained over the last ten years, however, make me feel that, whilst I do not wish any child to be born with Down's syndrome, if it had happened to me, it would not have been the tragedy that I used to imagine.

Even so, I am not in a position truly to understand the feelings of parents who have a baby with the condition. All I can do is draw together the experiences of parents, and the observations of other professionals, and try to show the feelings that parents seem to have in common.

When I finally decided to write this book I rather simple-mindedly thought that all I had to do was put down the information that I gave to parents during my visits to their homes. It proved not to be that easy.

When I am face-to-face with the parents, they can indicate to me what questions are most urgent and how much detail they want. I can also shape my answers to meet what I see as their particular needs and, of course, relate them to the baby who is present.

But all babies and children with Down's syndrome are so different from each other that it is almost impossible to make any general statements without noting a list of exceptions. Also, all families are different and have different needs and reactions.

I was also very conscious that parents often become frustrated when trying to extract answers to their immediate questions from long and complex general explanations. Further, I know how distressing they often find medical books, which, by necessity, concentrate on the pathological and abnormal aspects of the condition; and since the photographs and illustrations in such books must clearly show the major characteristics of a condition, the examples chosen tend to be extreme.

I have tried to solve these problems as follows:

1 I have provided a detailed list of contents and an index which you can use to look up specific information to questions.
2 When applicable, I have listed the main points in each chapter at the end of the chapter. You can use this as a checklist, to decide whether or not you need to go into more detail.
3 I have tried to make each chapter stand on its own, so that you do not need to read the book in a specific order. This does lead to some repetition but, as a teacher, I have learnt that repetition is not always detrimental.
4 In selecting photographs and quotes from parents I have tried to avoid extremes and include those which seemed to me to be representative.

This book would not have been written if the parents had not asked the questions and forced me to find the answers. Neither would it have been written if they had not been persistent. However, it is not a comprehensive textbook. It is merely the collection of answers and explanations which I have built up over the years. Because the parents have been mainly parents of babies and young children, it is biased towards the interests of this group and may not meet the demands of the later years. This new edition does, however, include more information about older children and adults.

Whilst I have tried to draw attention to medical and educational treatments, I have not gone into detail on how to carry them out. With most medical treatments it is obviously best to seek advice from your doctor or nurse.

In the case of early stimulation, educational and management programmes I have listed sources and books in the appendix which might be helpful.

Finally, it is impossible to give a truly representative picture. I ask that you use the information here to add to your own understanding of your child and of the effects that she or he may have—happy, sad, joyful, difficult—on you and your family. But never forget, your own child is an individual: as different from others as any child is; your reactions and feelings, and those of your family, will be your own.

# Chapter One

## 'WILL WE COPE?' 'WHAT ARE THEY LIKE?'

Will we cope with our feelings? Will we cope with our spouse's feelings? Will we cope with the baby? Will we cope with the family, relatives, friends? What are children with Down's syndrome like? How do they grow up? What sort of people do they become?

This whole book is an attempt to answer these questions, and also to indicate *how* you can learn to cope and help the child. But in this chapter I shall try briefly to give some answers which you may find reassuring.

**Will we cope?**

All the studies of families with a baby who has Down's syndrome, and also the reports from the families who have themselves faced this problem, *confirm that the chances of coping with the situation are far greater than the chances that you will not.*

Not only that: between 50 and 75 per cent of parents who have had a baby with Down's syndrome report that, once over the initial shock, they found the experience rewarding and strengthening.

A few studies have asked mothers of young children with Down's syndrome, and other mothers in similar circumstances with ordinary children, whether they felt they coped with the baby and young child. Over two-thirds of *both* groups said they coped, and just under a third said they experienced difficulties. There was no difference in overall response between mothers whose babies or young children had Down's syndrome and mothers whose children were 'normal'.

As the children grow older, some will indeed develop problems which will cause stress and difficulties for the family. But this cannot be predicted from examining the baby in the first months of life *nor* from knowing that he or she has Down's syndrome. Even so, well over half of the parents of older children who have been studied report that they cope, and most say they have much happiness with the child.

> When we found out she was a Down's syndrome, I thought it would just be an endless burden . . . I didn't expect any joy or anything good. Of course we didn't know any better. We had no experience and the way we was told just made you think of all the problems . . . Over the years that changed . . . She did things and every little gain was such a joy . . . I felt so proud, like the day she walked straight into the playgroup . . . head held high and just started to play like any kid . . . none of the other children bothered . . . it was really me feeling all up tight. That's all gone now. She's herself and one of the family. She's sort of brought us all closer together and whenever she's around somehow she soon cheers you up and gets people friendly.

These figures are based on families whose babies were born several years ago. There have been many advances since then, and we believe that these changes will result in *more* parents finding *more* pleasure in their child with Down's syndrome. The changes include better attitudes in society, better medical and health care, better educational techniques, better social services and better support for families. There is of course still much more to be done, and better services are still available in some areas and not in others.

**'What are they like?'**

Our studies tell us that there is a greater chance that children with Down's syndrome will grow up pleasant children, who are no more difficult to manage than other children, than there is that they will develop behaviour difficulties. There is a much greater chance that they will learn to walk (the average age is about two years, with a range of one to five years plus), that they will learn to dress and feed themselves and be toilet trained before the age of five, that they will be able to talk and hold conversations with people, that they will make friends and develop a range of interests, than that they will be severely mentally handicapped with little speech, poor skills and few interests. There is a greater chance that they will be good natured and attractive young people than that they will be hostile, aggressive, sullen and difficult.

All these factors depend greatly on the opportunities they are given to develop their potential, and you, the parents, will need to learn ways of teaching and management which are not always necessary with ordinary children. For example, because they develop more slowly and have difficulties in learning and making sense of their environment, parents generally find that they have to act in a more supervisory role and for much longer. You have to learn to give them time to interpret and understand what you want them to do. You have to learn to prompt and make things simpler by breaking them down into their component parts.

> When we go swimming I have to make sure I give him an extra five minutes to get out and get dressed—with his brothers I just say O.K., let's go, but I say to D——, dry yourself, then I check him, then I say put on your shirt . . . sort of prompting and checking each step . . . it takes longer but it's worth making him do it himself. (Father, of boy, 13 years)

You will also have to learn how to work with and use the services to get the best for yourselves and your child. And you will probably have to learn to adapt your hopes and attitudes, your ways of organising the family routines, the ways you react to others and the way you deal with your own feelings. Therefore there is likely to be a great deal of change in your life as a result of the baby. Many parents find that these changes *improve* the quality of their lives.

But not all parents cope. And for most parents, the first weeks after learning about the diagnosis are very stressful. About 20–30 per cent of parents in our area find they cannot face taking the baby home. They spend many agonising days or even weeks, trying to decide what to do. During this period, an accurate picture of the condition and up-to-date information is very important, to help them make a decision.

However, from my experience with these families, I have come to believe that, for most parents, the decision to take the baby home or not is not really an objective one, based on facts. It comes from the heart, not the head. There are those parents who just cannot take the baby home, no matter what they learn about the condition and the help available. There are others who cannot really leave the baby in the hospital—but are so shocked and frightened by the diagnosis they cannot take her home either. These parents find that good, accurate information, and the knowledge that they will be given help and support to cope with the baby, are reassuring.

There is no more tiring and stressful a situation than not being able to make this decision. This is partly *because* it cannot be solved by rational thinking alone. It is an emotional decision and, as discussed in the next chapter, mothers and fathers can have quite different reactions and may find themselves in conflict with each other. This increases the emotional stress. Sometimes parents get so worn out that they are unable to make a decision. It is also difficult to find out whether or not one can cope with the baby, while the baby is still in hospital.

I find that the situation tends to resolve itself in one of three ways:

1 The parents are reassured by the knowledge and information about Down's syndrome and the fact that they can get help and support; they breathe a sigh of relief and go and get the baby. In my experiences these parents never look back. They cope very well indeed.
2 The parents realise they cannot cope right now, and so they decide to have a break and stop talking about the problems until some time in the future.

> It did me good coming out of hospital and leaving the baby there . . . I had a chance to get over the birth . . .
>
> We decided not to talk about it for a few days. Then when we sat down we both knew we wanted to bring the baby home.

3 Some parents realise that they cannot resolve their problem and so take the baby home anyway. At least this puts an end to the emotional stress caused by trying to make the right decision. I have met only a small number of parents who made their decision in this way, but about half of

these found they could cope very easily, and enjoyed the baby.

Accurate figures are very difficult to get, and vary from place to place, but in our area about one in ten families find that they cannot take the baby home. As I said, I do not believe this is a cold, objective decision based on facts and figures. They just cannot face the prospect of having a baby with Down's syndrome. It is a most awesome decision to make, but I think, for the parents who make it, it is the right decision. I believe that most parents do make the right decision for themselves, provided they are not pressurised by outside influences. To take home a child whom you know you can never love or care for, that you might feel is repulsive, will not help the child or the family.

Please note that many, many parents feel like this when they are first told about the diagnosis (see Chapter Two). It takes time to readjust. Most find in time that it is not the baby that they reject, but the condition. But for some the feeling is so strong and so deep that they cannot cope with it. We cannot help ourselves in these reactions. To give up one's child is not easy, and those parents who do, need our understanding, not our criticism.

We are finding that as society learns more about Down's syndrome and old prejudices, myths and fears disappear, more people are willing to foster the children. If support and advice on managing and teaching the child are available, even more people appear to be willing. Thus in many parts of Great Britain, babies with Down's syndrome whose parents find they cannot take them home are found good long-term foster homes. We have met several foster families who have especially asked for a baby with Down's syndrome. Also, in recent years, there seems to be an increase in families willing to adopt a baby with Down's syndrome.

A small number of parents who do take the baby home, are never really able to come to terms with the handicap. Even given all the possible support, advice, information and help from friends, relatives and professionals, they do not appear to get beyond the handicap and see the child. They care for the child, but I do not feel they get very much joy or reward from her. Instead they seem to see the whole thing as a burden.

Again I think this is an instinctive emotional reaction, and there is little we can do to help except try to understand and respect their feelings.

The remainder, however, do learn to live with the child and the handicap, and to find enjoyment and happiness. The rest of the book is about this. It is about the things that we, and the parents who work with us, feel are helpful in this process of learning to live with the child.

In our research, when we first meet a family who has a baby with Down's syndrome, we ask them if they would like to see some photographs of children and young people who also have Down's syndrome. We do this to try to give them some idea of the tremendous differences among children with the condition. All too often, parents may have a stereotyped image of Down's syndrome. As one parent described it, this is an image 'of some sort of monster—a person with tongue hanging out, head drooping forward with dull, sullen eyes'. This seems to me to be the outdated image of the 'mongol' who has lived his or her life in a large institution, with little help or stimulation. My own image of the young person with Down's syndrome is one of a smiling, gentle person with an interest and curiosity in the world around her. I know some will not be like this, but far more people with Down's syndrome can be if we give them good health care, opportunities to learn about and experience the world, and special teaching to help overcome some of their learning difficulties.

The photographs are about this. Many are from the family albums of our parents: so they are happy pictures and tend to show the best in the children. But just as I have not selected photographs which characterise the extreme features or difficulties, I have also not selected only the best. I have tried to offer you a range.

WARNING Whilst most parents find looking at the photographs helps to dispel their worst fears and images, some find photographs distressing—especially if they have only recently learnt about the diagnosis. I find fathers are often less inclined to look at the photographs than mothers: I have seen many a dad increasingly irritated as mother thrusts more pictures under his nose. *If you feel you want to look at the pictures, do so; if not, skip to other chapters. Let other members of your family make their own decision.*

You will find the photographs in the centre of the book. With the exception of parents, brothers and sisters and Mrs Rothwell, all the children and people in the photographs have Down's syndrome.

## *Chapter Two*

# FEELINGS AND REACTIONS

People, families and children are all so very different that it is impossible to say what effect the birth of the baby will have on you and your family. It will depend upon your resources, the services and support provided where you live, your background and experiences, your plans and dreams for your children and the things you value in life.

What we can do is bring together the observations of parents who have faced the same situation, the observations of professionals who have been concerned with the families and the findings of research studies of groups of families. From these it is possible to describe some of the common reactions and feelings of parents, children and relatives. I believe that the parents of a baby with Down's syndrome can find some comfort in the knowledge that their reactions are similar to the reactions of others who have been through the same experience, and that there are ways of dealing with the problems that arise. But if you are a parent of a baby with Down's syndrome, *you will have to decide which parts of the general description below are important to you.* You will have to take an honest look at your feelings and reactions. You will have to act upon them and work through the process of change that follows from the birth. Understanding can only come from within yourself. Be patient with yourself and others. It takes weeks or months, and sometimes years, before the process is complete. You will certainly not experience all of the feelings or reactions, and the strength of those you do experience will vary considerably from time to time.

**Coming to terms with the handicap**

The first goal is to achieve what I call a *functional acceptance.* You get to grips with the diagnosis; you accept that it is

Down's syndrome and will not go away. Then, you begin to function as well as you can; you get on with your life and you start to help the baby to grow and develop to the best of his or her abilities. For most parents this takes up to two or three months.

For some parents it comes with little effort:

> We didn't need much information for us to accept her, other than that she was a Down's baby and how it came about.
>
> It didn't occur to us that we shouldn't take him home. He was ours no matter what he had got.

Other parents have to work consciously and energetically at first:

> It did me good coming out of hospital and leaving the baby there. We had time to settle our feelings and talk without getting overwhelmed . . . we feel we did not get rushed into a hasty decision and so when we brought her home, it was right for all of us.

For other parents time must be allowed to be the healer:

> I joined the human race again when she was four months old.

Some parents talk about accepting the child but rejecting the handicap:

> I don't resent the baby, I resent the Down's syndrome.

Some feel they *have* to reject the handicap in order to keep fighting against it for the sake of the child:

> I thought to myself, he may be a mongol but he'll be the brightest one anyone around here has seen.
>
> No, I didn't tell the neighbours she had Down's syndrome. I felt they would treat her more normally if they didn't know.

I collected these last two quotes when the babies were only a few months old. When the children were five years old, I talked to the parents again about their feelings. The first couple said they had not come to terms with the handicap for at least two years:

> I looked out the back and he was playing in the sand. I thought, well he's happy enough and so are we. After all, he wouldn't be himself if he didn't have Down's syndrome. He would be someone different . . . if you see what I mean.

The other couple still felt that they had not come to terms with the handicap. They tended to avoid situations like school meetings, holidays and family occasions that made them aware of the handicap.

Often parents complain that people, especially well meaning professionals and relatives, insist that they must accept their handicapped child in a 'nothing can be done' sort of way. This approach often simply adds to one's depression. Whilst parents do on the whole 'accept' the child, many cannot accept the handicap in this fatalistic way. Instead they want to seek constructive ways of trying to overcome the handicap. This is why I prefer to talk about 'coming to terms' with the handicap: one realises that it is there but looks for ways of coping with it and helping the child.

I am not sure what marks the 'final coming to terms', or if it ever really happens. Many parents do not find it a problem.

> About the second week after having him home I told myself to forget all about the Down's syndrome and treat him like any child. I sort of shrugged my shoulders and took each day as it came. If a problem arose, I sorted it out, but I thought there was no point sitting and worrying about problems that might never happen.

I think 'coming to terms' means seeing the child for him or herself—a unique person with his own special problems and special qualities.

> I hardly know what to wish for for Thomas. It makes no sense to wish he was well, without problems or like the other children. I love Thomas the way he is.

In our more recent studies, when the children were aged between eight and 13 years, we asked parents if they would like to change anything about the family. Except for parents of children with severe behaviour difficulties or health problems, hardly any said they wanted to change the child with Down's syndrome. In fact most described how the child with Down's syndrome was a benefit to the family and many were adamant that they would not change the child for any reason.

## First reactions and feelings

We say of pregnant women that they are 'expecting a baby'. By this we usually mean that they are looking forward to a healthy baby who will fulfil some of their dreams for the future. Fathers also have these dreams, and both parents will probably have strong feelings of affection for the baby even before it is born. It is true that most parents have occasional fears that something might go wrong. These are usually put aside and are only recalled when later problems occur—thus the premonition appears to be proved.

Most parents, especially if it is their first baby, are optimistic. They dream that the baby will be the best ever. In their imagination they plan the child's future, what they will do together, how the child will grow. Many of these plans reflect the parents' own ambitions or lost opportunities—the father who wants a son who will be a sportsman, the mother who wants a son or daughter who will go to University, the parents who want a beautiful daughter and so on.

A father of an eight-year-old girl with Down's syndrome wrote to me about this:

> . . . the cosy picture of stages of development of my little girl. I had never questioned that she would be intelligent and pretty, with a sweet nature and the object of universal admiration. These mental pictures now lay shattered at my feet. I was yet to learn that Louise would fulfil all these aspirations but in ways different and more wonderful than anything that my tormented mind, at that moment, could envisage . . .

*Even though the parent is aware that this child is a product of his imagination and fantasy, the dream is no less real for that.*

## Shock and disbelief

When parents are first told that the baby has Down's syndrome they are all deeply shocked. Many talk of 'going numb' and 'being unable to think straight'. 'I heard the word "mongol" and from then on I just remember his (the doctor's) mouth moving. I think I asked him if he was sure'. Other parents remember everything as 'crystal clear', but 'it was like it was happening to someone else. I was up in the corner watching it all but it was me he was talking to'. Parents often become irrational and confused and do not believe what they are being told.

> I told him there must be a mistake. I have just been feeding the baby and she's all right.
>
> I thought he must have mixed my baby up with someone else's—I was too young to have a mongol.

This state of shock can last for seconds or on and off for days. When parents begin to react to the news, they have a range of feelings which seem to come and go and to change in strength from moment to moment.

**Instinctive reactions***

Most of the parents that I have met seem to have two fundamental instinctive feelings: they feel protective toward the helpless child, and a parallel revulsion at the thought of the abnormality.

> We both looked at the baby and instinctively I was aware that we were thinking the same thing—poor little thing lying so peacefully, causing no trouble for anyone, as unwittingly you have done through all the dramatics of the last few days—totally unaware of the explosive effects of your birth. I think both my wife and I felt the same surge of love for her at that moment. Sarah, as a unique person, had entered our lives.
>
> I felt sick when he told me. I looked at the baby and I could see it . . . I could see the mongol look . . . I didn't even want to touch him . . . not then. I sat looking at him for hours in hospital . . . there was no one I could talk to because my husband wasn't coming in 'til later. How could I tell him? How do you tell anyone you feel like that

* The model of feelings and reactions is taken from Mackeith, R. (1973), 'The feelings and behaviour of parents of handicapped children', in *Developmental Medicine and Child Neurology*, **15**, 24–7.

> about your own child? Slowly I pulled myself together and changed him and then I started to feed him. It didn't feel so bad then but I still don't like to think about it—him being a mongol, I mean.
>
> (This mother told me about these feelings when the baby was a month old. By the time he was six months old she was very happy with him.)

Both these reactions are perfectly normal. 'By 'normal' I mean most people share them to a greater or lesser degree. It is important to recognise the reactions and their consequences. Feelings of protectiveness toward the baby will usually lead to warm loving care. But they can make one very sensitive to any threat from others. Any remark about the baby or his or her condition which seems to be critical can be seen out of all proportion. Sometimes the feeling can be so strong that one protects the baby, and oneself, from the necessary everyday experiences required for normal living.

> Looking back I was so sensitive and touchy in those first weeks . . . my brother-in-law said in fun (to the baby), 'What a little button nose you've got'—and I felt myself get red hot—and every time someone said things like 'he'll be a bit slower' or 'he'll need special help', I kept thinking they were being critical and somehow getting at him.

Also as a father of a 13-year-old boy told me recently,

> His brothers and sisters tend to do things for him . . . he can get crisps out of the machine but if they are around they do it—and he lets them. I suppose it's some kind of instinctive protection but it stops him doing it.

Feelings of revulsion are also normal, but, as the mother indicated earlier, many people find it difficult to talk about them. In our society one is not supposed to admit to such feelings. The feelings usually result in some form of rejection. 70 to 80 per cent of the mothers in our research admit to having had some feeling of rejection in the first months. Many have told me how they wished for the baby to die, and in some cases thought of ways by which this could happen. Fathers also have mixed feelings:

> My wife and I wished that Michael had a heart disease that would lead to his death. What I found very disturbing was that I actually entertained notions of murdering him in some way. The thing that made me most wretched about all that was that I could actually entertain such notions about my own son.

Many parents feel very shocked, not just about the diagnosis of Down's syndrome, but about the very intense feelings they can have toward the child and themselves and their spouses and their other children. It is a very intense and sensitive time when great changes in one's thinking are taking place. It is also a time when many parents see-saw between their feelings of protectiveness and rejection, trying to find a balance. In some cases parents will feel guilty about the feelings of rejection and over-compensate for them by extremes of lavish care: nothing is too much trouble for the baby, and all the family's needs are placed second to his.

Such feelings may even persist into later life. Parents remain very protective and over indulgent toward the handicapped child. This can have repercussions on the other children. It can create an imbalance in the family, with all the parents' energy being directed toward one child. Since mother and father are likely to have these contradictory feelings in different proportions, they may develop different ways of treating the handicapped child, and this in turn may create conflict between parents.

Please note that whether we have a handicapped child or not, most parents get into conflict at some time about how to treat the children. Such conflict can be useful, and through it we learn. But the potential for conflict is considerably higher when a child is handicapped, and these feelings about the child and oneself can often operate beneath the surface, causing anxiety. The best place for any handicapped child is in a family, but he or she should be a *part* of the family—a participant in the family and not merely the recipient of family aid. It is important therefore to think about such feelings and recognise their consequences. It is important to recognise that they are *quite normal reactions* and one need not feel guilty about them. Guilt can only lead to depression.

You will therefore need to work towards a balance within

the family, with the handicapped member receiving his or her fair share of family resources. Of course this is easier said than done: there are times in every family when one member requires more help and attention than another. But be aware of the need to keep a balance.

Recognising these two instinctive feelings of protectiveness and rejection can also help us to understand how on the one hand we can love and care for the child, and on the other reject the abnormality. It may well be that here, too, one needs to seek a balance. As I noted earlier, the feelings of rejection of the handicap may be necessary for some parents to take up the challenge and try to help the child, and not fatalistically to accept it and feel nothing can be done.

## Feelings of grief

Most parents experience a sense of grief and loss when they are told that the baby has Down's syndrome. Their hopes and dreams for the expected child are taken away in an instant. For many parents it is as though the child they were expecting is dead:

> I was just shattered when he told me. I could feel this great emptiness inside. A great feeling of having lost something. It was like when my mother died.

Many doctors think that it is important for parents to recognise these feelings and to go through a period of mourning for their lost imaginary baby. This can help to free them from using up their energy thinking about what should have been. Once over this, they can begin to get to know the baby they have. Some parents have also made this point:

> For three or four weeks I didn't do anything with the baby except wash her, change and feed her. I kept finding myself thinking about all the things I had hoped she would do . . . I would pick up the little cardigan I had knitted when I was expecting and remember all the thoughts that I had had when I was knitting it. After a while I started to tell myself to stop thinking about it. I made myself think about doing things with her. The exercises and games to help her develop were very good as they kept me busy.

**Feelings of inadequacy**

Many other feelings may also be experienced. Some parents have an overwhelming feeling of inadequacy, as though their ability to reproduce is in question. This can have great effects on their self-esteem and can cause depression.

> I felt I had failed as a human being. I got so angry that all these young girls in the ward could produce healthy babies and I couldn't even do that.

Sexual relationships between partners can be affected, too. Rather naturally, many parents do not wish to discuss this, and so it is not possible to provide much detailed information. But in the few cases I have come across who have mentioned it, parents have found it a relief to realise that it is not an uncommon phenomenon—in fact it is not uncommon after the birth of any baby.

These feelings of inadequacy appear to be stronger when the baby is the first born, and often parents talk about them only when they have had a second baby who has no abnormality.

If parents are experiencing difficulties, they need to try to talk to each other about them as soon as possible. The longer they leave it the more difficult it can become. But sometimes a parent will find it easier to talk to a close friend or to their doctor or social worker than to their partner. This, too, is not uncommon and should not be seen as any slight or criticism of the relative or partner. We all feel sometimes that it is easier to talk to 'a stranger'. Both the doctor and social worker are usually knowledgeable about these problems, and parents who can discuss their feelings with them usually find it a great help.

Such feelings can strike very deep, and in some cases will lead to severe depression. I should insist here that only a relatively few parents who have a baby with Down's syndrome do become severely depressed and suffer from deep feelings of worthlessness and helplessness. But some do, and they will need help. Often people feel that because they know why they are depressed—e.g. they have had a baby with Down's syndrome—then they do not require help. When one has a deep depression, whether one knows why or not, one can be treated.

**Feelings of uncertainty**

Whilst the baby that was expected was imaginary, the baby that is born is real enough. But most parents have very little idea of what the future holds—what the condition 'Down's syndrome' means.

> I knew she had Down's syndrome but somehow she wasn't a person but a big question mark.

Most parents have to use their imagination and past experience to fill in this question mark. In fact they create yet another imaginary child. Much suffering and difficulty can be avoided if one tries to control one's imagination, and instead seek out accurate information from reliable sources. Unfortunately, it is not unusual for parents to be given inaccurate and conflicting information. Also, parents often expect the doctor to have all the information, and become frustrated and angry when they realise he or she may not know very much. You should try to appreciate that whilst Down's syndrome is one of the most common causes of mental handicap, it is still not a very common problem. Most doctors will have far more people with heart problems or infectious diseases on their panel than children with Down's syndrome; so it is necessary for the parents to seek out specialists in this area whenever possible.

To reduce these feelings of uncertainty, parents will often look for comparisons. They will try to meet parents who also have a child with Down's syndrome. We find around half of our parents wish to do this in the first few weeks or months, though others prefer to wait to get to know the baby and their own feelings first. If you do meet another family who has a child with Down's syndrome, you may find it very useful, or you may find it very hurtful: it will depend in part on how you get on with them, and how you react to their child. You should try to remember that all children and all families are different, and whilst you will have some experiences in common you cannot generalise from one case.

Feelings of uncertainty are also associated with feelings of inadequacy in helping the child. Will we cope? I said in Chapter One that most families do. You will need to learn about various ways of doing this, and I have listed some useful books at the end of this book. But uncertainties can lead to a lack of confidence in dealing with the child. In turn this can lead to inconsistency: one moment you deal with him one way, the next, another. Again, parents can differ in their treatment of the child because both are uncertain.

Here are some quotes from our parents:

> When you first have a handicapped child you think they're all the same.
>
> We didn't get told much in hospital at all, and especially with him being our first we don't know whether something is a normal reaction or is typical of the Down's group of children.
>
> I just couldn't think what was best. I felt so inadequate . . . I would try to do something with him but I usually gave up because I wasn't sure what to do.

Here are quotes from the same parents when they got involved in our support programme. Similar quotes can be found from parents in many such programmes:

> My husband and I felt that when we were doing something, we didn't feel so inadequate.
>
> Just knowing that other people, experts or even other parents, found it was useful to do something gave me all the confidence I needed to keep going.
>
> They [i.e. my colleagues and me C. C.] never really told me anything new . . . it was often just common sense . . . but it was very important because I just dithered around at first . . . I didn't feel confident in myself because I knew he was handicapped.
>
> My husband was a lot better than me at helping Jamie at first. He enjoyed being able to contribute something positive. That's why working out a set of activities to do kept us both busy . . . we did it together and it was nice.

Finding out about the nature of Down's syndrome and how to help the child can reduce these feelings of uncertainty. If you are able to carry out activities, such as exercises to stimulate physical growth and games to stimulate mental activity, this can be very helpful in the process of 'coming to terms' and dealing with your feelings of distress. Some parents on the other hand find these activities difficult. The exercises are seen as a constant and painful reminder of the baby's condition. The fact that no activities can actually cure the baby, that he or she will always have Down's syndrome, makes it all seem so hopeless and unworthwhile. Such conflicts can be dealt with only by taking a long hard look at one's values, and at what we think life is all about.

We might start by asking ourselves another question, almost as impossible; why do we have children? How we answer such a question will reflect the extent to which we can accept the child's handicap. In our society many of us are raised to value intelligence and/or physical ability above all, and to seek after the material benefits that come with 'successful' jobs. A mentally handicapped child will not aspire to these goals. In our society most of us no longer live with death and disease, as was common fifty or sixty years ago. We grow up believing that 'science will solve our problems', that if we do this and that we can expect the good things in life. It is a terrible shock to meet a problem which cannot be corrected. Many of us plan our families to meet our financial, social or career requirements. What a shock when our plans go wrong! We may have planned for two children so that they can both be given 'the best'—but if one is handicapped, what do we do?

> If we hadn't had a handicapped child we would have had two children, everything pre-planned, under control . . . instead we have four kids and a really lively time . . . the carpet was yanked from under our feet by his birth but it has given us a tremendous amount of pleasure. It brought out our fighting qualities, has given us lots of friends —affiliations that are stronger than non-handicapped friends; it makes us value the important things in life as opposed to achievement and financial success, we are less inclined to worry about silly things.

It is my impression that the more parents feel in control of their destiny, and the more they have tried to plan their future, the greater the shock of the birth of the handicapped baby and the greater their difficulties can be in coming to terms with events. The more ambitious parents are for their children, the more difficult they can find it to relate to the handicapped child and to feel that his or her life is as important and worthwhile as the lives of other children. Very rarely, I also find parents who put unconscious pressure on the other children in the family as though to compensate for the handicapped one. Here is a quote from a father of a baby with Down's syndrome, who had a brother who was severely handicapped (not with Down's syndrome):

> Looking back, I realise I never did lots of things the other boys at school did. I never really got into trouble or fought. I worked very hard at school to please my father . . . I think I tried to do the work for two sons.

**Feelings of anger and hostility**

To some extent, the strength of one's hopes and ambitions will influence the degree to which one experiences feelings of anger and bitterness, and of being 'cheated' by having a baby with Down's syndrome. Most parents ask, 'Why did it happen to me?' They need a reason and look for one. Often they will think first of things that they did which might have caused the condition. This can again lead to feelings of guilt. This is why it is so important for parents to understand the cause of Down's syndrome and the fact that nothing they did, or did not do, caused it to happen (see Chapter Four).

But even when one knows the cause, one can still feel angry and bitter. Some of our parents tell us that they got over it all, yet when a brother or sister had a 'normal' baby some months later, they felt very bitter. 'It seemed so unfair.' I don't know how one works through this anger and bitterness—it seems that it gets less with time. One does need to face it and see it as an honest, normal reaction, but one which is best controlled. The danger is that it needs an outlet. One can release the anger by directing it at oneself, one's partners and relatives, or at the medical staff or therapists involved with one. Sometimes this hostility is even deserved by those to whom it is directed, but in most cases it will not be very productive. You may find that because of your hostility you are unable to use the services of relatives and friends when you most need them. You may have upset them so much they will not help—which shows a lack of understanding on their part—or you may be too embarrassed to ask them. This hostility can also be directed at the baby, and build up into long-term resentment. Fortunately most people are able to come to terms with their anger. They recognise it and talk about it, and this can reduce it.

**Feelings of embarrassment**

Having a child who is 'different'—who looks different, who can behave differently and sometimes needs to be treated differently—from the norm, can be embarrassing. If parents do not learn to live with this embarrassment, however, it can lead to withdrawal from social contacts and eventual isolation. In the first weeks you may well need to get over the initial shock in the company only of close friends and relatives. But you will have to fight this feeling as soon as possible: take your courage in both hands and get out! In the later section on social activities I have discussed this more fully. Most parents do manage, and once they get out into the community things are usually not as bad as they thought they would be.

**Changes over time**

During the period of adjustment—the change from what things were like before the new baby, to what they need to be like if the family is to survive, grow and prosper—most parents find that they seem to move 'two steps forward and one step back'; that 'some days are fine' and they think it's all over and 'the next day is dark despair'. At the time, you may not be able to see an end to it, but it does improve.

Often the changes are due to changes in the baby as well as the parent. Once the initial crisis or shock over the news is moving further behind you, you will begin to adjust to the new situation and adapt to the baby. You will become less inclined to see the handicap and more inclined to see the baby—a baby who is not that different from other babies.

Parents now begin to call the baby by his or her name. He or she is becoming a person. This will often coincide with changes in the baby. Parents find they get eye contact—the baby looks straight into their eyes. Smiles appear, and often the baby will smile when tickled. These behaviours do appear a little later in most babies with Down's syndrome than in ordinary babies. Sometimes it is around ten or 12 weeks before they occur reasonably frequently—but they will seem all the more transforming when they do.

From this time on we find that many parents tell us that the baby seems 'quite normal'; that he or she is 'just like their other babies', or may be 'even quicker at doing things'. Many parents feel their attachment to the baby gets much stronger at this time.

Whilst talking about attachment, I should note that many people think that mothers should have an immediate surge of maternal love and attachment for the baby—they should 'bond' together. In my experience many mothers do *not* feel this immediately, whether the baby is 'normal' or not. Instead they gradually develop feelings of attachment and love over time. Some mothers get upset because they did not feel immediately 'bonded' to the baby, even before they discovered the Down's syndrome. Sometimes babies need to go into intensive care or special treatment due to complications. This can mean a period of separation between parents and baby, and mothers and fathers can find that it takes longer for feelings of attachment to develop. In other words, lack of strong feelings for the baby may not be due to the diagnosis but to other factors as well.

The period from around two to three months can be quite euphoric for the parents. The baby is not as bad as they thought; they have managed to get over the shock and they are hopeful and optimistic. However, somewhere between six and twelve months, many parents also begin to see the reality of the baby's handicap. He is a little slow to sit up or reach for toys; he may not appear as lively and as interested as other babies. Parents often 'see' this quite suddenly. They are at the clinic or at a friend's house, where there is a baby of similar age. Suddenly one can see the difference. This can produce another shock, and many of the 'old' feelings come back. Thus whilst one might adjust quite quickly and well to the initial shock, later problems—sometimes problems that are nothing to do with the child—can cause upset, and one has to work through the feelings all over again. One also has to recognise that one's partner or other members of the family may have similar reactions at different times.

But please, do not be afraid to be optimistic and hopeful. All parents have the right and the need to be hopeful for all their children. But at the same time try to understand that the child will have limitations as well as strengths. We can't all have brilliant, sweet natured children, and we can't all have the brightest child with Down's syndrome. We have our own children. They are themselves, and all we can do is try to provide them with the help and opportunities they need to realise the potential that they were born with. Children with Down's syndrome will probably need, and benefit from, our help far more than those who are more able. You will have to find out about how to do this. No one should doubt that this can be difficult. It is a challenge. But never forget that perhaps as much as 70 to 80 per cent of the child's potential will be brought out by providing him or her with the same sort of parenting that we would give to any child. You try to treat him not as normal—but as normally as possible. A parent is not a professional. I am a professional when I deal with other people's children. This means I try to be reasonably objective and objectively reasonable in my dealings with them. But as a parent my children can make unreasonable demands on me (seen from the professional viewpoint) and I will make unreasonable demands on them. The other day my son asked me (actually he told me) to mend his bicycle. I said, 'Why should I? I'm busy'; he said, 'Because you're my Dad!' Also, being a child's parent gives you the socially legitimate right to make unreasonable demands for the sake of the child. *We* are *their* parents.

I am emphasising this because in learning how to help and manage our children, we parents are shown, and often expected to carry out, many of the methods that professionals use. As explained in Chapter Five, doing this has helped children with Down's syndrome to achieve higher levels of skill and independence than previously thought possible. But do not lose sight of the fact that the child needs a parent—not another professional. Sometimes, in their desire to help the child or as a reaction to feelings of guilt, fear for the future, or rejection of the handicap, parents can become too professional.

**Summary of the main points**

All parents find the birth of the Down's syndrome baby a great shock. They often feel confused and disorganised and cannot believe it is true. Depending on their experience, personality, value judgements about life and children, they may have a number of reactions to the birth.

They may have strong feelings of protectiveness to the baby and/or towards the family. Many will have feelings of rejection. For some both feelings are present: they accept the child but reject the handicap.

Many will have a sense of loss and grief for the baby they had wanted. They will often feel angry and bitter and need to seek out reasons to explain why it happened.

Some will have feelings of inadequacy in their ability to produce children. Very common is the feeling of uncertainty about what to do and how they will cope.

These feelings come and go over the first weeks, and may diminish in time so that the parents can come to terms with the fact that the baby has Down's syndrome and can then begin to help the baby develop. Doing things to help the baby can also help some parents to get over this crisis period.

But sometimes the feelings can return at later stages, especially if a new shock or set of difficulties arise. These may involve the baby or be due to things which are nothing to do with the child.

Parents need to recognise that such feelings are common and normal. They need to try to understand them, and to be patient with themselves and others during this very sensitive and volatile period when they are adapting to the new circumstances. It is really about making sense of what has happened and getting information so as to make sense of what will happen. When one feels able to predict the future with some certainty and know that one will cope, then the first stage of adaptation is complete. But we all adapt in our own way and in our own time.

## *Chapter Three*

# WHAT EFFECTS WILL IT HAVE ON THE FAMILY?

There is no substantial evidence that having a brother or sister with Down's syndrome has any major or permanent ill effect on the large majority of children. In fact, if you ask older brothers and sisters how they feel about it, their replies suggest that there is more reason to believe in a beneficial effect. In my experience, siblings of children with Down's syndrome are often very tolerant young people, with remarkable understanding and maturity in their dealings with others.

There are some exceptions. If the parents find it difficult to come to terms with the child's handicap, brothers and sisters also tend to find it difficult. If the parents feel resentment toward the child with Down's syndrome, and are constantly drawing attention to the difficulties and restrictions the handicap imposes on their lives, then the other children will often develop the same feelings. After all, who else can they look to and learn from, if not their parents?

Where parents have these difficulties, they may, consciously or unconsciously, avoid discussion about the child; they may feel embarrassment at taking the child out or inviting neighbours into the home. Such feelings are common at first, but most parents come to terms with them within the first months. If these feelings and behaviours persist, however, the other children will also tend not to invite friends in, and in extreme cases may become isolated from the neighbourhood children and the children at school. But I should say that we have found no instances of this extreme in our own research and the cases noted in the past may be largely due to the general negative attitudes of society.

Of course, there will always be an occasion when some child taunts the children about their brother or sister, and while at the time this is painful for all concerned, it does not appear to have any permanent ill effects. Indeed, if one can discuss why it happens—because of ignorance and insecurity—then such incidents can be used to help us learn about ourselves and others. Thus where parents have been able to adapt to the knowledge of the child's condition, and have been able to be open and honest about it, the other children can gain, not lose, by the experience.

At the beginning, when the news of the diagnosis is first given, the whole family is likely to be under some strain. Sometimes brothers and sisters are teenagers or adults, and conflict can arise between their views about what is best and those of the parents. Some will feel protective toward their parents and resent the upheaval and pain caused by the birth of the baby. This is usually only temporary, and as the parents adjust the older children will follow suit. Many parents find the older children are far more understanding and helpful than they would ever have expected. This often increases their respect for their other children, and strengthens the family bonds. Sometimes the parents' feelings of rejection towards the new baby will shock and disturb an older child, and he or she will need time to adjust, and perhaps some trusted person to explain the complexities of feelings at this time.

Other children can also become upset if parents have to take the decision, in later life, to place the child with Down's syndrome, who has grown up with his brothers and sisters, in a residential school or home. It is possible that the brothers and sisters will feel then that the child is being rejected, and fear for their own relationship with their parents. Or sometimes the reason given for the decision is that it is for the *sake* of the other children. This can induce guilt in the brothers and sisters, because it suggests that they are the cause of the child being placed in care.

However, these appear to be temporary difficulties, especially if there are good relationships within the family, and time and care is taken to talk about the problems. When this is done, a great deal of pain and stress can be avoided. I would like to emphasise that it is a case of talking *with* the other children; one has to listen to and respect their ideas and then give them time to adjust. It is not just a case of explaining one's own reasons—no matter how sound. If the parents are in conflict over what to do, then this can put stress on the other children, who may feel they are expected to take sides.

One interesting fact that has emerged from the limited number of studies of parents, brothers and sisters of children with Down's syndrome, is that if parents are asked whether having a child with Down's syndrome has had any ill effects on the other children, many feel it has. In most cases, they feel they have been unable to give the other children as much attention as they might have; that they have had to restrict family events such as holidays and outings; or, in the case of some mothers, they have been unable to return to work and help with family resources. These problems can relate to:

1 the degree of independence (social and self-help skills) that the child with Down's syndrome has—the more able he or she is, the fewer the difficulties;
2 the presence of behaviour disorders: these not only disrupt the home routine, but can lead to social embarrassment for all members of the family;
3 the resources in the community to help the family. Where nurseries, schools, hostels, short-stay residential facilities, youth classes, local societies and self-help parents' groups are available, these can greatly relieve the problems if parents are willing and able to use them.

However, the problems for the other children as seen from the parents' point of view are often quite different from the way the children themselves see them. If one asks the brothers and sisters about their difficulties, they usually say that they do not think their lives have been particularly restricted, compared to those of their friends. Indeed, most studies find that the majority of brothers and sisters develop strong bonds of affection for their brother or sister with Down's syndrome, and feel that they have benefited from growing up with him or her.

The extent to which brothers and sisters experience problems generally relates particularly to how much the handicapped member of the family interferes with everyday activities. If the brothers or sisters have to 'take him everywhere', or feel they are 'always looking after her', they naturally feel resentment. Many older brothers and sisters feel similarly about looking after the younger children in the family. Also, if they cannot get their homework done, or can never leave their toys, models and books around without them getting damaged, this can cause great difficulties. But such difficulties happen in all families—especially to older children who have younger brothers and sisters. In the case of the child with Down's syndrome, he or she will simply be at this interfering stage for longer. Hence the problem lasts for longer, and can become very tiring. Many parents learn to organise the family routine and home to cope with this. Mothers with children who have Down's syndrome, especially those who are growing and learning very slowly, do need to organise the routines at home carefully, particularly at 'crisis' times such as getting off to school or work, and between 4.00 and 8.00 p.m. in the evening. In our studies of behaviour difficulties we have not found any evidence that brothers and sisters of children with Down's syndrome have more problems than those with non-handicapped brothers and sisters.

Running a family is not always an easy business, and having a handicapped member does not make it any easier. However, it would seem that for the majority of families with a child with Down's syndrome there is no reason to suppose the other children will automatically suffer. But even in those cases where the brother or sister with Down's syndrome is very mentally handicapped and has behaviour disorders, parents are likely to believe the ill effects are far greater than the other children in fact experience. I think this is an important point. Many parents who seek residential care for their baby with Down's syndrome list as a major reason for the decision their fear that such a child in the family will be detrimental to existing or future children. As noted earlier, this reasoning carries the danger of inducing feelings of guilt in the other children.

**'How will I tell the other children?'**

No parent can find it easy to tell his or her children that the new baby has Down's syndrome. We will all find reasons for putting off telling them until some other time. Doctors have similar problems when breaking the news to parents. Yet most parents complain if they are not given the diagnosis fairly quickly, and certainly get upset if they notice that routines in the hospital are 'different' for them and their new baby.

Children are equally sensitive to disturbances in the household. Conversations suddenly cease when they are around; there is some tension in the family; the new baby stays in hospital longer, or goes to the doctor more often, than the babies of friends and relatives. It is very difficult to hide these things, and in doing so one is in danger of indicating to the other children that there is something to hide. Therefore it is best to tell them as soon as you can.

If the other children are at the age when they understand that people and children can be different—around four to seven years onwards—then you can tell them that there is something *different* about the new baby. (I prefer the word 'different', because if one says 'there is something wrong with the baby' this is a judgement which can be misunderstood.) Explain that the new baby will not find it as easy as they did to learn about things and will need extra-special care and help.

The older the child, the more information he or she will understand. I think it is best not to try to push too much information at the child, but to explain it simply without too much detail, and answer her questions honestly. But we are still inclined to underestimate our children at times. A friend who has a very severely handicapped baby told me this story recently. A neighbour—in all kindness—had gone through the rather harrowing—'How are you?', 'How is the poor little girl?', 'What a shame'—set of inquiries, when the three-and-a-half-year-old brother looked up and said, 'But we still love her, you know.'

The majority of six-to-ten-year-olds seem to take the news in their stride and carry on as before. As they grow, they will learn new facts and information as they want it, providing it is easily accessible. Depending on their age and understanding, some children do get upset and they do need to express their feelings just as you did. Some will protest that it cannot be true because the baby looks fine and is very happy and alert. This can hurt, as it is of course what parents want to believe despite all evidence to the contrary. However, try to understand their need to express their shock and grief, and give them the same help and understanding that you wanted when you were told. Some will want time on their own to think about it. Also, try to be together, mother and father, when you tell them. I have no strong evidence about how important this is, but an eighteen-year-old brother of a girl with Down's syndrome recently told me how, when she was born and he was twelve, his mother told him about his sister. He knew his father was out in the garden and, at the time, could not think why he did not tell him as well. It was a year or two before he ever discussed his sister's condition with his father, and they were both profoundly relieved when it happened. At eighteen, he said he understood why his father had not been able to tell him, but he felt sad that there had been some tension, something to be avoided, in what otherwise was a very close relationship.

If both parents cannot be present when the other children are told, then try to explain to the older ones why. An honest reason can often prevent misunderstanding.

It is often nice to be holding the baby when you tell them. This shows them that you are treating the baby just the same, caring for him or her just the same, as when they did not know something was wrong. With younger children, this is often the best thing to do. You are getting the baby ready for a visit to the clinic or hospital and you mention that he or she is not quite the same as we are and needs some special help. As the child grows up, hearing you talk openly about the condition, it will all be quite natural.

The same is true for children born *after* the baby with Down's syndrome. They will pick up comments they hear when you talk with others. At some stage they will ask questions. These are best answered simply. Do not pounce on the first question and drown the child in complex explanations. A similar problem can arise when talking to small children about sex. Too often we parents over-react to the first casual question about sex, and explain all sorts of details that the children really did not want and cannot understand.

When children who were little when the baby with Down's syndrome was born are older, say around ten to 15 years, it is worthwhile asking them if they want more detailed information about the condition. Sometimes one forgets that they do not know as much as we do, and are not sure how to get hold of the information. This is important if they are to understand the possible risks of themselves having children with the condition. In the very rare case of one of the other children being a translocation carrier of the condition (see p. 86) one really has to try to explain the implications. You may find that the adolescent child would like to receive counselling from a geneticist (see p. 98).

Finally, all parents find it a great relief once they have told the other children. They are usually very surprised by, and very proud of how well the children respond. Indeed, the greatest difficulty is getting up the courage to tell them!

**'Telling the relatives?'**

As with the other children, most parents find it a great relief when they have told friends and relatives and neighbours. Again, the longer one leaves it the harder it can become. Sometimes, if a relative is unwell or very old, parents do not tell them. I have not heard of any instances where this has caused stress: in one case I do know, when the great-grandmother recognised the condition as the child grew, she fully understood why the family had not wished to distress or worry her.

The telling of the diagnosis to relatives and friends—particularly grandparents—usually falls on father. Mother and baby are in hospital and everyone wants to know from father if all is well.

It is not easy to break the news, especially when one is in a state of shock oneself. The grandparents, friends and relatives also have to work through their feelings of shock, disbelief and anger when they hear the news. They may ask 'Are you sure?', 'Have they made a mistake?'. These are hurtful questions, even though they are asked with the best intentions. They are hurtful because, as I said earlier, it is what one wants to believe oneself. It can take grandparents a few minutes or many months to work through these feelings. If you can understand how you felt or feel, then you will know how they are likely to feel. A father recently told me that when he and his wife were being told about the diagnosis of Down's syndrome for their baby, he suddenly realised he would have to tell his mother and father.

> It was their first granddaughter . . . they had always wanted a girl. They had been getting really excited. Mum had been knitting and Dad had helped me wallpaper the bedroom. Well, the doctor who told us was so good I thought it best to do as he did. I went to their house and

sat them down together and said straight out, 'I've got some bad news, the little girl has got Down's syndrome —that's what they used to call mongols—she's a mongol baby . . .' They reacted just like we did. Mum cried and Dad said are you sure, there must be a mistake. I wanted to shout—How do I know if they're sure—I could feel my temper rising just like it had when I left the hospital. I told him that the doctor said he was 99.9 per cent certain but would do a chromosome test and we would know the results in a couple of weeks.

I told them that the doctor said it wasn't like it used to be . . . there was lots of things one could do to help . . . schools and exercises for the baby. But I can see them now, they were so sad and helpless . . . Mum asked how was J. . . . taking it and I said, not too bad. Then I looked at her and said we'll need your help, Mum, if we are going to get through. Well that was it. She just came over and hugged me and said of course we'll help, won't we, Dad? We'll manage and don't you worry about the baby she's still one of the family . . . Well somehow after that things looked better. I found it easier to tell friends and my brother. It was best just to say—'she's got Down's syndrome—that's mongolism.' Once I had said it everything was usually okay and every time I said it, it got easier. But you soon find out who your friends are. I was surprised just how kind people were—even people in our street who we only ever said Hello to . . . I was also surprised to find out just how many people in our street had a relative or a friend with Down's syndrome . . .

During the same home visit, the mother told me that it was such a relief to come out of hospital with the baby knowing that A. . . . had told most of their friends and relatives.

One should also be aware that brothers and sisters find it difficult to tell people.

I was always embarrassed about informing people about Peter's mental handicap. Explaining mental handicap to people when you are only young can be overwhelmingly difficult—even if you understand it yourself. It was also difficult coping with questions like—What does your brother do? Where does he go to school? etc., etc. It was

> only as I became older that I ceased to use 'mental handicap' as an excuse for Peter's behaviour and was able to explain that he hasn't learnt to do it yet.

Sometimes a brother or sister will not admit or mention their handicapped brother or sister. Often, this is not because they wish to deny his existence—they may well have a very close relationship. It is because they find giving the explanations difficult and embarrassing. Parents need to help their other children learn how to answer these questions.

**Reactions of grandparents**

It is quite clear from what parents tell me that grandparents have a very special role to play when the baby is born. However, they can also be the cause of many difficulties, so I think it worthwhile to try to share the experience of our parents with you, and to make some particular points.

One of the best ways of helping people who find themselves in a crisis is to show them what they can do to help. Something useful and positive. For example, we find that many parents of babies with Down's syndrome get great comfort from starting to play stimulating games and exercises to help the baby's development. Brothers and sisters can find it very satisfying to help with the baby—to make a contribution. No one likes to feel useless or left out. Grandparents are no different. If you can involve them in caring for the baby, helping with the stimulation activities, and if you can provide them with the information you felt you needed, this can help them and you. How much this can be done will depend upon different family circumstances. But do remember, you have the baby and family to keep you busy and occupied. It can take your mind off things for a while. Often grandparents have little to do but sit at home and brood and worry about you and the baby. So a little understanding on all sides can help.

Some grandparents are very bewildered and upset, and if they do not understand about the condition they can really cause problems. The main ones reported by parents are:

1 Grandparents find it difficult to accept or appreciate the consequences of the condition. As I have already mentioned, they may question whether the doctors are sure of the diagnosis. Even when they accept it, some grand-

parents still talk about the child 'growing out of it', or insist 'Just look at her, she can't be that bad, someone has got it wrong'. Even comments such as 'Just see how well he is doing, I am sure he is going to be a bright boy even if he has got Down's syndrome' can upset parents who are trying to be more realistic and let go of their own dreams.

In the first months many parents are frightened to be hopeful, and are trying to find a balance between their fears of the worst and their dreams for the best. Relatives and friends may say things which *they* think will make the parents feel better—it is their way of trying to help, and if you can see it as such it can reduce the tensions. But sometimes parents think that grandparents have not understood or accepted the condition. I should tell you that many professionals appear to have the same difficulty. If they hear the parent being optimistic and hopeful and talking about how well the baby is getting on, they sometimes conclude that the parent 'has not really accepted the diagnosis'. It is rather sad that people have to concentrate on the negative aspect of the condition in order to convince others that they are not being unrealistic! It is because they fear that the hopes of parents will be dashed in the future, that parents will be sadly disappointed when the child does not live up to their expectations. On the other hand, the parent who remains in a morbid state with few expectations or hopes for the future runs the risk of increasing the child's difficulties by not providing an *environment of opportunity*. As one of our parents wrote: 'We need to learn to build on things they can do instead of perhaps dwelling on the things they might never do.'

Parents can also be distressed when grandparents take too pessimistic a view and, using their knowledge and experiences of people with Down's syndrome from the past, predict a grim future. In extreme cases grandparents will press you to consider residential care or having the baby fostered. We have a number of families where the grandparents actually arranged residential care *before* the mother and baby even got out of hospital.

Such extremes can be avoided if grandparents can have access to the information that parents have. They, too, need books and information sources. If you have someone, another parent or professional, who can tell you about the facts and figures of Down's syndrome and the future hopes and possibilities, then try to arrange for him or her to meet the grandparents as soon as possible. My experience with grandparents in these matters is that they are usually as upset and bewildered as the parents, but they tend often to be forgotten in all the attempts to help the immediate family. It is often easier for someone not in the family to talk to them.

2 More serious problems arise when grandparents start hinting that they have never had anything like this before in *their* half of the family. These comments can be very hurtful to the son-in-law or daughter-in-law. Often they are quite blatantly meant as an accusation—and at the same time a protection of their own child.

The effects can be devastating. Parents of any child born with a handicap can feel at some time that there is something 'wrong' about them, that they have perhaps 'let down' their partner, that people will think there is something 'wrong' with them. A proper understanding of what causes the condition, especially in the case of Down's syndrome, will usually do much to get rid of these feelings. But even then, the remarks still hurt.

Worse still, they can create tension between the parents. The son or daughter of the grandparent making the comments is usually less critical and more accepting of such comments than the son-in-law or daughter-in-law. This can then start arguments between the two. If you are a grandparent reading this, and find yourself inclined to make such remarks, please find out a lot more about the causes, and please think about the consequences of whatever you say. Over 40 per cent of the families who have worked with us complain about problems with grandparents! Learning to live with the baby who has Down's syndrome is difficult enough without this kind of extra stress. There is so much good and positive help that you grandparents can give, if only you try not to be too influential, too knowing, too protective. Offer your help and understanding, then let your sons and daughters accept and direct it according to their needs.

If you are a parent who is on the receiving end of such

remarks, try to understand that they usually reflect the grandparents' own difficulties in learning to live with the fact that they have a grandson or granddaughter with Down's syndrome and their protectiveness towards you as your parent.

3 The last and most difficult problem arises when there is conflict between the parents over whether to care for the baby themselves or seek fostering. This is not common, but when it happens it can produce such anguish for all concerned that grandparents need to tread very carefully. My one hope is that grandparents will *let the mother and father arrive at the right decision for themselves.*

> I felt as if I had let them down. My mother used to say to me—'I don't know why you're sending him to nursery so soon'—you'd have thought I was sending him to prison.

> My mother was not much help. She felt the baby was being messed around with by all the doctors. I know she was just trying to support me . . . but she would not let the baby do anything. She'd prefer her (the baby) to just sit there. She always asks—'Why does she (the baby) have to do these exercises, she'll do them in time herself'.

> We would not have survived without Mum and Dad. From the beginning they loved him and could never do enough to help. They wanted to learn all about what the doctors told us and about how to do the exercises. Dad was great at them. We could call on them any time. I never ever felt they resented the baby.

**Does the presence of a child with Down's syndrome disrupt the marriage?**

You may read, or be told, that having a handicapped child causes great stress in marriages and leads to a greater number of separations than among families with no handicapped child. In cases of severe physical and mental handicap or severe behaviour disorders, there is some evidence to support this. But the few research studies with families who have a child with Down's syndrome have not found the same problem. All agree that for early childhood at least, there is no evidence to show more marital difficulties than in similar groups of families who do not have a handicapped child. If anything, the families in our research have a lower rate of marital breakdown than one would expect from national figures. Frequently, when asked what effect having a handicapped child has had on them, they reply that it has brought them closer together. Also, we have no evidence to show that as the child gets older (i.e. up to early teens) more difficulty or stress is found, as is often supposed. In fact, many parents are saying things are getting easier, especially as the children become more independent and the child with Down's syndrome improves in communication abilities and self-help skills. One can find individual cases, usually where the child is severely mentally handicapped and has some behaviour disorder, in which marital difficulties have occurred. Such problems are often due to the strain of coping with the child, and at the same time with conflict between parents about what to do. However, this is rare in my experience of children with Down's syndrome and in all cases there have been other difficulties. We should see fewer cases like this in the coming years, as we improve our help and support for families. For example, there are:

1 increased facilities for older children and adults, such as Adult Training Centres, Youth Clubs, Holiday Schemes, Recreation Groups, Residential Hostels in the community;
2 parents more and more are given guidance on management and education, which should prevent many of the children from developing serious behaviour disorders and help them to be more skilled and independent; and help parents avoid becoming isolated and making the child too dependent upon them.

By this last comment I do *not* mean to imply that the parent becomes 'over-protective'. This term is really a judgement of the care provided, and not of the parent. The word is too widely used by professionals and parents, and becomes yet another 'label', and interpreted as meaning that mothers are smothering their child with love, or caring too much for the child. Surely what we should be paying attention to is the possibility that a parent (in her or his concern and love for the child) is not providing enough opportunities for the child to grow up as independently as possible. Therefore I feel that as society changes its attitudes and as we increase our community care for handicapped people, parents will find far more support and less strain with the older child and young person—provided the parents can take an outward looking approach and encourage the child to be independent wherever possible.

As noted earlier, the studies on marriage, together with observations by parents and professionals, consistently report that many marriages are strengthened by the birth of a child with Down's syndrome. The shock and crisis of the birth increases the need for each other. When the couple respond to this, and can give each other the necessary emotional and practical support, it often enhances the relationship. An old college tutor of mine once told me that marriages stay together because the partners learn to trust each other and respect each other. I think this is what happens when a couple find themselves with the baby. It provides an opportunity to demonstrate each other's qualities and concern as never before.

> The doctor told me he was a mongol . . . I had to tell Frank, I was dreading it. I thought he would blame me and not want anything to do with the baby. Well, for the first few days after I told him he didn't say anything about the baby. I was still in hospital. He came in with some flowers and said 'Sorry', that's all—just sorry. After a minute he looked at me and said, 'I haven't been much help, but it's over. He's our baby and I think we will cope. We'll have a damn good try'. You know, we had been married for five years and I didn't think he had it in him . . . but we never looked back from that day. This little one really brought us together . . . he's brought a lot of love into this family.

It would be nice if all couples found this. But unfortunately it is true that the birth of the baby can be a catastrophe for some. When one examines these marriages more closely, however, one usually finds that there have been difficulties *before* the baby was born. Therefore it seems that if the parents have a good relationship, the birth of the baby will bring them even closer, but if the relationship is poor then the birth can cause considerable disruption. One also finds that it is in the unhappy marriages that there is conflict between parents over the treatment of the infant, and that the parents find it most difficult to come to terms with the baby's condition.

I believe this information is important, as it is very common to hear people lay the blame for family stress or marriage breakdown on the fact that a child in the family has Down's syndrome. Because the condition is so obvious and can cause distress and concern to parents, people assume far too easily that it is responsible for all the ills that happen. This is the problem in focusing all one's attention on the handicap, instead of trying to step back a little and examine the whole situation.

Finally, my experience suggests that parents have to work at building up their relationship. They have to examine their own feelings, discuss them honestly with their partner and try to see other points of view. It is a time for tolerance and gentleness and patience.

**Possible conflicts between partners**

I have hesitated about writing this section for a long time. Relationships between husbands and wives are very complex, and I do not feel at all competent or confident in talking about them. However, I made a promise that this book should be as honest as I can make it and I have tried not to avoid areas of difficulty.

Our observations indicate that about one in five couples do experience some conflict. These observations are mainly based on what mothers tell us, because it has been more difficult to meet the fathers, who tend to be out at work. Also I think mothers are more willing than fathers to discuss problems. At the risk of over simplifying, I feel that women find that talking over problems is therapeutic. Many more mothers seem willing to join groups—usually of other mothers—and talk about their feelings, than fathers do. This may be just a case of having more opportunity, but I know many fathers, like myself, who recoil from the idea of meeting with a group. As one father said to me, 'My wife likes nothing better than to talk a problem to death. She keeps on and on—it drives me round the bend.' I do feel that many men like to go straight at a problem and solve it, and if they can't, they see no point in talking about it. Sometimes their wives feel they are uninterested, uncaring or trying to avoid an issue.

As I say, this may just reflect my own reactions and not those of men in general. But we recognise that men and women do react differently; are even expected to react differently by our society. We all feel more embarrassed if a man weeps than if a woman does so.

I also feel that men and women differ in their reactions to the handicap. Fathers are more likely to ask me questions about the effect of the child on the family and on the mother. They are more likely to ask about provision of residential care, and seem more often to make a decision to use residential care. I do not think that this is because they are less humane. I am beginning to think that it is instinctive for the father to try to protect his family, whereas the mother is more likely to feel protective towards the new baby. I know this is very simplified and there will be many exceptions. I also know that society is changing rapidly, and that more and more fathers are very involved with their babies. Fathers also tell me that they are more objective and less emotional than mothers.

In fact a common source of conflict—though usually not serious—is that mothers feel the baby is achieving more than the fathers think is true. One explanation for this is that development of new behaviours is not a steady process. By this I mean you do not find that a baby learns a new behaviour suddenly and completely, and then goes on to the next. Development is uneven (see Chapter Seven). A behaviour will appear and you think it is learnt, and then it disappears for a few days. Then it reappears and lasts a bit longer, and so on until it becomes well established. Mothers are likely to see the first emergence of the behaviour because they are more often with the baby. When I ask mothers and fathers to tick off what the baby can do on a developmental checklist, and then compare it with my list, I usually find that mothers tick most, fathers the next and myself least. As the child grows older, we seem to find less difference between parents but even so, one father, when filling in a checklist on his teenage daughter, remarked, 'I'm not at home enough to know about all those—the wife will know better.' Is this wishful thinking on the part of the parents, or is it merely the result of the different opportunities we have to see what the child can do?

Unfortunately parents can get into conflict over the future education of the child. One parent may feel the other has unrealistic expectations of the child's ability. This conflict can be reduced if parents recognise that it is difficult to assess abilities, and they are quite likely to disagree. They should seek the best professional advice they can, and then use the professional person's findings to prove one or the other was right. Bringing up a child with Down's syndrome is very much a matter of trial and error. We do not have normal experiences on which to make judgements. (By normal I mean having things in common at similar ages.) Therefore no one can be too sure of what is 'right' or 'wrong'.

A more serious potential for conflict arises when parents' deeper feelings are involved.

For example, one parent may feel the need to have another child; the other parent does not, perhaps for fear that a subsequent child would be handicapped, too, or perhaps out of a wish to devote his or her energies to the child with Down's syndrome. I can only suggest that such parents try to examine their own feelings and seek professional help if no solution is found. I think I should add that this is not a common problem, but it can be difficult to handle.

A more common difficulty arises when parents differ in their degree of acceptance of the handicap. If one parent, for instance, reacts as though nothing is wrong, it can be very painful for the other. Or if one parent needs to care for the child, while the other cannot help rejecting or resenting the child, then conflict will also arise. Couples resolve such conflicts in their own way. I know many mothers who do so by taking over the main responsibilities for the care and treatment of the child, while the fathers direct their energies into their work. These mothers recognise that the father has great difficulty in dealing with the child:

> I know he loves John but he just can't bring himself to do things with him. So I do all the work with schools and hospitals and look after John and he (the husband) gets on with the business and the other children. We all understand the problems and it works all right for us. I did resent it at first but if you are going to keep your family together it is worthwhile—you have to make some compromises.

**Do families with a child with Down's syndrome suffer more ill-health than other families?**

Many parents who have a severely handicapped child—particularly if the child requires much lifting and physical handling or has behaviour disorders—are likely to be under great stress and so require more medical attention than the rest of us. Do families with a child with Down's syndrome have similar difficulties? Such limited information as is available suggests that groups of families with children with Down's syndrome do *not* have more ill-health than similar families with ordinary children. At several times in the life of our research, when the children were around 2–7 years, 5–10 years, 7–13 years, we have measured stress and health in the mothers and lately the fathers. The average rating for the group was not significantly higher than that found in groups without handicapped children. As with families of non-handicapped children, we found that about 20–30 per cent had high ratings and these were usually associated with such things as unemployment, ill-health, poor family relationships, stress at work. If the child with Down's syndrome also had very severe behaviour difficulties like high levels of activity, poor concentration and unpredictable behaviour, then there was more chance of the parents having high stress ratings.

Also, there are stressful times and specific worries related to the handicap: for example, coming to terms with diagnoses, coping with any additional medical problem and, of course, selecting schools and planning for the future. However, compared to families without handicapped children, these things appear to create different rather than heavier strains. Indeed, from our studies it appears three out of four families do not have additional major strain and, of the rest, only about one in three is primarily due to the child's handicap. It should be remembered that these families have had reasonable support from the early years and most make use of the local services. Families in the past and those with poor local services may well have higher levels of strain.

Thus it seems, as we found in the case of marriage problems, the presence of the child can be seen as the cause of problems which in fact have quite different causes. However, if the parents have difficulty in coming to terms with the child's condition, or the partners are in conflict over the child, or there is stress arising from difficulties with relatives, some parents *will* be under extra emotional strain, and we know that this can lead to ill-health.

**Does the presence of the child restrict social activities?**

This question is rather difficult to answer because families are so different in what they do, and what they want to do. Families who have a car, for example, have different social habits from families who do not.

It is not uncommon to read that parents of handicapped children often feel isolated. I think there are two types of isolation: social and emotional. Social isolation is not being able to get out and do things because of the child. Emotional isolation is when parents feel they have no one to share their worries and concerns with, and no one who understands what it is like to have a child with a handicap. I have not yet been able to find out how extensive this emotional isolation is. It changes, often coming and going, and can be related to other things that get one down. What I have noticed over the years is how parents of children with Down's syndrome often find talking to each other beneficial and supportive. Therefore if you feel this sort of isolation, the best advice is to try to contact other parents or a parent-to-parent support group.

Overall, the few studies that have compared families with a young child with Down's syndrome with families with ordinary children do not find any major differences in social aspects. Most mothers do not find themselves isolated and lonely because of the child. In fact many tell us that they have met more people and have wider contacts because of the child's condition.

In the first weeks or months some mothers do feel shut off, but most say that this was because they did not want to mix. This is what a young single mother told us:

> At first I just stayed in all the time. Then one of the lads from the youth club came round. He's got no hand (Thalidomide) and said, 'What's up with you!' I could have hit him but I just cried. After I told him why I hadn't been out he said, 'Don't be bloody stupid! . . . Look at me, I've got no hand and they've accepted me all right.

> 'Course they'll accept the baby, there's not much wrong with him!'
>
> That night they all came round. Now they spoil him rotten! I've no trouble getting baby-sitters, but I wouldn't leave him with them—they're all mad!

Once they get over the first hurdle and take the baby out, parents are often quite amazed at the friendly reactions of people. But you may have to work to overcome your initial reluctance. You will have to take your courage in your hands, get the baby dressed, put him in the pram and go for a walk or visit your friends. You are most likely to find that people will stop and talk, they will tickle the baby and ask questions. Tell them as soon as possible that he or she has Down's syndrome. If you do not take the chance on the first occasion, it will be more difficult next time: people may become embarrassed and avoid you. But if you can tell them at once, you will find that most people are immediately interested, and will take a special delight in future in asking how the baby is. Of course you will encounter occasional tactless remarks. Try to see them as well-intentioned, then forget them. Also, remember that when you talk to people about the child and his or her condition, you will be doing something to educate the public in general, and eventually to produce a more tolerant society which encourages community care for its handicapped members rather than segregation.

Because the baby with Down's syndrome can be particularly susceptible to illnesses, and if he does catch a childhood illness, such as measles, it will tend to be more severe than for ordinary children, mothers may find that they visit the doctor more than usual, or nurse the child for longer periods. However, this will probably be true only in the first few years of life. Parents may also find they spend a fair amount of time visiting clinics for treatment and advice, and attending lectures or parent groups. Again this can take up time, but only a few seem to find it a problem. Most find these outings and meetings actually extend their social life.

When the child is young, most parents do not appear to have any more difficulties with baby-sitting, getting out and holidays than families with ordinary children. A few have noted that the holiday can disturb the young child's routine, and he takes a while to settle down afterwards. But this may not be a bad thing, since in the end it should help the child to become more adaptable.

Initially, however, parents may be reluctant to ask a friend or neighbour to baby-sit:

> We hadn't been out since he was born—nearly eight months. I kept finding excuses why I couldn't go. One night my husband looked at me and said—'Are we going to sit at home like this with him for the rest of our lives? We have to make a move sometime.' I could see he was right, so there and then we asked our neighbour if she would just come in for an hour or two. She was so pleased I had asked her, as she had wanted to suggest it but didn't like to. I worried for the whole two hours we were out. Now we get out just the same as we did for the other children, and most of our friends or relatives are quite happy to sit for us. They usually say he's easier than the other kids.

Two points: first, restrictions on social activities are usually due to parents' own difficulties in coming to terms with the child's condition, not to the condition itself.

Second, during the life-time of the child there are likely to be periods at least when the family will require help from the Social Services. In some areas specially trained 'foster' parents are available, who will get to know the family and the child and look after him or her for weekends or holidays. In some areas, there are small, friendly, residential homes that will care for the child. The Social Service departments or Voluntary Parent Societies will usually have information on these. For many parents the greatest problem is *using* the facilities. They feel guilty about 'putting the child away' or admitting that they 'cannot cope', or they imagine that people will think they do not love the child—even that their relatives may condemn them for using these facilities.

These ideas arise from outdated attitudes to handicap, and traditional and justifiable fears of the large, old institutions. They are negative attitudes and no longer appropriate.

I like to take a positive view.

There are periods when a handicapped child may produce great strain on the family. For example, in the early stages of the family, to have an eight-year-old who is still at the toddler stage, active and very exploratory, is likely to be tiring, especially if you have other children around the same age. Or in middle family years you may wish to take the children on active holidays—walking, fishing, boating—in which the handicapped member may not be able to take part. Or it may be, as the child gets older, that he or she becomes increasingly difficult to manage. You cannot go to family gatherings because the child will be disruptive. You cannot take a holiday in a hotel for similar reasons. Or it may simply be that the sort of activities you want to do on your holiday are not those that the young handicapped person wants to do.

In these situations either you can sacrifice your own needs, or you can make alternative arrangements. You can also carry on until you become too tired to cope and a crisis arises. The problem with getting tired and carrying on is that it is not until the crisis is upon you that you realise you need to do something. Unfortunately by then you may be too tired to make any decisions and act.

One way to avoid this is to take regular breaks, whether you feel like it or not. These breaks will give you the opportunity to re-examine how things are going and re-charge your energy banks. If the handicapped member of the family tends to take up a lot of time and attention, these breaks will provide the opportunity to give attention to the other members of the family and yourself.

Regular breaks may allow you to get to know your children again. I find that my children change so quickly between holidays, it is difficult to keep up with them. Especially in mid-family years when they are adolescents, you may have to rearrange your activities so that you can find time to be with them individually. For instance, while one of the children goes off to camp or on a school holiday, you can spend more time with the other children. And the handicapped member needs her turn to be away from the family, too.

If things are very difficult at home, you can assess the situation best when you are free of the everyday routine. How nice to have a break and still look forward to having the children together at the end. If after your break you find you still cannot cope with the handicapped child, you will be aware that there is a problem and you need help. Far better that you

EXHIBITION

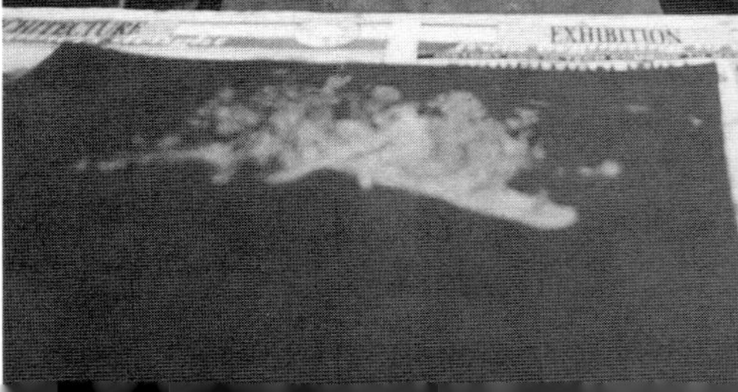

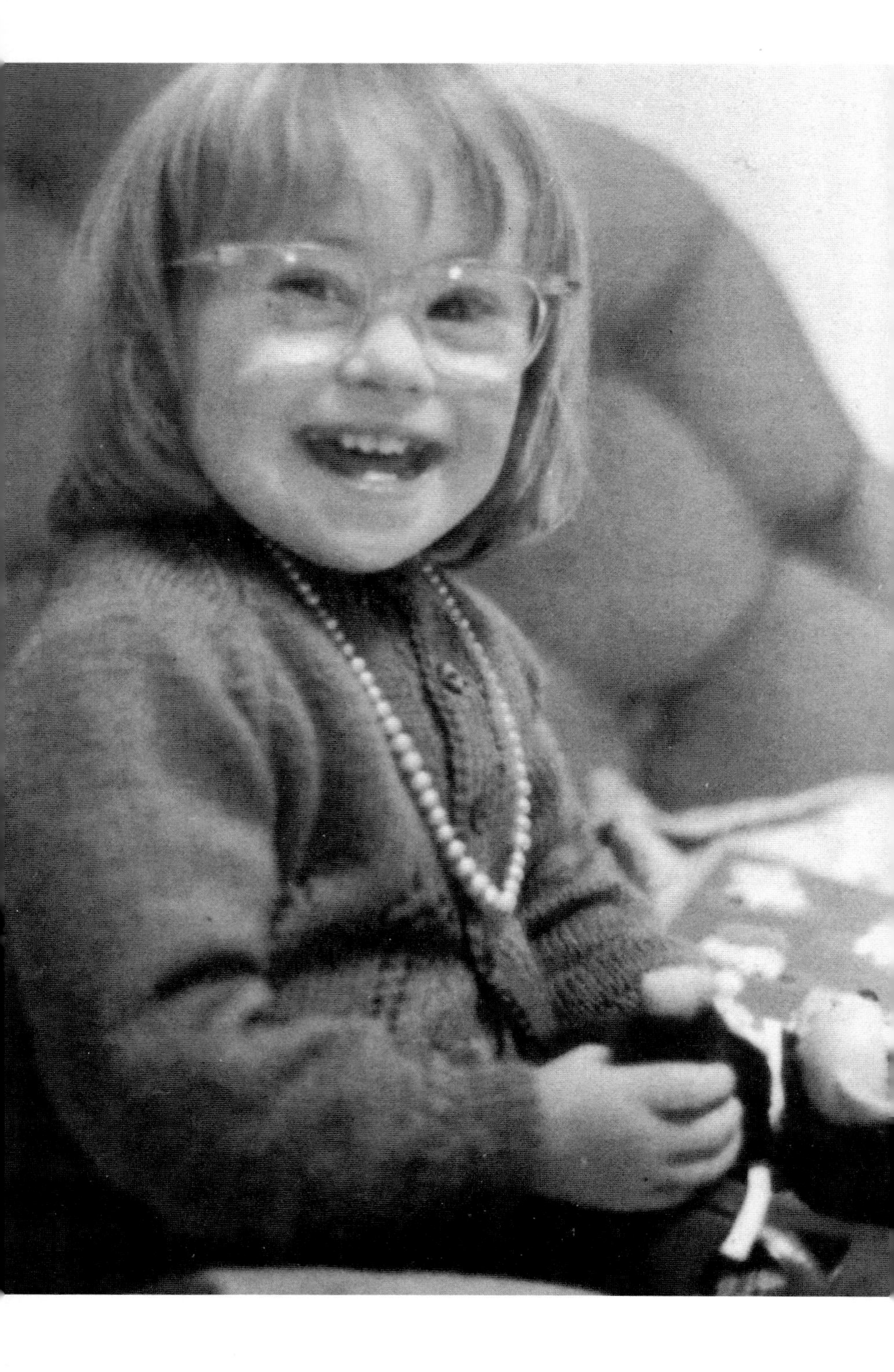

Kate with her brother Matthew.

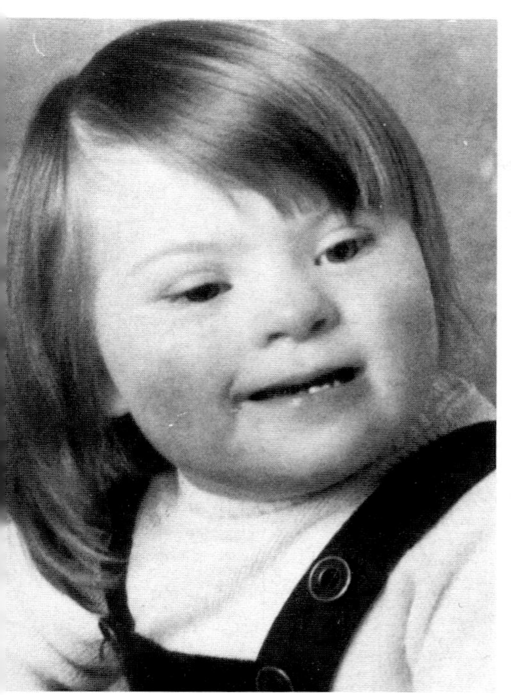

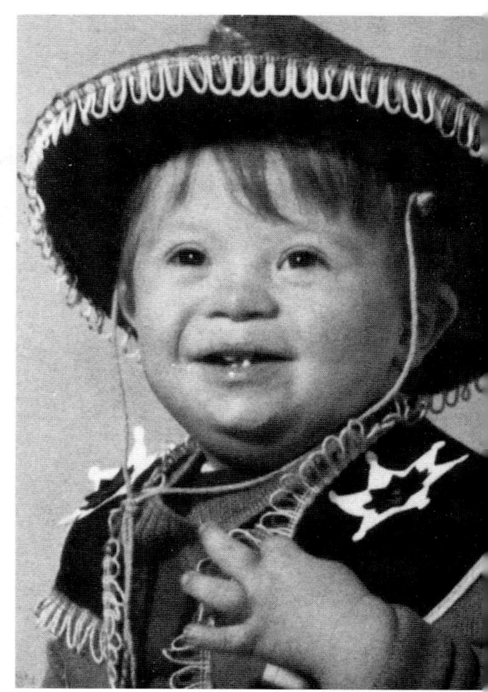

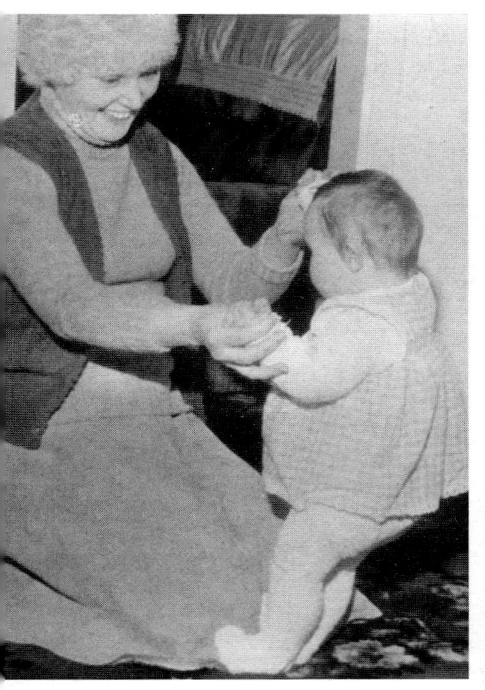

Mother and baby groups.

Photo courtesy of Belinda Whiting.

come to the realisation this way, than to wait until some crisis overwhelms you.

From the handicapped child's point of view, the breaks from the family can be of great benefit. First, a change in routine and meeting different people can stimulate development and learning. I have often heard mothers marvel about how much the child 'came on' after staying with grandmother for a week. Changes challenge the child's behaviour by providing different routines and experiences. Of course, if the challenge is so great that the child becomes confused or cannot make sense of what is happening, then one can expect some anxiety and emotional reactions. Therefore, as parents, you have to programme the extent of the challenge in small stages.

Second, the aim for all of our children must be that they grow up to become independent, that they learn to manage without us. By getting the child used to short separations and then holidays, or short stays in residential settings, one can begin this preparation. It helps the child to learn to be adaptable.

A major worry for many parents of children with Down's syndrome is—What will happen when we die? It is no good ignoring or worrying about this. One has to try to plan for it—one has to help the child toward independence. By this I do not mean just teaching him to dress and feed himself, but also encouraging emotional independence. Yet it is often the parents who *prevent* this growing independence. I am reminded of a conversation I had with a 28-year-old lady who has Down's syndrome. When I asked her how she was getting on, and how her mother and father were, she replied, 'Just the same, thank you. They still won't let me get my own place. I look after them too well. I do all the shopping and tidying. They'd be lost without me—that's what they keep saying.'

Furthermore, where a family takes a positive view of temporary care, and uses it regularly, I have the impression that brothers and sisters find it easier to accept permanent residential care if it is needed in later life, and feel less obliged to insist that they will look after their handicapped brother or sister when their parents die. At the moment I have no factual information to support this belief, but the impression is a strong one.

I should point out that the large majority of parents of

children with Down's syndrome do not find it necessary to seek temporary care during the childhood years. Even during adolescence the majority still manage at home. For many families, bringing up a child with Down's syndrome is very like bringing up any other child. The problems are different rather than greater. Therefore, arranging for the child to spend time away with others should not be seen merely as a respite or preparing him or her to be 'put away'. It has the same purpose as for our other children. Certainly, it can relieve the extra supervisory role that many parents experience and also give time for themselves and the other children.

**Do mothers find they can go out to work?**

In our research sample, quite a number of mothers do get employment. They are usually mothers with older children at school, or mothers with a first baby. Several resume their careers, but the majority take part-time work. Often the baby is cared for by a relative or a child minder, and an older child attends a nursery. We find that the relatives or child minders are keen to learn how to help the baby, and will often carry out exercises and games to stimulate the child. Only a few mothers say they took the job to get away from the baby. The majority take it for financial reasons, or because they are anxious not to lose touch with a profession. All mothers interviewed so far, who have part-time work, have felt it to be beneficial to themselves and the family. They say they do not get too 'engrossed in the baby and his problems', and that work gives them a wider range of interests. Some argue that this helps them keep things in perspective:

> People react to handicapped children very differently now. The first job I went to, they just wouldn't talk to me after I told them. I had to tell them 'cos I feel that I'm deceiving them in one way, making them believe that nothing was wrong and you feel as if you're not telling them the whole truth . . . But in my new job they're great! I don't feel like an outcast.

We found that at the pre-school age the mothers in our research group were less likely to have a job than mothers of ordinary children. Other studies have also found mothers of handicapped children less likely to be in employment compared to the national figures. However, when we looked at the employment of our mothers when the children were five years of age or older, we found no difference compared to the national figures. An interesting finding was that significantly more mothers in our group had jobs than in a similar group of families who had not received regular early support. Since the ability level, type of school or behaviour difficulties of the children in the groups were the same, we felt that the difference in mothers' work must be due to attitude and support. Perhaps the fact that they had had our team and other mothers to confer with gave them the impetus and confidence to try to get work.

It seems, then, that having a baby with Down's syndrome does not necessarily restrain mothers from employment. But some mothers of older children do find that the child's lack of independence—e.g. being unable to travel by him or herself, or to be left in the home on his or her own—can restrict the type of employment they are able to take up.

**Summary of points in this chapter**

There is no evidence that having a child in the family automatically produces ill effects in the other children.

There is no evidence that couples who have a child with Down's syndrome are more likely to separate than other couples.

In fact there is evidence that many families gain from the experience.

Conflict between couples and relatives, particularly grandparents, can arise. Much of this can be avoided if parents recognise their own feelings and those of others and discuss them.

For the parents of young children with Down's syndrome, there is no evidence to show that their social life or working life is automatically restricted. However, as the child grows, some families can experience difficulties. This will depend upon the child's level of independence, whether or not he or she becomes difficult to manage, and upon the available local resources for support of the family.

Parents can be forewarned about potential difficulties and action can be taken to avoid many of them.

Here are some of the pieces of advice that parents have

told us have helped them to come to terms with the handicap.

1 Try to take each day as it comes and do not dwell too much on the future.
2 Get to know your child. Look for those individual ways he or she has of showing his or her uniqueness.
3 Try to tackle the situation as a partnership and let the family be involved and give support.
4 Avoid letting the handicapped child become the focus of the family life. Try to keep the organisation and social life of yourselves and the family as close to normal as possible. Do not avoid your friends and relatives.
5 Take the initiative and tell your friends, relatives and neighbours about the child as soon as possible. The longer you leave it the harder it becomes.
6 Do not hide the facts from other children in the family. This will only cause stress later on. If the children are old enough, explain simply that the baby is different, will be slower in growing up and so on. If they are young, talk about it in front of them, and as they grow and begin to ask questions, answer them honestly.
7 Remember that friends and relatives will take their cue from you. If you are embarrassed and ashamed in talking about the baby, they will act accordingly. They will also believe there is something to be ashamed about and to hide. When this happens, you can lose a great deal of support and help. As one parent told us, 'We found a fund of goodwill in our friends and relatives. We needed to harness it and direct it.'
8 Also, take your baby out and do not be afraid of people seeing him. On most occasions people are understanding.
9 Get used to the tactless and hurtful remarks that people make without thinking. In fact, teach them the truth.
10 Try to find out accurate information from people who know. Beware of myths and superstitions. Be cautious about 'cures' or exciting new treatments. Get professional advice (see pp. 132–5).
11 Talk to people, especially other parents of children with similar handicaps. They are usually very helpful.
12 Remember that all the family, and particularly your

spouse, will feel upset and irritable. Try to be calm and tolerant with each other. The first months are a sensitive time of rapid change.

13 Start to learn how to help the baby, and begin to stimulate and play with him or her as soon as you feel able.

And remember, as time passes and your expertise with the baby grows, it will become easier to cope both practically and emotionally.

*Chapter Four*

# WHAT CAUSES DOWN'S SYNDROME?

This is one of the first questions parents ask. But it is really two questions—'What is it that produces the condition in the baby?' and 'How and why did it happen to us?'

These questions are usually followed by: 'What are the chances of having another baby with Down's syndrome?' and 'How common is Down's syndrome?'.

This chapter will deal with these questions and others. But we should begin by stressing that Down's syndrome was *not* caused by anything that happened during the pregnancy. The condition began either when the egg or sperm cells were being produced, or just after the egg was fertilised by the sperm and began to divide and grow. As we shall see, somehow during the production of the sperm or egg, or in the first division of the fertilised egg, an extra chromosome appears. It is this extra chromosome material that leads to the differences in physical and mental growth of the child with Down's syndrome compared with other children.

Once one understands about the chromosomal fault, many other questions are easier to answer.

Let us begin, then, by dealing with the first of our questions.

## 1 What produces the condition in the baby?

To answer this question we must first understand the make-up of our bodies. Just like bricks make up a building, our bodies are made up of thousands of cells. These cells are of different types: there are skin cells, blood cells, nerve cells, etc. The cells group together to produce the different parts of the body—the bones and skull, the muscles, the heart, liver, kidneys and so on. All these parts fit and work together in harmony in the healthy body. The development of this complex machine from a single, tiny cell is a constant source of wonder. How do the cells know when to divide and what sort of cells to become? How do the legs, arms, heart, eyes get into the right place? Why do babies usually sit up at about the same age and walk, talk, run at similar times?

There must obviously be a master plan which controls and programmes this development. And it is the job of the chromosomes to carry this master plan from generation to generation, and from cell to cell. If something happens to alter the plan, like an extra chromosome, then the developing person must be different.

*Where are the chromosomes found? What are they?*

With the exception of the red blood cells, each cell has two parts—the nucleus and the cytoplasm (Figure 1). The nucleus can be thought of as the control centre of the cell. In it are found the chromosomes. The word chromosome comes from the Greek meaning *Chromo*—colour—and *soma*—body. The chromosomes get their name because, during certain phases of cell division, they can be stained with dye and thus be easily seen with a microscope (Figure 2). As you can see in the photograph, the chromosomes look like tiny threads. When stained and magnified these threads show up as long strands of light and dark bands.

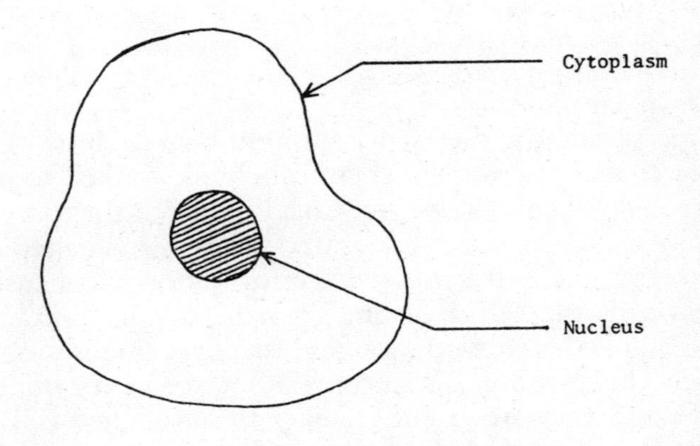


Fig 1. A typical cell from the inside of the cheek.

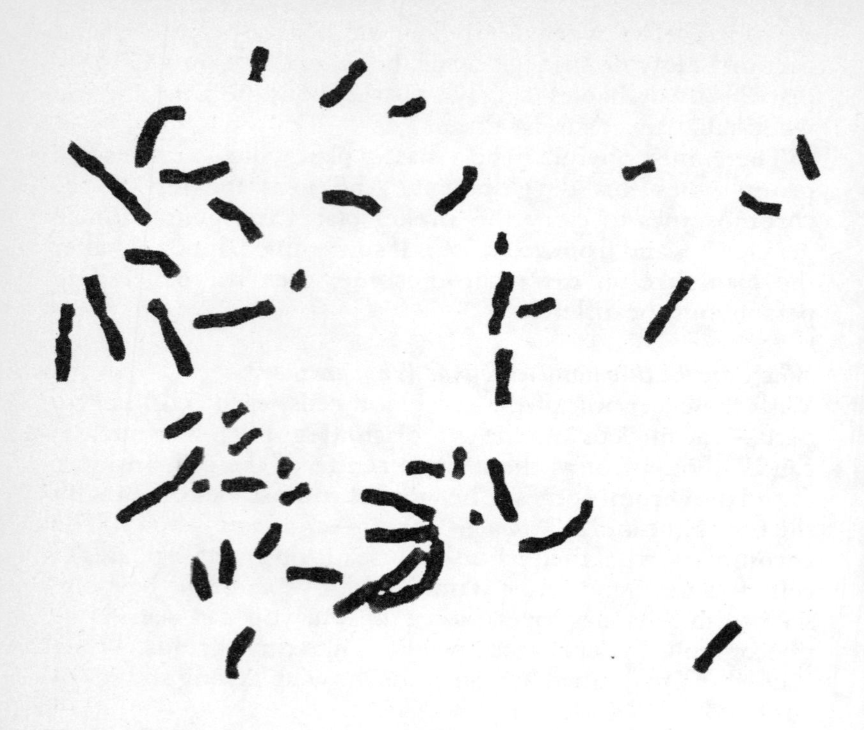

Fig 2. Human chromosomes.

*How do chromosomes work?*
To understand how they work it might help to think of them as long chains of complex chemical chunks linked together. Unlike most chains, however, each link is not the same as its neighbour. Many of the links carry information coded in the chemical structure. It is this coded information which instructs and controls the cell division, growth and function. These 'coded chunks' are called *genes* and there are many thousands on each chromosome. But you cannot see genes under the microscope, they are just complex patterns of chemicals. The information carried by the genes is called the *genetic code*.

Each species of animal has its own genetic code carried by its own special set of chromosomes. The size, shape and number of chromosomes generally differs from species to species. Thus the tiny fruit fly has four giant chromosomes, whilst we human beings typically have 46 chromosomes of different sizes. This is why different species cannot usually cross-fertilise—the chromosomes are special to each and will not work together. Therefore human chromosomes are special to human beings and carry the plan for new people from generation to generation. You cannot get non-human chromosomes in any human being.

As I write this it looks rather obvious, but I have been asked, more than once, if the mental and physical differences of children with an imbalance in their chromosomes is due to a throw-back to the time when we were monkeys! The answer is no, and neither is the extra chromosome a throw-back to a more primitive type of human being.

You may think these are rather far-fetched ideas, but the nick-name 'mongol' came about because Langdon Down —the doctor who first identified people as having Down's syndrome—believed they were a 'throw-back' to a more primitive racial type. He was impressed by the Oriental appearance about the eyes and thought that his patients looked like Mongolians, whom he apparently believed to be 'primitive'. Thus the condition became known as 'mongolism'. This was in 1866 and Darwin had not long put forward his theory of evolution. Not only that, but Langdon Down was apparently related to Darwin by marriage. I do not know if they ever met, but I cannot resist the idea of the two of them chatting over the port on some family occasion; Down wonders aloud what causes this condition—could it be that the different ethnic races represent different evolutionary stages in man? If so, then people with 'mongolism' could be throw-backs, or representative of arrested development at some earlier evolutionary stage. I do not know how Darwin would have reacted to this idea, but when you realise what little was known of genetics at this time, and what confident superiority most Victorians felt, Down's is not such a far-fetched idea. But it is less easy to understand how, as late as 1924, a book was published in England called *The Mongol in Our Midst* which argued that the condition was a reversion to the Orang-utan!

Fortunately, the discovery of the extra chromosome in 1959 and our better understanding of genetics has meant that these theories, together with many others, especially those which blamed events during pregnancy, have once and for all been laid to rest.

It is partly for this reason that many people object to calling this condition 'mongolism' and to using the nick-name 'mongol'. Not only is this name inaccurate, it tends also to be associated with an image from the past of people with Down's syndrome who have been cared for in large institutions. Nowadays we are all aware of the ill effects—particularly on appearance and behaviour—that such large institutions had upon the people who lived in them.

We hope that the increasing use of the term 'Down's syndrome' will begin to get rid of these 'old images'. However, I am reminded in this connection of the mother of one of our infants. I had, rather badly, tried to explain that most people no longer use the name mongol but instead use the name Down's syndrome. 'If I talk about Down's babies,' I said, 'that is what I mean.' After a pause she looked at me and said, 'I don't think that is very nice—all babies have their ups and downs.'

This forced me once more to realise that a label is a label whatever you try to do with it, and also that the children are not Down's children but they are children—children with Down's syndrome.

After this digression, let us return to how chromosomes work, and how they permit individuality.

Whilst people may be very similar, they are never identical. There are differences between races, families and individuals. Thus the genetic code allows for plenty of variation even within a species.

Individuality comes about because the genetic code of each person is *unique*. It is a combination of chromosomes from the mother and chromosomes from the father. Also, most characteristics of a person are not programmed by one gene but result from the interaction of several genes. Height, for example, is controlled by a number of genes from different chromosomes; some will be more dominant than others, and how they interact determines how tall you will be. Thus whilst tallness may run in a family, a new member may inherit a gene for shortness which in that person is dominant.

Within the broad plan carried by the genetic code there is thus a great deal of room for individual difference. You do need, however, the right amount of chromosome material or coded information to programme a person with normal physical and mental characteristics. (By 'normal', I mean the characteristics that most human beings tend to have in common.) If for any reason someone has too much or too little chromosome material, then we can expect a disruption to the programme. This is the case in Down's syndrome and other chromosomal abnormalities. But before we discuss the details, we need first to understand how nature tries to ensure that, while each new human being is given a unique plan for development, the balance in genetic material is maintained.

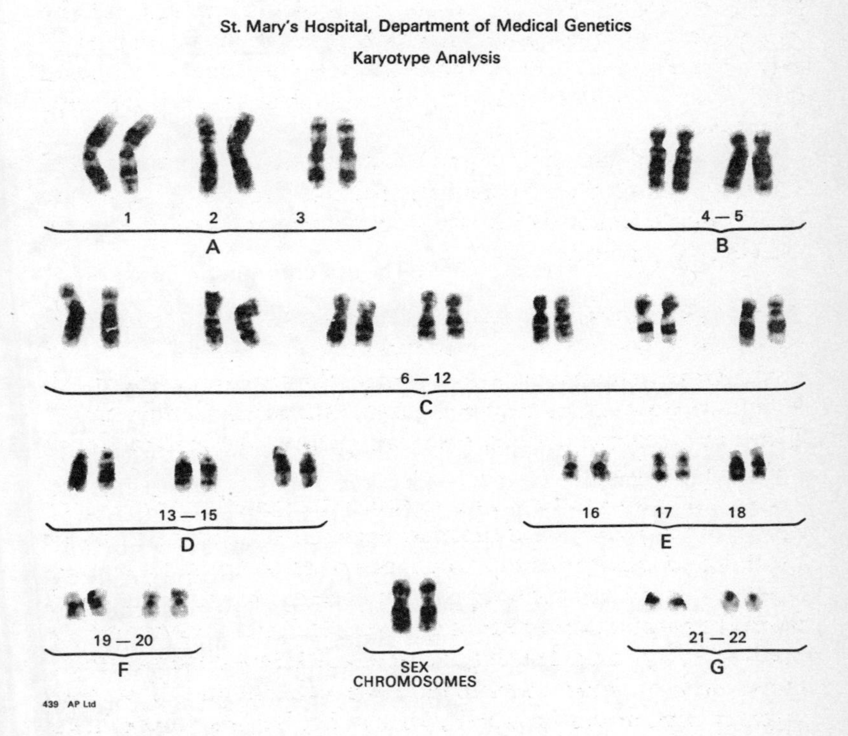


Fig 3. Karyotype of a normal female. The sex chromosomes are XX.

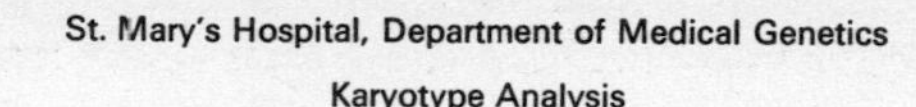


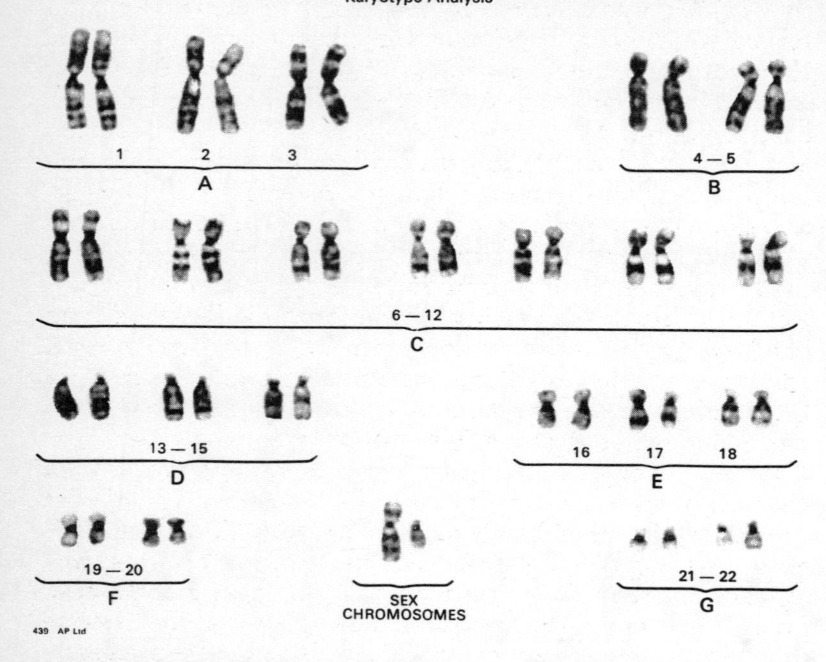


**Fig 4. Karyotype of a normal male. The sex chromosomes are XY.**

*A normal set of chromosomes (the Karyotype)*

During the stages of cell division it is possible to stain the chromosomes. To do this a sample of cells—usually blood, but skin cells can also be used—is taken and grown in a culture for several days. For a blood sample, it is the large white blood cells that are used, as the red blood cells do not have a nucleus and hence no chromosomes. The division of the cells is stopped and the cells broken down so that the cromosomes are released. These are then put on a slide, stained and examined with a microscope. Photographs can be taken (Figure 2), which are then cut up so that the chromosomes can be arranged in order (Figures 3 and 4). This is called the karyotype, i.e. the person's number and arrangement of chromosomes.

As I said earlier, human beings have 46 chromosomes in all cells except the red blood cells and the germ cells (the sperm or the egg).* These 46 chromosomes consist of 22 matched pairs (called autosomes) and two sex chromosomes. The sex chromosomes determine whether the new person will be male or female. In Figure 3 you will see a photograph of a normal karyotype with the chromosome which will produce a female, and in Figure 4 the XY pair that will produce a male. For the purpose of identification, scientists label the pairs 1 to 22 according to size and length of arms. For the same reason they put the chromosomes in groups A to G; the six biggest being in A group, the next four in size in the B group and so on. Recently, the development of techniques to allow different bands on the chromosomes to be seen has meant that the band patterns can be used to identity the chromosomes, so the A to G grouping is no longer necessary. However, you may see it referred to in books about Down's syndrome.

As each new human being needs a complement of 46 chromosomes—matched in pairs—it is necessary for the mother and father to donate half, i.e. 23, each. Thus, when the germ cells (egg or sperm) are made, the pairs of chromosomes separate, and one chromosome of each pair goes into the new germ cell. Each egg and each sperm therefore usually contains 23 chromosomes—one of each pair. When they combine, they produce a cell with 23 pairs, 22 of which will be matched (the autosomes) and the two sex chromosomes will be paired.

This new cell, the fertilised egg, then begins to divide into two cells, the first cell division; then into four cells in the second cell division, then into eight in the third cell division and so on.

It is important that each cell gets an identical set of chromosomes and hence the same coded instructions. To make sure of this, before the cell divides each chromosome splits down the middle and each half takes up chemicals from the cell to make two identical chromosomes. One copy of every chromosome

*In some books written before 1956 you may find reference to 48 chromosomes in man. The development of new techniques for study has since established that the true number in man is 46. Because of this technical development, the extra chromosome in Down's syndrome was identified in 1959.

goes into each of the two new daughter cells. *This means that every cell will have a matching set of chromosomes and therefore the same unique genetic code as the first cell.*

*How does the extra chromosome get into the cell?*
Sometimes the chromosomes of a pair will not separate and remain 'stuck together'. This is called 'nondisjunction' because the two chromosomes fail to disjoin or split up. It can happen in the production of a germ cell, and so the egg or the sperm will have 24 instead of 23 chromosomes. When this germ cell combines with another to form the fertilised egg, the new cell will have 47 chromosomes and not 46 (Figure 5).

Less commonly, it can happen when a cell divides. One of the chromosome pairs may not separate, and so one of the new cells receives 45 chromosomes and the other receives 47 (Figure 6). The cell with 45 does not usually survive, but the cell with 47 can, and will divide forming two new cells each with 47 chromosomes. If this fault in chromosome distribution occurs late in growth, when there are many thousands of cells already developed, it is unlikely to have any major effect unless it coincides with a critical time in the growth programme. If it occurs in early cell division, however, when there are only a few cells, it will have a severe effect. If it happens during the first division of the fertilised egg, then all the cells produced from it are likely to have 47 chromosomes —just as in the case of an extra chromosome being present in the sperm or egg.

A cell with 47 chromosomes will therefore have three which match. There will be the two that did not separate plus a matched one from the other germ cell. This is known as a trisomy (*tri* meaning 'three', *soma* meaning 'of the body').

*Down's syndrome: Trisomy 21*
When the number 21 pair stick together, a person has trisomy 21. People with trisomy 21 have a special set of physical and mental characteristics which collectively are called Down's syndrome. (A syndrome is a collection of signs or characteristics, and Down, as we have seen, was the doctor who put them together and suggested they were related to the same problem.)

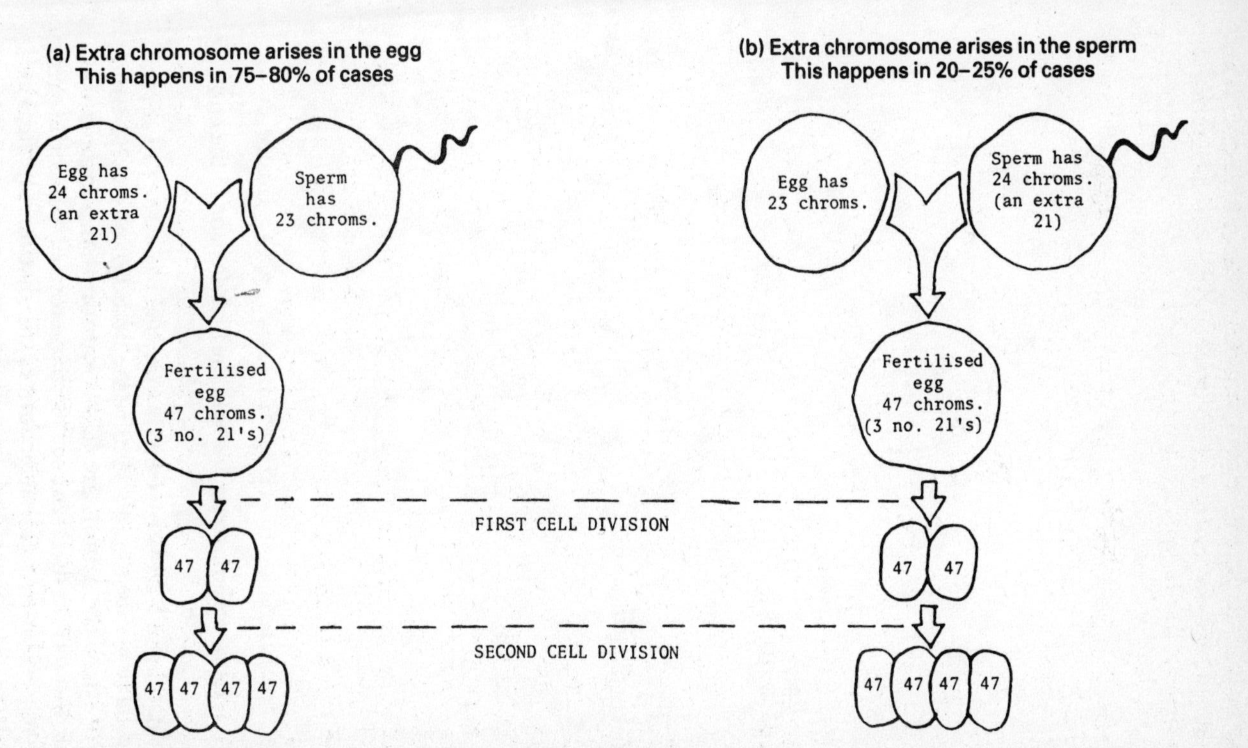


Fig 5. Faulty distribution of chromosome 21 leading to standard trisomy 21. 90–95 per cent of people with Down's syndrome have this form of chromosome distribution.

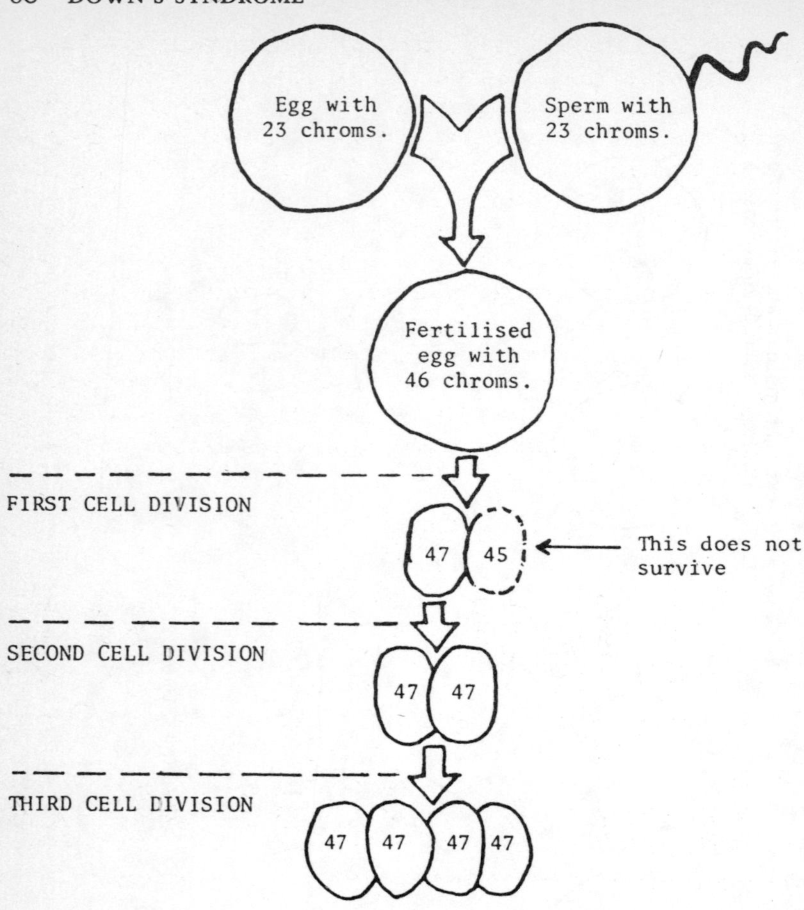


The child will have an extra chromosome in all future cells

**Fig 6. Extra chromosome arises in the first division of the egg.**

If it had been a trisomy of pair number 13 or 18, the person would have either Patau's syndrome or Edward's syndrome. Both of these conditions are less common than Down's syndrome and have a different set of characteristics. It is the *extra 21 chromosome* material that produces the distinct physical and mental characteristics and development known as Down's syndrome. In Figure 7 you can see the extra number 21 chromosome for a boy with Down's syndrome.

It is important to note that the extra chromosome producing the condition is a perfectly normal 21 chromosome which *can only come from either the mother or the father*. It is not a strange or unhealthy chromosome.

This is why family resemblances can be clearly seen in children with Down's syndrome. I have often heard both parents and professionals note with surprise that the child with Down's syndrome looks like his brothers or sisters. Yet since the child has inherited the genetic code of the family (with an extra set of family genes) the likelihood of him or her being similar to the rest of the family must be high. If we are surprised it is because we do not fully understand the genetic

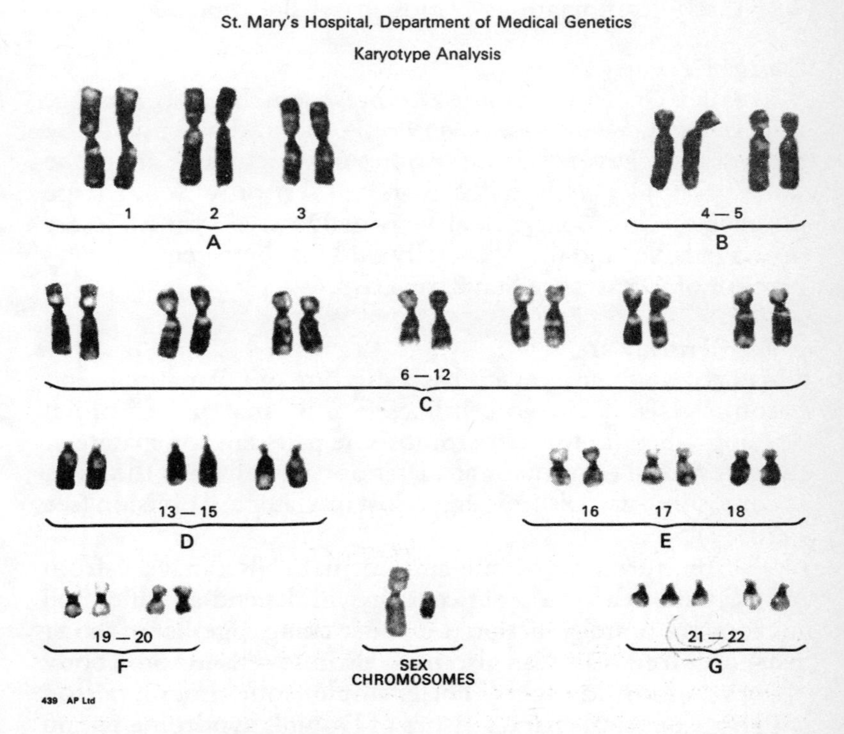


**Fig 7. The chromosomes of a boy with Down's syndrome. You can see the extra chromosome 21 in the G group.**

base of the condition, and are still thinking of these children as strange or alien!

There can also be a great deal of difference among brothers and sisters, so it is not surprising that the child with Down's syndrome should have individual differences. Indeed, given the fact that the extra 21 chromosome could disrupt all the planned development based on the coded information of the genes of the 21 chromosome, it is surprising that people with Down's syndrome do not differ even more than they do from the ordinary, everyday model!

*Are there different types of Down's syndrome?*

There are three distinctive karyotypes related to Down's syndrome: *Standard Trisomy 21, Mosaicism and Translocation.* Within these one can find different types of translocation and, very rarely, combinations of mosaic translocation.

*Standard Trisomy 21*

When the extra chromosome 21 is present in the sperm or egg, or in the first cell division, every cell produced will usually be trisomic (i.e. have 47 chromosomes of which three are in the same group). This is called Standard Trisomy 21. A large number of chromosomal surveys of Down's syndrome are now available, and they generally find that between 90 and 95 per cent of all cases are Standard Trisomy 21.

*Mosaic Trisomy 21*

This occurs when a person has a mixture of normal cells and trisomic cells. The two cell lines (i.e. normal and trisomic) develop when (a) the 21 chromosome pairs fail to separate at the second cell division or at a later one; or (b) when the extra chromosome in a trisomic egg is lost in a later cell division (see Figure 8).

The mixture of trisomic and normal cells can vary from very few to nearly 100 per cent. It will depend at which cell division the nondisjunction (i.e. the sticking together of the 21 pair) occurred. One can also find trisomic cells in some body tissues and not in others. For example, sometimes a person will have physical characteristics of Down's syndrome but no trisomic cells are found in the chromosome test using blood cells. Usually one then tests skin cells, and the trisomic cells are

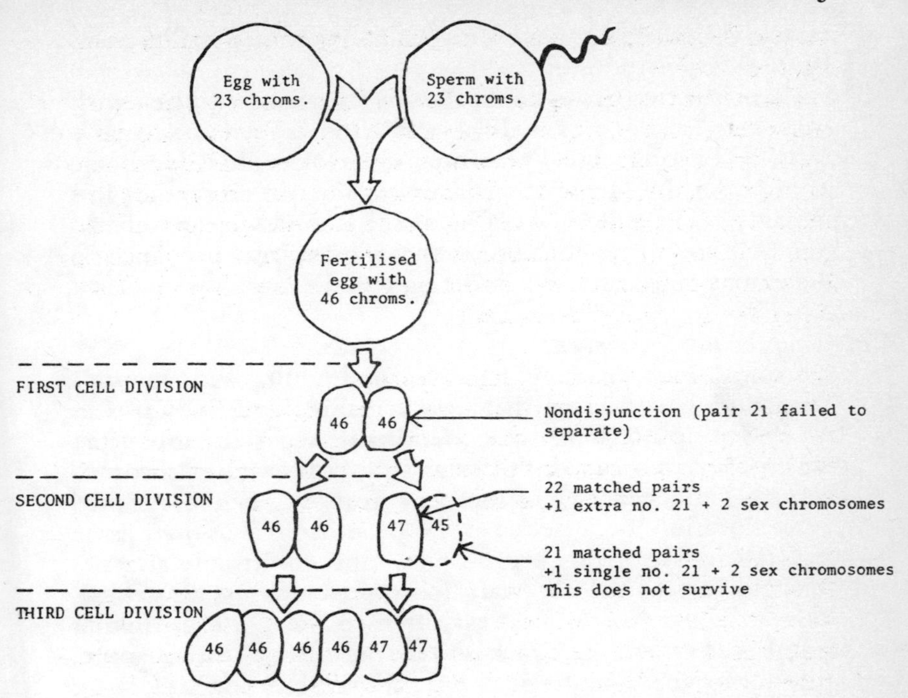


**Fig 8. Faulty chromosome distribution leading to mosaic trisomy 21. Found in 2–5 per cent of all cases of Down's syndrome.**

found. Mosaic Trisomy 21 is rare. Studies vary in their estimates, finding between two and five in every 100 cases of Down's syndrome.

The question arises whether people with Mosaic Trisomy 21 differ from people with other types of Down's syndrome. However because of the rarity of mosaicism it is difficult to collect enough cases together to study. Even when this is done, the studies involve many technical difficulties and the results are often disputed. However the majority of surveys suggest that, as a group, children with Mosaic Trisomy 21 generally have less marked or fewer of the physical characteristics of Down's syndrome, and slightly higher mental performance and language development, than those with

Standard Trisomy 21. The differences in group performances are not large, though, and there is a good deal of overlap between the two groups. This means that many children with Standard Trisomy 21 will be less handicapped than many Mosaic Trisomy 21. Therefore, at an individual level one cannot use the fact that the baby is mosaic to predict less handicap. The child is what he or she is, and we can only do our best to ensure that he or she is given every chance to develop to the best of his or her potential.

*Translocation Trisomy 21*

Chromosomal studies of children and adults with Down's syndrome have shown that between three and five cases in every 100 do not have three identifiable separate number 21 chromosomes. Instead, the long arm of the extra 21 chromosome has attached itself to another chromosome. This is called a translocation, because the extra chromosome has *trans*ferred its *location*. The extra chromosome most commonly attaches itself to one of the D group (chromosomes 13, 14 or 15), usually number 14*, and less often to the G group (either number 21 or 22). If it attaches to the number 14 chromosome, the karyotype will be written as Translocation 14/21, or Translocation D–G (14–21).

A translocation 14/21 happens when both the number 21 and the number 14 chromosomes break at the point where chromosomes are joined together. The two broken arms then fuse together. This produces a pair of chromosomes that do not fit into the size scale. As can be seen in the photograph (Figure 9) there are 46 pairs of chromosomes, but there is one that is larger than the rest of the group. There is, therefore, extra 21 chromosome material which will disrupt the development and growth and produce the characteristics of Down's syndrome. Studies have been carried out to see if children with Translocation Trisomy 21 differ from those with Standard

* You may find some early text books state that it is more common for the extra chromosome to attach itself to No. 15 chromosome. The development of new techniques has suggested otherwise; however, whether it is 14 or 15 is of academic interest. This is another example of the changing nature of facts and ideas about Down's syndrome due to new techniques and research.

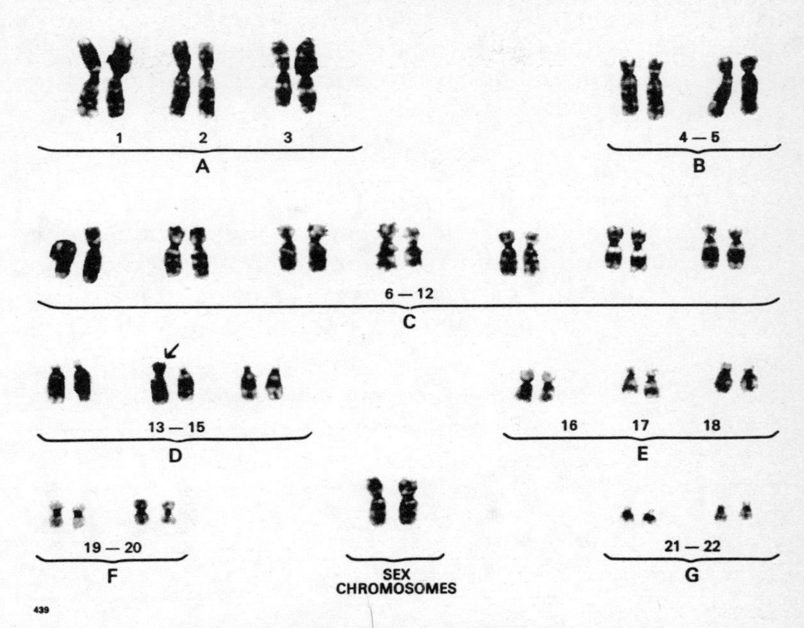


Fig 9. The karyotype of a girl with translocation trisomy 21. [46XXt(14:21)] The arrow points to the extra chromosome 21 material that has attached itself to chromosome 14.

Trisomy 21 or Mosaic Trisomy 21. Overall, there are no conclusive results one way or another, and as in the case of mosaicism, there is no practical purpose in trying to predict differences.

However, as we will see in the next section, if the baby has Translocation Trisomy 21, this can have special importance for the parents and family.

To complete the picture and give some idea of how complicated karyotypes can become, there have been reports of translocation mosaics, and combinations of trisomy 21 and other extra chromosomes—such as an extra sex chromosome. In all these cases, and in all translocations, it is wise to seek advice from a genetic counsellor.

## 2 What are the chances of having another baby with Down's syndrome?

The answer to this question will depend on the baby's karyotype and the age of the parents. I will begin with the facts about karyotype and discuss maternal age in the next section, as it begins to overlap with causes.

*Is Down's syndrome inherited?*

The vast majority of cases of Down's syndrome are not inherited. In only about one in every 100 cases can it be shown that the condition was inherited from the mother or the father. In all these cases the baby will have a Translocation Trisomy 21 karyotype. But only about one third, and not all, Trans-

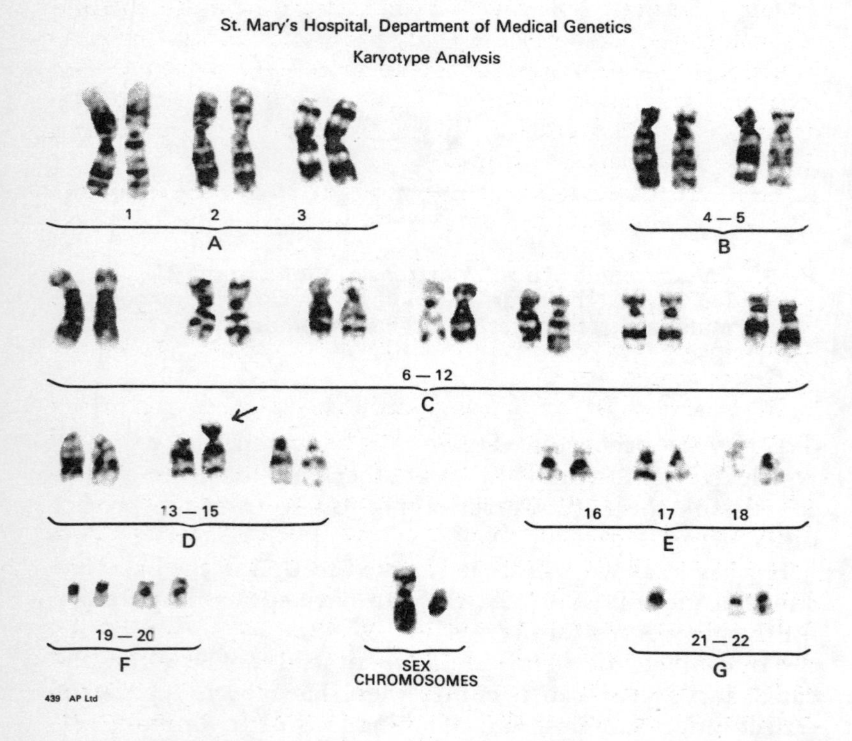


Fig 10. The karyotype of a male balanced translocation carrier. [45XYt(14:21)] The arrow shows the chromosome 21 attached to chromosome 14.

location Trisomy 21 will be inherited. The inherited cases occur because either mother or father is a 'carrier'. This parent will be physically and mentally normal and will be a genetically balanced carrier of the translocation chromosome. This means that whilst he or she has two number 21 chromosomes, one will be attached to another chromosome and the person will only have 45 chromosomes overall. However, the balance of chromosome material is not upset; *the carrier will not have more or less chromosome material than normal.* This is why the person can have an unusual karyotype and yet be quite normal (Figure 10). If the translocation chromosome and the number 21 chromosome of the carrier are both passed on to the egg or sperm cell, then this will result in a fertilised egg with two 21 chromosomes and a translocation chromosome. Consequently the baby will have Down's syndrome in the form of Translocation Trisomy 21. Only parents of babies with the translocation need have chromosome tests to see if they are carriers. Several variations of Translocation Trisomy 21 are found, and each involves a different level of risk of producing a baby with Down's syndrome.

First, the translocation can be between the D and G group (a D/G), i.e. chromosome 21 and chromosomes 13, 14 or 15 (14:21 is most common and 13:21 most rare).

Second, the translocation can be within the G group (a G/G), i.e. when the extra 21 chromosome has attached itself either to a number 22 chromosome (21/22) or to another 21 chromosome (21:21).

In the case of any D/G translocation and the 21/22 G group translocation, the couple could have (i) a baby with a normal complement of 46 chromosomes; (ii) a baby who is also physically and mentally normal but is a balanced carrier; (iii) a baby with Down's syndrome; or (iv) the conception could result in a fertilised egg with a missing chromosome, and this will not survive. This suggests that the chance of having a baby with the condition is one in four. In practice the odds are about one in five if mother is the carrier, and one in 20 to 50 if father is the carrier. The reduced risk if father is the carrier is thought to be due to the fact that thousands of sperm are present in each emission of semen, and those with an incorrect set of chromosomes may be less likely to fertilise the egg.

If the translocation is the 21/21 type, then every baby born will have Translocation Trisomy 21. This is because the carrier does not have a normal, unattached chromosome 21 to pass on to the germ cell.

Translocation Trisomy 21 is more common in parents under 30. Some studies find as high as nine per cent of babies with Down's syndrome born to mothers under 30 have a translocation, compared to one to two per cent of those over 30. *If the infant has translocation Down's syndrome then it is advisable for both parents to have chromosome tests carried out. If either parent is found to be a balanced carrier, it is advisable to have tests carried out on other offspring and on the blood relations of the carrier parent.*

In cases of Standard Trisomy 21 it is not usually necessary to carry out a chromosome test on the parents, unless there is a history of Down's syndrome births in the family. By family, I mean the kindred group including grandparents, aunts, uncles, sisters and brothers.

*Is there a tendency for some families to have Down's syndrome babies?*

Several studies of families who have a child with Down's syndrome have reported that between five per cent and 10 per cent have had other babies with the condition in their immediate family or kindred group. When chromosome tests became available it was found that some of these cases included translocation carriers. However, the majority were Standard Trisomy 21 and could not be explained by the karyotype. No explanation is available at present, except that there might be some genetic tendency to nondisjunction (i.e. the chromosome pairs failing to separate).

A second factor which might increase the risk of a mother or father having more than one Down's syndrome child is related to mosaicism. As noted earlier, many of us may have some trisomic cells without knowing it. If trisomic cells are in the ovary or testes, then they are more likely to produce trisomic sperms or eggs, and hence babies with a trisomy. There is very little hard evidence on this point, but it is a possibility.

*What is the risk of having another baby with Down's syndrome?*

From the previous sections, you will have gathered that the risk varies depending upon the karyotype of the baby and the history of the family. If one rules out inherited Down's syndrome through carriers, and providing one knows the karyotype of the baby, then the risk usually quoted is one in 100 for parents under 30–35 years of age. I have summarised the commonly given risk rates in Table 1.

The likelihood of giving birth to a baby with Down's syndrome varies with the age of the parent (see next section). Some experts will thus use the age of the parent to work out the risk rate of having another baby with Down's syndrome. For parents under 30–35, use of the age factor can decrease the overall one in 100 risk figure.

| **Present baby has:** | | **Risk:** |
|---|---|---|
| 1 Standard Trisomy 21 | | |
| (a) parents under 30–35 | | 1 in 100 |
| (b) parents over 35 | | Depends on age (see Table 2) |
| 2 Mosaic Trisomy 21 and Translocation Trisomy 21 where a parent is not a carrier | not related to age but so rare that accurate figures are not available | Small |
| 3 Translocation Trisomy 21 | | |
| (a) D/G translocation (13, 14 or 15/21) | | between |
| when mother is carrier | | 1 in 5 and 1 in 10 |
| when father is carrier | | 1 in 20 and 1 in 50 |
| (b) a G/G translocation 21/22 | | |
| when mother is carrier | | 1 in 5 and 1 in 10 |
| when father is carrier | | 1 in 20 and 1 in 50 |
| (c) a G/G translocation 21/21 | | |
| when mother is carrier | | 1 in 1 |
| when father is carrier | | 1 in 1 |

Table 1 Commonly quoted risks of having a second baby with Down's syndrome

### 3 Why did it happen to us? What causes it?

So far, I have tried to explain how the condition arises in the infant—it is produced by a chromosome fault. But this does not tell us how this fault came about—except perhaps for translocation cases. To find out about causes, one tries to prove an association between the birth of a baby with Down's syndrome and some other factor. Usually one asks if more births are found in different countries, races, ages or when parents have had different illnesses, etc. Because no one knew the chromosomal cause until the early 1960s, many theories were put forward. These were often quite wrong and produced much distress to parents who had a child with Down's syndrome.

### *Is the likelihood of having a baby with Down's syndrome different for different races, social and economic levels, countries and geographic areas?*

Trisomic chromosomal abnormalities like Down's syndrome are found in all races of people, all countries of the world, and are distributed across all social and economic levels. This suggests that such things as poor diet, climatic conditions or geographic area are not particularly associated with the syndrome. By contrast, other handicapping conditions, such as Spina Bifida, are found more often in some geographic areas than others; are more common among people in poor circumstances; and are likely to be related to poor diet and vitamin deficiencies prior to pregnancy.

There are, however, a small number of studies which suggest that the birth incidence of Down's syndrome (i.e. the number of babies born with the syndrome compared with all births in a given geographic area) varies in three- to six-year cycles, and possibly between geographic areas. A number of environmental factors have been put forward to explain these suggested variations, but none has been substantiated. Even the variation in incidence is still disputed.

At present, therefore, there is no single environmental factor, such as an illness or vitamin deficiency, that is accepted by the majority of experts as an explanation of why the chromosome fault arises to cause Down's syndrome.

I should also note that trisomic conditions have also recently been found in some animals bred in captivity. Thus it is possible that trisomic abnormalities are quite common in all animal species. The science of genetics is a relatively new field and is discovering new facts and advancing its technology at a rapid rate, so more insights may well be discovered in the next few years.

*Is it true that older mothers are more likely to have a baby with Down's syndrome?*

It has been established that the chance of having a baby with Down's syndrome increases with the age of the mother. Different studies quote slightly different figures and these are summarised in Table 2.

All studies agree that there is a sharp rise in risk around 35 to 40 years of age.

*Why should older mothers have more Down's syndrome babies?*

The eggs are formed in the mother before she is born. They remain dormant until puberty, when they mature and are released at monthly intervals. Thus, the eggs have been exposed for many years to the possibility of injury or damage from environmental factors such as irradiation, chemicals, viruses. Under experimental conditions many such factors have been shown to produce chromosomal faults. Thus it may be that there are many different environmental causes which can result in a trisomy—and Trisomy 21 is the commonest outcome. If this is so it will be very difficult to establish a causal relationship between any one factor and the births of Down's syndrome babies. One study in Australia has found a degree of association between the frequency of Down's syndrome births and the frequency of infectious hepatitis—but this has not been substantiated and is in dispute.

It has also been suggested that the ageing of the egg, which may relate to changes in the mother's metabolism, is a contributory factor. Similarly, it has been suggested that the last

| Mother's Age | No. of Down's syndrome births per total no. of live births |
|---|---|
| under 20 years | less than 1 in 2000 |
| 20–30 years | less than 1 to 1500 |
| 30–34 years | between 1 in 750 to 880 |
| 35–40 years | about 1 in 280 to 290 |
| 40–44 years | about 1 in 130 to 150 |
| Over 45 years | between 1 in 20 to 65 |

Table 2 Age of mother and frequency of Down's syndrome births. (These figures do not apply to Translocation or Mosaic Trisomy 21)

eggs laid down in the mother are also the last to 'ripen', and may be inferior. They are also the last to emerge so it could be that inferior eggs and ageing and environmental factors act together to produce the trisomic cells.

However, this concentration on mother's age as the main factor has been seriously questioned by recent evidence on father's contribution. Also, as we shall see, the majority of infants with Down's syndrome are born to mothers under 35.

*Is Down's syndrome related to the father's age?*

Until the mid-1970s, no evidence could be found to link the increased risk of having a baby with Down's syndrome with the father's age. Up to this time, it was generally assumed that the chromosome fault causing the condition occurred mainly in mothers. However, the improvement in techniques for staining and banding chromosomes in recent years has meant that in many cases, but not all, one can now trace whether the extra chromosome in the baby came from the mother or the father. Present studies are showing that in 20 per cent to 25 per cent of cases, the extra chromosome has come from the father.*

Since a large proportion of Down's syndrome births are associated with the father, and since, unlike the egg, the sperm are newly generated, other factors than 'the ageing of the egg' clearly need consideration. Further, a number of studies have looked at the age of the father and there is some suggestion of an increased risk with fathers over 55. But there are not many fathers over 55, so it is difficult to assemble sufficient numbers to prove or disprove this.

*The first time I explained this new information to a couple with a three-month-old Down's syndrome baby, the father—who until this time had been really supportive and caring to his wife and new baby—went to pieces. He said later that he had really admired his wife for the way she responded to producing the baby but when he 'realised it may have been my fault' he felt profoundly guilty and upset. Nowadays I try to explain and emphasise that it is *no one's fault*.

*Why do so many young mothers have Down's syndrome babies? Are more younger mothers having Down's syndrome babies?*

Many people get confused by this age-related risk and cannot understand why so many young mothers have babies with Down's syndrome. The facts are, first, that most babies are born to mothers under 30, the peak being around 24–27 years of age—therefore many babies with Down's syndrome are born to this age group by virtue of the large number of births; and second, that the mother's age is only one factor that may be associated with Down's syndrome.

The answer to the second question is not so simple. Some studies have suggested a slight increase in Down's syndrome births in young mothers in recent years, but again no clear facts are available. These days, however, there are certainly more mothers under 35 with Down's syndrome babies than mothers over 35. Estimates in the 1960s showed that whereas 85 to 90 per cent of *all* births were to mothers *under* 35 years of age, over half of Down's syndrome births were to mothers *over* 35. Recent estimates, in such countries as Britain, Denmark, Japan, USA and Canada, show that between 65 and 80 per cent of babies with Down's syndrome are now being born to mothers under 35. This change is largely due to the increased use of family planning techniques in developed countries, and to the tendency for mothers to complete their families earlier. To a much smaller extent it may be due to the use of pre-natal tests for mothers over 35. These tests (see Appendix) can show if the foetus has a chromosome anomaly, and the parents can then choose to end the pregnancy.

## 4 How common is Down's syndrome?

This apparently simple question has three parts: How common are Trisomy 21 conceptions? How common are births of babies with Down's syndrome? How common is Down's syndrome in the population?

These questions are closely associated with chances of survival and life-span, and so these problems, too, will be dealt with in this section. I appreciate that this can be painful for parents, but I am assuming that most will probably prefer to know the facts.

*How common are conceptions of Trisomy 21?*

It has been well established that many spontaneously aborted foetuses (miscarriages) have a chromosomal abnormality. Some studies have suggested that as many as one in every 200 conceptions may be a Trisomy 21. Others have estimated that between 60 and 75 per cent of Trisomy 21 conceptions abort spontaneously during pregnancy. For this reason, some mothers who have had a Down's syndrome birth may have experienced more miscarriages than average. However, miscarriages are very common and there are many factors other than an abnormal foetus which can produce them.

*How common are births of babies with Down's syndrome?*

Many studies have been carried out over the years and in different countries to answer this question. They have reported figures as high as one Down's syndrome birth in every 520 births and as low as one in 1,000. Most report a figure between one in 600 and one in 700. No differences between incidence figures (i.e. number of Down's syndrome births per total number of births during a given period in a given place) have been reported between different races or countries. The variations among the figures are mainly caused by difficulties in collecting the information. For example, before chromosomal analysis was available, occasional misdiagnoses were made. Initially the baby is *clinically diagnosed* as having Down's syndrome according to certain physical characteristics (see page 103). The limited information available indicates that 85 to 95 per cent of cases can be confidently judged from these characteristics in the first days of life. Thus very few are missed who are later diagnosed. On the other hand, about eight per cent are clinically diagnosed as having Down's syndrome yet are not confirmed so by the chromosome test. However, in half of these cases, other abnormalities are found and mental handicap may be expected.

Because of these unusual cases, doctors will occasionally feel compelled to withhold their suspicion of Down's syndrome from parents until the chromosome test has been completed.

Variations in incidence figures also arise from failure in the past to report Down's syndrome in stillborn births. However, the greatest effect is due to fluctuations in the births to older or younger mothers. The low incidence figures of one in

900 are reported from recent studies in developed countries where there has been a rapid decrease in births to older mothers.

*How many adults and children are there with Down's syndrome? What is the* **prevalence** *of the condition?*

**Prevalence** is the number of individuals with the condition at the same age, time and place of all other individuals. If the survival rates of people with the condition are different from the average, then the prevalence can vary with age. The most commonly quoted prevalence figure for Down's syndrome is around 1.1 to 1.2 per 1000 of the population. However, this figure was based on studies carried out in the 1960s in developed countries and for the 0–14-year-old age range. Changes in survival and life-span have certainly altered it, and a higher prevalence can now be expected.

Chances of survival have improved considerably in the last 100 years for all people in developed countries. This is particularly due to the decline in mortality from such diseases as diphtheria, measles, whooping cough and tuberculosis through the use of immunisation. Another major influence has been the improved treatment and control of respiratory disorders. For example, deaths of all infants under one year of age dropped from 29.7 per 1,000 in 1951 to 16.3 per 1,000 in 1974 in England and Wales.

Before discussing the chances for infants with Down's syndrome I would like to emphasise that the figures I will quote are overall figures. But many infants who die are very poorly babies from the beginning, and have medical complications other than the Down's syndrome. Therefore if you have a thriving, energetic baby with Down's syndrome these figures are not directly applicable.

Studies between 1940–1950 reported that over 60 per cent of these infants died in their first year of life; in the 1950–1960 period the reported rates varied between 40 and 55 per cent. In the early 1960s rates fell to 25–40 per cent and studies in the mid-sixties were reporting levels of 16–20 per cent. The estimate for our study of infants born between 1973–1980 is just under eight per cent in the first year and about 14 per cent by the age of five years. Such figures will vary according to the availability of medical treatment, general health standards and possibly climatic conditions of the area (in the case of respiratory problems).

This dramatic drop in the mortality rates of Down's syndrome infants appears to be levelling out, and I feel that it will remain around the ten per cent level in the first four years. This probably represents those very poorly babies who survive the birth but have too many added complications to cope with.

People used to think that children with Down's syndrome never survived adolescence. This is untrue, many did survive until old age. However the average life-expectancy figure was about nine years in the 1930s, 12 years in the 1940s, 18 years in the 1950s and it is well beyond this now. The trouble with these figures is that people do not understand that they are based on the number of years survived by a group of Down's syndrome individuals, i.e. they are the *average* for the group.

Precise, up-to-date figures are very difficult to obtain as so much change is taking place. For example, it is often quoted, even in recent books, that about 50 per cent of these children do not survive the first five years of life; that 25 per cent will reach their early thirties and a few will reach 50. These figures are certainly out of date. Today's figures suggest that fewer than 15 per cent have died before five years of age. But this is changing. In the last years we have noted more open heart surgery being carried out on children with Down's syndrome and so preventing early death from severe heart conditions. If a child survives the first five years, he or she would seem to have about the same chances of survival, until about 40 years of age, as any other child unless there is a major heart problem. However, there is a definite increase in deaths after 40. Some studies suggest that this could be as much as 30 per cent higher than for the population as a whole. Again, this is changing all the time. However, just as there appears to be a slower development in the early years, there appears to be faster ageing in the late years. One finds a high proportion of conditions associated with old age in Down's syndrome people in their late thirties and onwards. (See p. 130.)

Finally, on balance, the studies carried out suggest that, in the early years, girls are more at risk than boys. So far as I know, there is no explanation for this, and it is the opposite of the normal trend, where boys tend to be more at risk than girls.

Far more children and people with Down's syndrome are alive and well than ever before. The majority can expect to live well into middle age, if not old age. Thus we can no longer think about them as having short lives. Instead we must make provision to equip them, like any children, to live lives as independent and fulfilled as possible.

**Facts in this chapter**

1 Down's syndrome is a set of special characteristics produced by extra chromosome 21 material. In 90–95 per cent of all cases this is in the form of Standard Trisomy 21, in which every cell in the body will usually have an extra number 21 chromosome. In 2–5 per cent of the cases a mixture of trisomic cells, containing the extra 21 chromosome, and normal cells are found. This is called Mosaic Trisomy 21. In another 2–5 per cent of cases the extra chromosome 21 is attached to another chromosome and this is called Translocation Trisomy 21.

2 In all cases of Down's syndrome the extra chromosome 21 is present in either the sperm or the egg before fertilisation takes place, or it arises in the first division of the fertilised egg. Thus *nothing that took place during pregnancy was the cause.*

3 The extra chromosome 21 is a normal healthy chromosome and a copy of the mother's 21 or father's 21 chromosome. It is not an alien chromosome, nor a 'throwback' to a more primitive evolutionary stage.

4 Thus the special physical and mental characteristics associated with Down's syndrome arise from an imbalance in genetic material which disrupts the normal programme of development and growth.

5 The majority of cases of Down's syndrome (about 90 per cent) are not associated with a family tendency towards having babies with this condition.

6 About one third of all translocation trisomies are inherited, either the mother or father being a balanced carrier. Therefore about one in 100 cases of Down's syndrome is inherited. Parents whose infant has this form of chromosome abnormality should seek genetic counselling.

7 Down's syndrome is found in all races of people, in all

social and economic classes and all countries. Trisomies have also been found in other animal species.

8 No relationship between diet, illness, geographic area or climate and the occurrence of the syndrome has been substantiated.
9 Some recent research has shown that in 20 to 25 per cent of all cases the extra chromosome has come from the father.
10 Estimates of the incidence vary between one in 500 and one in over 900 births. These have altered in some countries because the use of family planning has reduced the number of babies born to mothers over 40.
11 The one consistent relationship established is the increasing risk of having a baby with Down's syndrome as parents get older. The risk for mothers in their early twenties is about one in 2,000, at 35 it is one in 800, and then sharply rises to around one in 45 or more at 45 years old.
12 There is no relationship between birth order and Down's syndrome. But these children are often first born to very young parents, or last born, due to the increased likelihood of older mothers having a baby with Down's syndrome.

## Genetic counselling

Knowing that an extra chromosome is responsible for the syndrome, however, does not explain how it actually makes the body different; how it causes learning problems or alters growth. At present we do not really know. The science of genetics is very new and needs a lot more time before such answers can be expected. Neither does knowing about the extra chromosome tell us why it happened. If you are in any doubt about the type of chromosome abnormality your infant has, ask your doctor or paediatrician for the information. You may also feel the need to ask to see a geneticist for further counselling.

The aims of genetic counselling are to help people understand:

what is known about the cause of Down's syndrome;
what type of trisomy 21 your child has;

what the chances are of you or your children or close relatives having a baby with Down's syndrome;
what can be done to prevent the birth of a child with Down's syndrome;
what choices are open to you.

Genetic counselling will not tell whether you should or should not have more children. That is a very personal decision which only you and your partner can make. The hope is that the counselling will help you make the choice that is best for you at the time.

Genetic counselling is usually given by medical doctors with special training in genetics and counselling. Most regions in Britain have a specialist department and your own doctor will advise you and arrange an appointment.

## *Chapter Five*

# CHARACTERISTICS OF DOWN'S SYNDROME

SYNDROME: when a number of signs or characteristics appear together.

*Warning*: This chapter emphasises the many characteristics and medical problems that have been associated with the condition. The majority of children with Down's syndrome will have only a small number of these characteristics, and will not be afflicted by all, if any, of the medical problems. Therefore please take care in relating the information to your baby or child.

In Chapter Four I emphasised four points:

(1) That Down's syndrome is the result of an upset in the master plan carried in the chromosomes. The extra chromosome 21 adds extra genetic information which upsets the 'normal' planning of growth and development. If the extra genes had been from a different chromosome the result would be a baby who had a different set of characteristics—a different syndrome. The fact that children with Down's syndrome have similar extra genetic material results in their having many physical and mental features in common and looking somewhat like each other.

(2) But the chromosomes—i.e. the genetic plan—for children with Down's syndrome are inherited from their mother and father, and like those of any child, are quite unique. Because of this the children will have many features in common with their family and resemble their brothers and sisters. They will also have a great degree of individuality in physical features, mental ability and personality. This can be confusing, since on the one hand emphasis is laid on their being the same—sharing the syndrome—while on the other we have to remember that great individual differences exist.

Therefore, *the child with Down's syndrome will not have all the signs or characteristics associated with the condition, and some characteristics will be more obvious in some children than in others.* Furthermore, *some of the physical features change as the child grows and can become more or less noticeable.*

(3) Because the extra chromosome is present from the first stages of growth and development, there is a potential for disrupting the planning from the beginning. This 'disruption' will only show when the information from the chromosome 21 is required. Hence we can expect widespread disruption to any system or aspect of the body which is associated with chromosome 21 information. However, this is not a total disruption, and people with Down's syndrome have far more 'normal' than 'abnormal' characteristics. You should try to keep this in mind when you read this chapter, because I will mainly be writing about what is different from the 'norm'. I do feel this is important. *Many of the parents in our research have told me they want to know all the physical and behavioural characteristics so that they can then stop asking themselves if 'such-and-such' is due to the Down's syndrome—they can forget about the syndrome and get on with the job of caring for and helping their baby.*

(4) Finally, whilst we know that the extra chromosome produces the condition, we do not know exactly how genes interact to produce the changes. We do not know, therefore, why some children with Down's syndrome have a heart problem whereas others do not; why some grow tall and thin and others short and squat; why some have relatively high mental ability and others are less able. All we do know is that whereas they share some of the characteristics of the syndrome, they are all very different from each other.

With these ideas *firmly in mind* we can now consider the characteristics of the syndrome.

These fall into three categories:

(1) physical characteristics and their implication for health and development;
(2) characteristics of personality and behaviour (Chapter Six);
(3) mental characteristics (Chapter Seven).

## Physical and medical characteristics

When in 1866 Langdon Down first recognised the syndrome, he identified fewer than a dozen characteristics. Since then, the number of clinical signs associated with the syndrome has multiplied at a great rate. Most text books suggest over 50 signs, many studies list over 80 and one Polish study has identified 120 clinical characteristics, and recently I have seen reference to 300, that might be related to Down's syndrome. The number of signs identified has gone hand in hand with developments in medicine. When X-rays became available, for example, many differences in the skeleton of Down's syndrome people were found, and as late as 1966 one study reported that about 18 per cent of adults with the syndrome, mainly women, did not have a twelfth rib. Recent advances in the study of the chemical make-up of the body are also increasing our knowledge of Down's syndrome. For example, there is an increased likelihood that some children with Down's syndrome will not have the antiseptic enzyme—lizone—in their tears. This then increases the chances of eye infection. We can certainly expect more discoveries about Down's syndrome as medical techniques advance.

*Many of the signs, however, are not common and are of minor importance—they do not really affect the child's growth, health or functioning.* For example, fewer than one in 100 children with Down's syndrome will have a webbed toe. Whilst this is more common than in ordinary children, it is still rare and has little or no effect on the child.

It is neither possible nor of much value to discuss all these signs here, and so I will concentrate on the main ones and their importance, and try to indicate how common they are in the condition. Before doing this, I would like to make one further warning point.

Having begun to recognise the physical signs of the syndrome, many parents become worried when they 'see' the signs in their other children or themselves. But many normal children and adults will have some of the signs. For example, the folds of skin on the inner side of the eye (epicanthic folds) are reported in 60 to 70 per cent of children and adults with Down's syndrome and the upward slant of the eyes in about 80 to 90 per cent. These folds are also seen in about 20 per cent of ordinary people and the slant of the eye in around 14 per cent.

*Down's syndrome is only present when an individual has a collection of the more common signs, and the extra chromosome 21 material.*

Let us begin with a common question: '*How could the doctor tell that the baby had Down's syndrome?*'

For many parents this question goes hand in hand with the need to see what the doctor sees, so that they can accept and believe that the diagnosis is true. Several studies have identified the most common signs (called cardinal signs) of the syndrome. These signs occur in at least 50 per cent of cases, and usually in 60–80 per cent. In the newborn infant these are:

a) The eyes have an upward and outward slant.
b) This is often exaggerated by a fold of skin on the inner side of the eye (the epicanthal fold).
c) The eye slit is often narrow and short (an oblique palpebral fissure).
d) In some 30 to 70 per cent of the babies, small white patches (Brushfield spots) can be seen on the edge of the iris. This is more obvious in blue-eyed babies.
e) The face has a flat appearance, because the bridge of the nose tends to be low and the cheekbones rather high. This also makes the nose look small and stubby.
f) The head is usually smaller than average and the back of the head (the occiput) tends to be flattened. This gives the head a round appearance. The soft spots (the fontanels) are usually larger than in most babies, and occasionally one finds an extra soft spot in the middle. This is because the baby is growing more slowly than ordinary babies, so the bones of the skull take longer to grow together.
g) The ears tend to be small and are usually low-set. Occasionally the top of the ear may be folded over, and in just under half of the babies the ear lobe may be very small or absent. But remember, absent or small ear lobes can also be a family trait.
h) The mouth of the baby tends to look small and the lips rather thin. In fact the inside of the mouth is usually smaller than that of other babies, and the roof of the mouth is flatter, with a high arch in the middle (a

'cathedral' or 'steeple' palate). Because of this smaller mouth space the tongue has less room and so tends to stick out. Also, the muscles of the jaw and tongue tend to be floppy and so the mouth is often open.

i) In the young baby the neck often appears slightly short, and loose folds of skin are seen at the sides and back. These disappear as the child grows.

j) The legs and arms are often short in relationship to the length of the torso. The hands of babies with Down's syndrome are often broad and flat and the fingers are short. The fifth or little finger is often rather short and has a single crease on it. Also it often curves in towards the other fingers (clinodactyly).

In about half of the children there is a single crease across the palm (the simian line). This can be found on both hands or only on one hand.

k) The feet also tend to be broad and the toes rather short. Very often there is a larger space than normal between the big toe and the other toes, and between the thumb and the fingers.

A crease can sometimes be seen on the sole of the foot running from the gap between the big toe and the other toes.

l) At birth most of the babies will have poor muscle tone (hypotonia) and will feel floppy. There is also a tendency for loose-jointedness (hypoflexibility), which adds to this feeling of floppiness.

m) The reflexes tend to be weaker and less easy to elicit. Also, in about two-thirds of the babies, the cry is weaker, being shorter in length and pitch. Many cry very little and, at first, do not cry for food or when they are uncomfortable.

These are the major observable signs at birth. The babies also tend to be born a week or two earlier than expected, and their birth weights, whilst in the normal range, tend to be lower than average—about 3.0 kg.

If the baby has six to ten of these common signs, it is almost certain that the syndrome is present. There are very few cases when the signs are present but the trisomy is not found in the chromosome test.

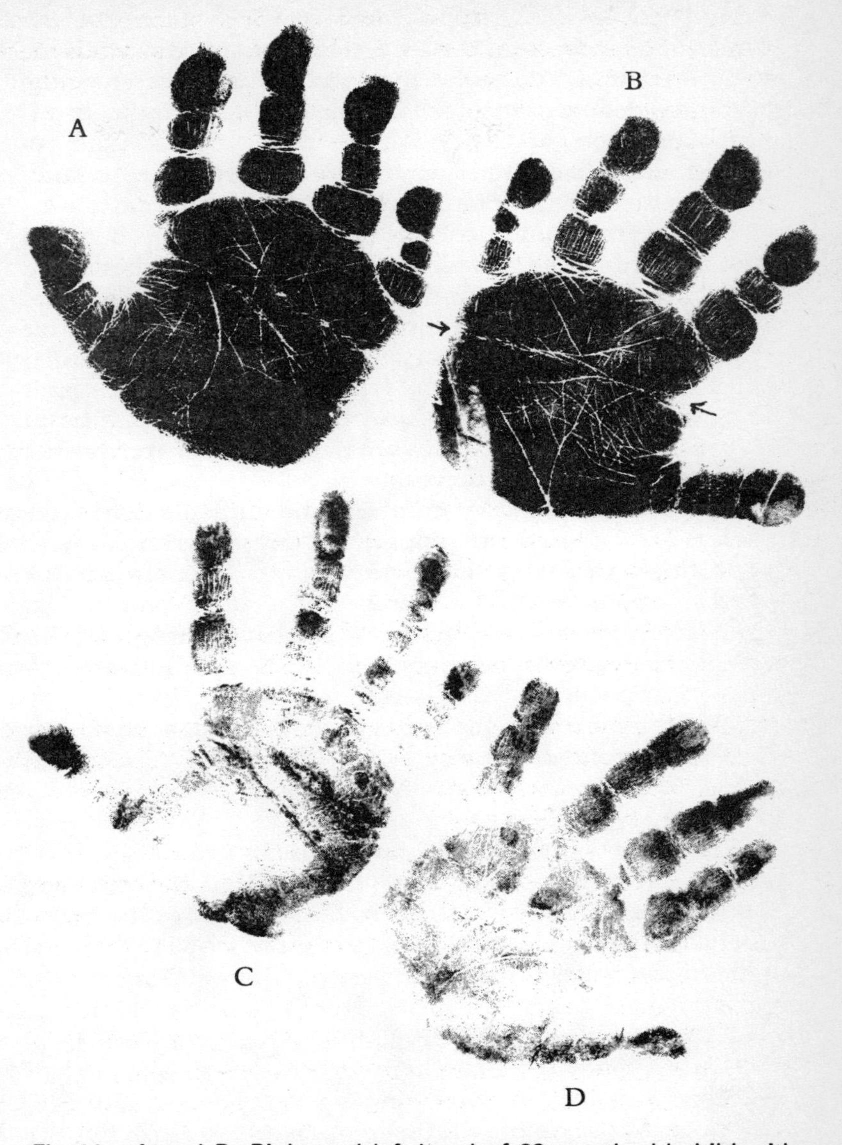


Fig 11. A and B: Right and left hand of 28-month-old child with Down's syndrome. C and D: Right and left hand of 18-month-old child.
Note simian crease in B (arrowed) and the curving little finger and shorter fingers of A and B compared to C and D.

*Do the baby's looks tell you how handicapped he or she will be?*
Parents of the young child often feel that the more obvious the physical features, the worse the condition and therefore the greater the degree of mental handicap. This is an understandable assumption, and they are not alone: doctors and researchers have been studying and arguing over the question since the turn of the century. In the late 1950s and 1960s, several research studies tried to find a relationship between physical features and mental functioning. Some studies found a small degree of association to suggest that the more features the person with Down's syndrome has, the greater the degree of mental handicap. One or two studies found the opposite, whilst the majority found no substantial relationship either way. Overall, the weight of the evidence is that no significant relationship can be found between the physical characteristics and the person's mental functioning.

These studies are very complex and difficult, and have usually been carried out with adult people with Down's syndrome who live in large institutions. It could be that different results would be found with children who live at home. Our own research has not looked at this in detail, but we have no strong impression that the general physical appearance of the baby is related to later mental ability. Therefore no one can really tell from the 'looks of the baby' how well he or she will grow and develop.

*Does the 'floppiness' in the new baby tell you how handicapped he or she will be?*
The few studies to look at this have not really been able to show that the degree of 'floppiness' in the first few months predicts later development. But very poor muscle tone at one, two and three years is associated with slow development. Therefore, one clue to later development is not the initial level of floppiness but whether it improves. For example, about half the babies with Down's syndrome appear to be rated as having very poor muscle tone in the first months and less than five per cent as having relatively good tone. By the time they are 18 months to two years old, less than five per cent appeared to be rated as having extremely poor muscle tone and over half as mild to normal muscle tone.

But of course, as you might expect with something as complex as a human being, it is not as simple as this.

Firstly, babies with severe heart problems usually have poorer muscle tone, as do babies who fail to thrive and have other medical complications. Second, in a recent study we found that when parents carried out physical activities to stimulate the babies' muscles and motor behaviours, the babies had 'sharper' reflexes and sat up and stood up a few weeks earlier than babies with less stimulation. But parents of babies who are frail or have severe heart problems are less likely to stimulate the baby physically.

Therefore, it is difficult to be certain whether it is muscle tone or heart problems plus less stimulation which may have some influence on later development. Some studies* found muscle tone to be important, whereas our work has not led to this conclusion. We found that heart problems were related to slower physical development but that, except in very frail and ill babies, many of which do not survive, muscle tone is not a major factor. The parents in our study appeared to be more likely to stimulate the babies even with severe heart problems than some of the other studies.

## Physical and medical characteristics in childhood and adulthood

As we have seen from the above, some characteristics change as the child grows. The floppiness certainly reduces and is not as serious a problem in later life. The inner folds of skin on the eyes tend to become less obvious as the head size increases. As teeth appear, the mouth alters shape and as the muscle tone of the jaws and tongue improve, many of the children will be able to keep the tongue in the mouth (I shall discuss how to help this in the next section). Many babies with Down's syndrome have a protruding navel (an umbilical hernia). Estimates of frequency vary from 12 to 90 per cent depending on the criteria used. Only a few cases will require surgery, as most close by themselves as the child grows and the muscle tone improves. Because of the poor muscle tone the young child often has a rounded belly which sticks out for longer than normal.

*Pueschel, S. M. (1984) (ed). *The Young Child with Down's Syndrome*. Human Sciences Press, Inc., New York.

However, most of the characteristics seen in the baby will persist and will be present in later life. I feel it is best to discuss these according to the systems of the body, and to consider the medical and practical implications at the same time. Because of the interactive nature of the body it will be necessary to discuss certain aspects across systems.

*The skull and face*

Many unusual characteristics of Down's syndrome are related to the differences in the skeleton, and clearly illustrate the effect of the extra genes on the body growth.

The characteristic facial features are mainly due to deficient growth and development of the skull. For example, the orbit holes for the eye are, and remain, egg shaped, giving the eye its slanting appearance. Also, the nasal bone remains underdeveloped, producing the flatness to the face. The jaw bones tend to be small and so the mouth is small. Of some importance is the absence or poor development of the air sinuses in the skull. Because of this, the sinuses can become easily blocked. The child will then breathe through the mouth. Mouth breathing will not only encourage the 'open-mouth, protruding tongue' look which is often associated with Down's syndrome, but will also increase chapped lips, dry tongue and possible infection. Thus whenever possible it is best to try to keep the nose and sinuses clean and free. Advice on nasal drops and nose cleaning for the baby should be got from your doctor, health visitor or nurse, as the baby can build up a resistance with continual use of nasal drops. As the child grows older, he or she should be encouraged to use a handkerchief frequently. Also, telling the child to 'keep his mouth closed', 'breathe through your nose', etc. at every opportunity in the early years can often alleviate the mouth breathing and 'tongue out' problem. These early efforts can also prevent later social problems, because most people do not feel attracted to gaping mouths and protruding tongues. However, early training does not always work. You may have to wait until the teeth appear and the child grows before the tongue will be kept in. In a few cases the physical abnormalities (i.e. small mouth, lack of air sinuses and infection) will be so great that the protruding tongue is unavoidable. But you will not know this unless you have persisted in the training.

*Upper airway obstruction**

Whilst discussing mouth breathing, it should also be noted that the tonsils and adenoids can also be relatively large in many children with Down's syndrome. This may contribute to the tongue protrusion and open-mouth appearance and also may cause difficulties in breathing and hearing.

In recent years a number of medical practitioners have become interested in the problem and treatment of upper airway obstruction in children with Down's syndrome. *Severe* upper airway obstruction is uncommon in children with Down's syndrome but can happen. The children have difficulty sucking air into their lungs because the air passages behind the nose and tongue may be narrow and can become partly blocked or obstructed by the tonsils, adenoids or a floppy tongue. When this happens one can see the pressure in the breast bone (sternum) as it is pulled in at each breath. At night, when the child is asleep and the breathing drive is more relaxed, difficulties can arise if he is unable to suck in as much oxygen as he needs. In this situation he will wake, often with a startle, every time his blood becomes short of oxygen. He may therefore have very disturbed sleep.

Therefore, the signs to look for are: very noisy breathing, especially at night; the caving in of the lower end of the breastbone each time the child breathes in; frequent waking up at night with a startle; excessive daytime sleepiness, lack of energy, and failure to thrive. Of course this problem is more likely to be associated with blocked nasal passages, colds and excessive mucus.

If parents feel there may be a problem, then it is worthwhile checking with your doctor. It may be the doctor does not know about this area since it is only a recently recognised aspect. You may therefore need to get some information from voluntary bodies like the Down's Syndrome Association to help.

To find out if the child has an obstruction, small skin sensors are stuck onto the child to monitor oxygen and carbon dioxide levels and chest wall movement. This is not an intrusive or uncomfortable procedure and is done while the child is asleep.

* I am grateful to Dr Jennifer Dennis and Dr David Southall for advice on upper airway obstruction which is based on her current research project.

In some cases it is recommended that the tonsils and adenoids are removed. If the tongue is the main problem, surgery is possible in the more severe cases. Other things which can help are: placing the child on his or her front to sleep (in babies this also helps motor development); minimising the amount of nasal congestion; improving the muscle tone of the jaw and tongue.

*Hearing*
A second effect of the small skull is that the ear chambers and ear canals are small. This means they, too, can get blocked, which causes temporary deafness. This is usually a conductive hearing loss due to exudative otitis media. The middle ear chamber becomes filled with fluid instead of air. It is common in all children but generally disappears by around nine years of age. However, it does appear to be more persistent in children with Down's syndrome. For many, it not only persists into adult life, but sometimes is more difficult to get rid of. The thick, glue-like fluid can be removed but can come back—in some cases frequently.

Recent surveys have shown that 80–90 per cent of young children with Down's syndrome will have some hearing loss in one or both ears, especially during times when they have colds. In about a third of these cases the loss is only mild and is unlikely to hinder the child very much. However, because of the risks, it is important to have regular hearing checks beginning between six and 12 months of age. It is not just a case of checking if the child can hear noises. Some hearing losses are only found to high frequency noises. Therefore, the child hears but cannot decipher words if parts of the sound are high frequencies. Several studies have shown that some children with Down's syndrome develop high frequency sensori-neural loss as they get older. This type of loss is due to changes in the nerves concerned with hearing.

Ideally, it is best to have the child tested at an Audiological Clinic where they are more likely to determine the degree and nature of the loss. If any problem is found, then early treatment is required. It may be treatment with mild decongestants to reduce the amount of mucus. Surgery and hearing aids may also be required.

At this point, I would like to stress how important early

detection and treatment are. Children with Down's syndrome tend to have an additional delay in language development compared to their general development. Indeed, many appear to rely more on their visual system in learning about the world than on their hearing system. This could be due to many reasons, but one is that their early hearing difficulties incline them to opt out of that system and rely more on vision. In our research we have some rather tentative evidence that some ten to 20 per cent of the language delay may be related to the hearing difficulties. Of course, this is group data and for some individual children, the correction of a hearing problem has had marked effects on the language and speech. Therefore, although language delay due to cognitive difficulties is likely to be the main problem, hearing loss can contribute and can also effect the behaviour of the child.

A second reason to stress the importance of early detection and treatment comes from a series of studies which Dr Sheila Glenn and I carried out. We used apparatus which allowed the baby to show us what he or she liked to listen to most; the baby could touch either of two touch detector switches which switched on tape recorders. If the baby touched one a lot more than the other we gained some idea as to what he or she liked to listen to. By six to nine months, ordinary and Down's syndrome babies preferred to listen to speech or songs rather than noises, and to familiar nursery rhymes rather than the same rhymes sung backwards. This showed that *by this age* the babies were already recognising familiar words, which is the beginning of comprehension. Incidentally, they were very attracted to the rhythms which appear to be useful in getting the baby to pay attention to the words. So do use rhymes and rhythms in your play with the baby.

Therefore, although a good half of children with Down's syndrome may have some hearing problems, they can be helped with treatment. Parents and teachers can also be advised on how to talk with the child and this should help to reduce the degree of hearing handicap.

*Growth*

The under-development of the skull means that the child and young adult with Down's syndrome looks much younger than her age. This impression is compounded by the slow growth of the skeleton and body in general, and the shorter height. As was noted for the newborn babies, the arms and legs tend to be short in relation to the trunk but the overall length is usually within the normal range. By two to three years of age many children with the condition appear a little shorter than average. By four to six years, they are, on average, about five inches shorter than ordinary children, and range from about 35 to 42 inches (90–105 cms) in height. Some research studies report an acceleration of growth at six to eight years, and others note a growth spurt during adolescence, as is expected with most children. Even so, the average young man with Down's syndrome will be just over five feet tall, with a range from about 4′ 9″ to 5′ 6″; and the young women, like most young women, are a few inches shorter than the men, with an average of 4′ 7″, ranging from 4′ 4″ to 5′ 1″. However, there are plenty of exceptions who are tall and slender and well within the normal ranges for height.

The baby with Down's syndrome also tends to weigh slightly less than ordinary babies (on average about 3.00 to 3.10 kg), and does not gain weight as quickly. For this reason parents may become anxious about feeding the young baby. The average number of ounces given for bottle feeding are based on ordinary babies' age, weight and expected growth. If a baby is not growing at the expected rate, he will need less than average feeding. Provided the baby is reasonably active and is not showing any signs of dehydration, there is no need for great concern if he or she does not take all the 'ounces' stipulated for his or her age and weight at each feed. The main signs of dehydration are (i) the spot on the head (the fontenal) begins to dip inwards and (ii) the skin becomes loose and if gently pinched does not return to its original position quickly. But please ask your health visitor, nurse or doctor to explain this more fully.

Whilst the weight growth is less than average, height growth is proportionately even more reduced, and this, plus the short arms and legs, creates an appearance of roundness and plumpness. This weight-height difference is more pronounced for the girls than for the boys.

Many older children and adults with Down's syndrome show mild to moderate obesity. Whether this is directly due to the extra genes, family traits, metabolic problems or environ-

DAVID AND HIS FAMILY
Photographs by Dad

On holiday at the caravan – 18 months.

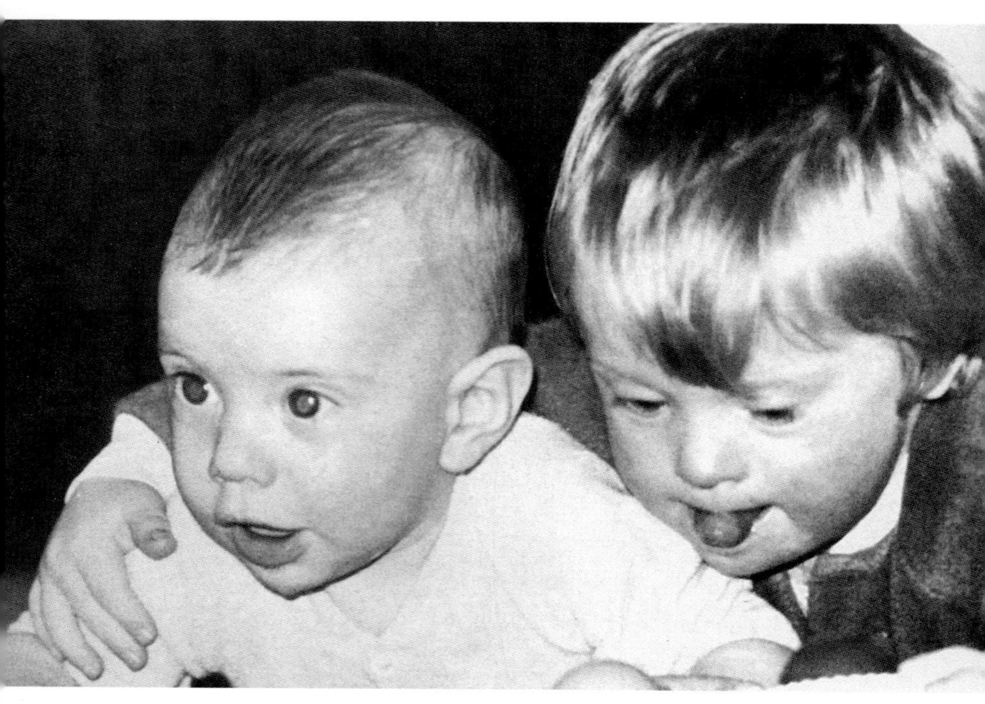

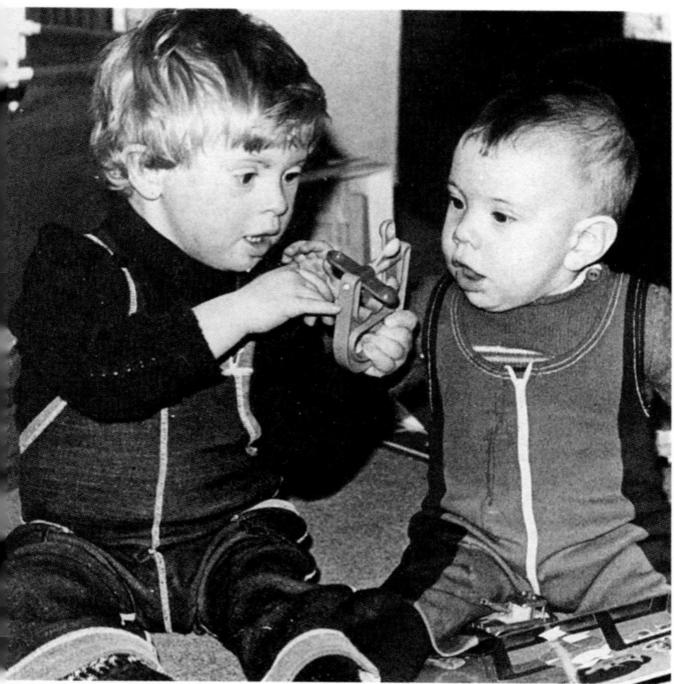

David and his brother Matthew.

With Matthew – David aged 5.

David with Mum, Grandma, Matthew and sister Emma on holiday.

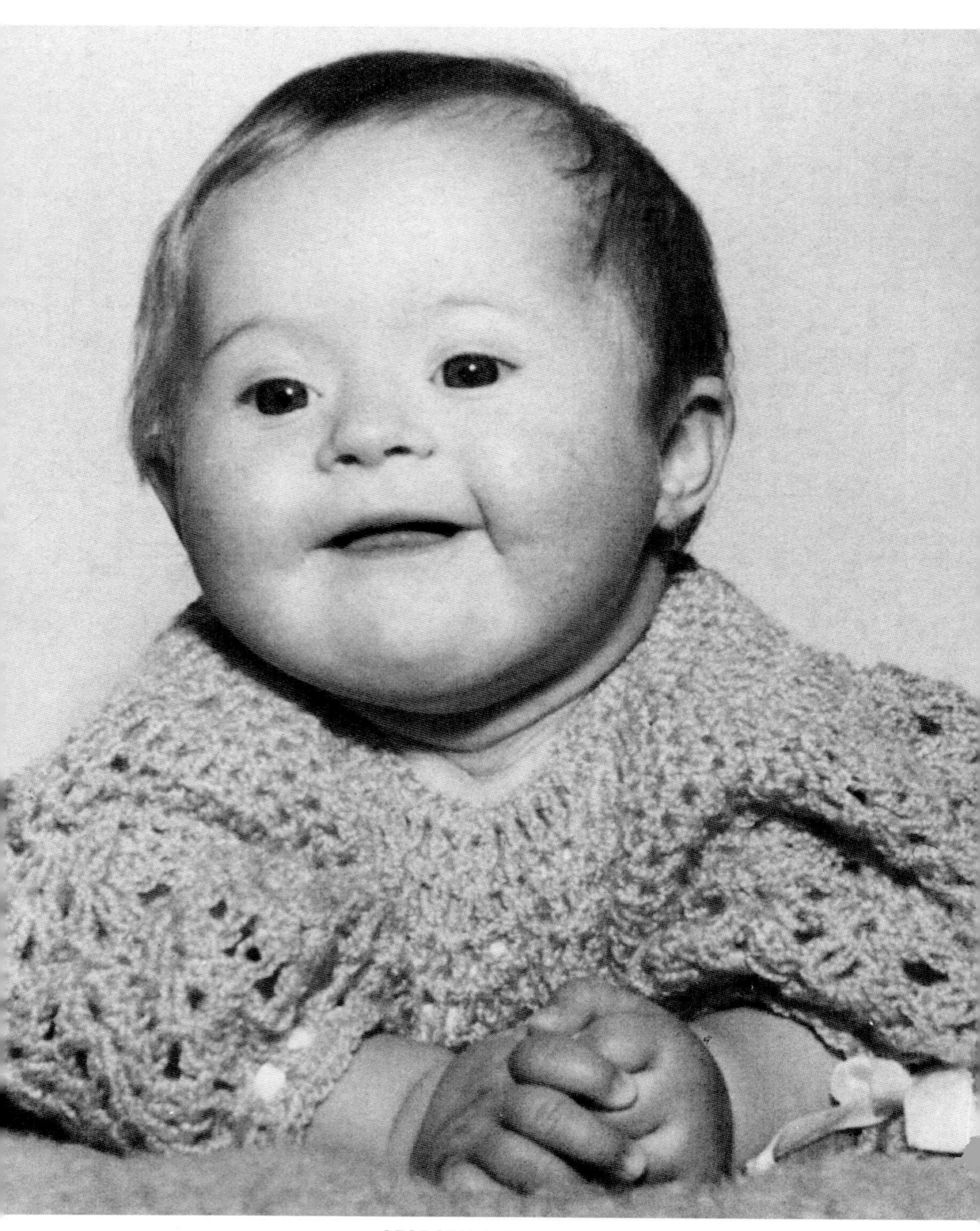

GEORGINA AND HER FAMILY

First steps, at 22 months

Georgie at the dentist.

CHRISTOPHER AND HIS FAMILY

Christopher – 17 years

mental circumstances is not known. However, it is true that many of these children generally tend to be less active than most children, and so do not burn up their food to the same extent. Some also tend to enjoy their food and to be very interested in it—possibly because they have a more limited range of interests than other children. Some people suggest they have a marked preference for sweet foods, but again it is difficult to tell whether this is inherited or caused by habit. Some parents do appear to indulge these children—possibly to compensate for their handicap or, in the early years, as an easy way to cope with frustrations and demands for attention. Many of the children are also passive eaters, preferring softer foods. This appears to be related to the hypotonia of muscles of the mouth. For example, it is not uncommon for mothers to complain that the baby spits out the solid foods when they begin mixed feeding. Sometimes this is no more than the baby thrusting his or her tongue forward in the action needed to suck from the teat. It can take longer for these babies *to learn to use the tongue* in the different action pattern required for solid feeding. However, some babies really do object to the 'lumpy' bits in food. Whether this is due to the small mouth size, difficulties in chewing or something else, is not known. Mothers often use the fine baby foods, which require little or no chewing, for much longer. If you have to do this, do not stop trying more lumpy foods every week or so in order to find out when you can introduce solids. If you delay too long it can cause problems. (See also p. 121.)

Since the muscles of the jaw are likely to be floppy, chewing is not likely to be easy. But to overcome the floppiness the muscles need exercising—i.e. chewing. Added to this, the *teeth* appear later than average and are often rather small, of irregular shape and can be placed in unusual positions. The first 'milk' teeth tend to appear between 12 and 20 months in these children, rather than between four and six months as in ordinary children. Not only is development later but there is more variation in developmental rate among the babies with Down's syndrome than among ordinary babies. The first 'milk' teeth (the deciduous dentition) may not be complete until the child is four or five years old. Often one finds the back teeth appearing before the front teeth. Variability is also found in the permanent teeth, and between 25 and 40 per cent of people with Down's syndrome are reported to have one or more congenitally missing teeth. On the positive side, there is less likelihood of dental decay, and hence need for fillings, in Down's syndrome than in the normal population. It is suggested that this might be due to slight chemical differences in the saliva. Even so, the habits of good oral hygiene should start in infancy, with the first tooth, because older people with Down's syndrome are more likely to suffer from disorders of the gums. This is thought to be due to their lower defences against infection (immunodeficiency), combined with the habit of mouth breathing, producing a drying and cracking of the lips, tongue and possibly gums. Again this suggests that we can prevent such problems if we take early precautions and provide positive care and training.

While there are many factors that contribute to increasing overweight, encouragement of physical activity, the development of good eating and chewing habits and a reasonably balanced diet from the first weeks of life will do much to prevent later obesity, the open-mouth look and poor breathing.

*Posture*

The posture of children and adults can also be characteristic. Some of this posture will be due to the differences in the skeleton and muscles, and the weight and height distribution. However, some recent work in schools shows clearly that the posture and movement of the children can be improved quite a lot with plenty of physical recreation and good training. If the child has a heart condition or is prone to respiratory problems you must first check with the doctor, but such difficulties do not necessarily preclude the child from taking part in physical activities. One of the boys in our research has taken up gymnastics and been selected for the Special Olympics even though he has a small hole in the heart.

It has to be remembered that the information on height, weight, breathing, and posture is often based on children and people born several years ago. Physical growth is affected by diet and exercise and, in recent years, the efforts of parents, teachers and sports people to provide opportunities for swimming, athletics, gymnastics, dancing, horse riding and so on, is making a lot of difference to the physical aspects of people with Down's syndrome. Even those with a weight and heart problem can learn not to walk with a 'hang-dog' posture, seen all too often in the past. This is usually the product of a poor exercise programme or inactive life-styles from early years, and also of living in an unstimulating and non-challenging environment, where they received little respect and were given few opportunities or encouragement to gain respect.

Many parents have found the child with Down's syndrome thoroughly enjoys swimming from the earliest years. They need to keep a watch, as the child gets cold quicker than brothers and sisters, but otherwise there are no major difficulties. Several of the girls in our research have begun dancing classes at three or four years, just like their friends. Some have gone on to pass examinations and win grades. Others are active in gymnastics clubs. Horse riding is not only proving to be great fun but really helps to overcome the poor sense of balance that is common in people with Down's syndrome and also gives confidence and a sense of pride and achievement.

*People with Down's syndrome may have a physical disability in terms of the stature, posture, balance and, for some, heart conditions, but these need not be barriers to their taking part in sport and leisure and achieving satisfaction and skill. The barriers are largely put up by our expectations and protectiveness, and by societies' lack of provision of resources and opportunities.*

*The skeleton*

As you will have realised by now, nearly every part of the body of people with Down's syndrome can have some variations, and this is understandable, given the presence of the extra genetic coding from the first moments of conception. There are, therefore, several more characteristic differences in the skeleton and muscle system. The absent twelfth rib I mentioned earlier; the pelvis is rather small and the bones less developed; the iliac wings of the pelvis tend to be flatter and wider than in the general population. However it is unlikely that these deviations will affect stance and posture to any great extent.

Because of the poor muscle tonus and flexibility in the tendons, Down's syndrome children are more than normally likely to have flat feet. About one in 100 will have a club-foot or a foot which is turned too far in or out. However, if diagnosed early these can be corrected with orthopaedic devices.

Congenital dislocation of the hip occurs more frequently than normal, but will affect only a few children. Fewer than one in 200 will have a cleft palate. There is a higher than normal frequency of 'funnel chests', when the chest bone is depressed, and of 'pigeon chests', when the chest bone sticks out.

Spasticity can be found in children with Down's syndrome, but this is not associated with the genetic disturbance. Like any baby, these children can suffer damage at birth, and if they do this will add to their handicap.

*Atlanto-axial dislocation*

Our spinal column (backbone) is really a pile of small bones stacked on top of one another. There is a hole in the middle of each to allow the spinal cord nerves, which take messages from the brain to the arms, trunk and legs, to pass through. The top two bones in the neck are very specialised. The very top one is the atlas with a saucer shaped surface which supports the skull. The second one is the axis, which has a peg-like protrusion which sticks through the hole in the middle of the atlas along with the spinal cord. Muscles and ligaments hold all the different bones firmly in place.

As we discussed earlier, children with Down's syndrome are more floppy than many ordinary children and their ligaments tend to be more lax. This allows one bone to move slightly more freely on the surface of the next. Usually this is of no importance, but very occasionally the axis is able to move considerably more easily on the atlas than usual. This is called atlanto-axial dislocation. In this case the peg-like protrusion of bone can cause the spinal cord to be squashed as it passes through the atlas. This is known as spinal cord compression. If it is recognised early by X-rays, damage to the nerves can be prevented by doing an operation to stabilise the bones on each other. Symptoms of trouble include difficulty with or painful neck movements, development of incontinence, stiff-leggedness or deterioration in walking.

It is not known exactly what proportion of children with Down's syndrome have such problems, but various studies put the level between nine and 30 per cent. Many may have a laxity but no symptoms, and in probably no more than one in 20 children over five years old does the problem require treatment or some care in management.

If the child engages in active sports such as trampolining, soccer, gymnastics, swimming and diving, then it is worth carrying out an X-ray to be sure. If abnormal laxity is discovered, then the child should be carefully monitored by parents and medical staff and, depending on the degree, it may be necessary to avoid certain sports such as trampolining and diving. However, before deciding on this, it is necessary to balance the possible risk against the loss of sporting activities. Engaging in physical activities and sport is very important as it reduces the likelihood of the child becoming obese and lethargic, and also promotes feelings of well-being, social interaction and self-esteem.

If symptomatic atlanto-axial instability and spinal cord compression is discovered (usually in no more than one or two per cent), then use of surgery to stabilise the bones may be needed.

Finally, the dangers of whiplash necks to car passengers involved in an accident are well known. If the child has a lax neck, then the use of supportive seats and seat belts is advisable.

*The skin*

I mentioned earlier the distinctive creases on hands and feet. As well as these, the actual lines and fingerprints (dermal ridges) are usually different from the norm in nearly all children with the condition. The patterns made by these lines are called dermatoglyphs, and tend to be fewer than usual, and the loops open more often to the ulner side (the left side looking at the palm) of the hand.

These differences do not affect the child in any way and are mainly of interest in diagnosis and study of the condition. More important for the child and parent is the nature of the skin. The skin appears to have less elasticity than in ordinary people, and in places can be quite firm, dry and rough. This is not very noticeable in the young baby, but increases with age. The circulation of the blood in the skin also tends to be poor, even in children who do not have a severe heart condition.

This can give the skin a 'marbled' look (marmoration) but it does not have any serious consequences. What is important is that the nature of the skin causes it to dry out and chap easily—particularly lips, cheeks and hands and feet—in many children with the condition. This tendency is compounded by the poor circulation, and in some cases possibly by reduced sensitivity to temperature changes. Thus the baby is less likely to be in control of his 'cooling' and 'heating' system and will rely more on parents to prevent him getting too hot or cold. Please do not go overboard in your anxiety for the baby on this. I often see babies so swamped with clothes that they cannot move and kick, and so will not be able to get themselves warm even if they want to. One important aspect of plenty of handling, such as rolling, rocking, bouncing and tickling, stroking and bathing, is that it can stimulate the circulation of blood.

The areas of dry skin and chapping can be treated with creams; and good cosmetic care of the hands, elbows and face should help combat the 'drying' of the skin that occurs with age. Thus again, early efforts at establishing regular habits in diet, hygiene and skin care are worthwhile and can compensate for some of the inherent problems of the condition.

Like the skin, the hair of children with Down's syndrome can be different. It can be rather fine and sparse. Since the scalp can also be dry, it is well worthwhile consulting a good hairdresser for advice on the use of shampoos and hair conditioners. For the older children, one should also try to find a hairdresser who can cut the hair well as it is sometimes not as easy as in ordinary children. Also, when the girls begin to use make-up, do get advice from a reputable beautician who understands skin.

Equally important is the dress and appearance of the growing child. Far too often one sees older children with Down's syndrome dressed in clothes more suitable for younger children. Such clothes may fit them, because they are smaller, and to some degree may relate to their mental and behavioural level; but they will do nothing to help the young person feel he or she is growing up. One needs to find clothes which fit into the appropriate age group, and do not accentuate physical differences.

Whilst on the subject of appearance, a note on the recent development of facial plastic surgery is needed.

*Facial plastic surgery*

Operations have been devised in recent years which remove the epicanthic fold on the inside of the eye, correct the slant of the eye, raise the flattened cheek bones, reduce the lower lip, make the small chin larger, shorten very large tongues and reduce fatty tissue in the neck. The idea is to make the child's appearance more 'normal', with the assumption that this will improve long-term functioning because people will treat the child more normally. Whilst the evidence clearly shows that the physical appearance can be altered, there is no real support for improved functioning.

I must admit, I find the idea that merely changing the facial appearance of a child with Down's syndrome will have a substantial effect on functioning, simplistic and over-generalised.

Firstly, it assumes that the general public either find the appearance of these children unattractive and so avoid them; or that they recognise the condition and then either avoid them or treat them in a less than optimal manner. From my experience and our research we cannot find any support for the first assumption. Indeed, in childhood at least, the openness of the facial features appears to be attractive. Furthermore, a large number of studies were conducted in the 1950s and '60s which investigated the relationship between the physical characteristics of people with Down's syndrome and the level of ability. None could be found.

In the case of the second assumption, it would seem more appropriate in the long term to make a concerted effort to change attitudes in society than to subject these children to surgery with the attendant risks to the child's physical well-being and possible behaviour. Young children do react to the trauma of hospitalisation and separation from home. In non-handicapped children this can be associated with later disturbances in behaviour, particularly when there are added stresses in the household and family relationships. Our own research has indicated similar results with children with Down's syndrome.

Thus, it is important for the parent to consider very

carefully the advantages and disadvantages of such procedures. A survey by Dr Pueschel, in 1984, found that parents were far less likely than physicians to regard the facial features of children with Down's syndrome as unpleasant, and conversely, physicians were more likely to favour the use of cosmetic surgery.

Finally, children tend to take little notice of physical features of their fellow playmates—at least up to eight to nine years and especially if the features are not very striking and disfiguring. Instead they make friends and create impressions most of all by who they are: their temperament, skills, behaviour and, when older, their interests and ability. Therefore, although facial appearance may have a small initial effect, it is not likely to cause major social isolation which prevents good social functioning. I have never come across studies or anecdotes of children with Down's syndrome in which the appearance has been cited as a major barrier to integration. Therefore, there is no scientifically valid evidence that facial surgery has positive effects on functioning for children with Down's syndrome.

However, there may be specific cases in which surgery is required. *The criteria for making the decision would be those which apply to any child*—not just because of the Down's syndrome. Thus the reduction of very large tongues which are affecting eating, breathing and possibly speech, may be needed. Such operations with children with Down's syndrome have been reported as leading to more normal mouth closure, fewer respiratory infections and improved eating. Some reports argue that speech also improves, but again this is a little oversimplified. Speech problems are likely to be due to a more central motor co-ordination deficit (see Chapter Seven), affecting mouth, tongue and lip movements. Current reports tend to rely on parents' perceptions and have not used more objective controlled measures to prove the point. Until these studies are available it is necessary to be cautious and fully explore each individual case by getting a range of professional views.

*The digestive system*

The large majority of children with Down's syndrome have a structurally normal gut. About four to five in a hundred will have blockages in the tube leading to the stomach, or more often in the duodenum (congenital duodenal atresia). Occasionally the large bowel will be abnormal (Hirschsprung's disease). In the case of such blockages the baby begins to vomit at most feeds. These serious conditions are discovered in the first days of life, and generally require surgery if the baby is to survive.

Do not think, however, because your baby vomits a little after a feed and has a round belly, that he has these difficulties. Many of our group of babies with Down's syndrome vomit after feeds. They certainly are more likely to vomit than ordinary children. This tendency generally diminishes as they grow, and by six months has usually disappeared. We feel that in most cases this is due to floppiness of the muscles of the stomach; as these strengthen, the vomiting reduces. Sometimes, however, the baby can be allergic to milk, and one needs to change the diet. Again we find that the frequency of vomiting is reduced with the gradual introduction of solids into the diet at two to six months. You should consult your doctor and health clinic if you have difficulties. About half of our families experienced some difficulties in feeding in the first days. This is more than one would expect with ordinary babies, and is usually due to immaturity and weakness of sucking and swallowing reflexes and muscles. However, with perseverance this can usually be overcome within a few days. Similarly, most of the mothers who wanted to breast-feed found that they could—again, they often needed to persist. Sometimes, as with any baby, it is not possible to breast-feed, but it is worthwhile finding out precisely why. It is not uncommon for mothers to be told they cannot breast-feed simply because the baby has Down's syndrome. In one or two per cent of cases, severe feeding difficulties are prolonged and parents do need special advice from the medical staff on particular problems.

The large majority of these babies have no difficulty moving on to solids, but it may take longer for them to learn to use the tongue to push the food to the back of the mouth and swallow, instead of thrusting the tongue back and forth as is done in sucking the teat. If you do experience difficulties, try pressing the spoon gently down on the tongue and gently pressing the chin upwards. This usually causes the tongue to move backwards—taking the food with it. And of course it encourages the child to close the mouth. If you still have difficulty after several days, try altering the size of the spoon, placing the food toward the edges of the tongue, or altering the texture and taste of the food. Do not assume too quickly that the baby is 'not ready' or 'does not like the food'.

Another problem encountered by just over three-quarters of our parents was that their babies seemed to strain a good deal when passing a motion. Even though the babies were not in distress, mothers often worried. We feel that for many children this difficulty is simply due to the hypotonia of gut muscles, and lack of activity. Usually it diminishes as the child gets older and moves around more, and it seldom becomes a serious problem. Several of our mothers found improvement when they increased the roughage in the child's diet. Other parents gave the babies mashed up raw fruit, or gave older children some bran sprinkled on their cereal. In the case of the young baby a little extra sugar in the feeds helped. Some parents have found that increasing the fluid intake helps, and also tickling the anus with a cotton wool bud dipped in Vasolene. *You should be aware that laxatives can become habit forming and increasingly larger doses are required.* So if you have increased the roughage or sugar and given the infant lots of exercise and activity and are *still* having problems, do consult your medical adviser.

On the positive side, many mothers find the babies become very regular, so they can 'catch' the stools at certain feeds and have clean nappies. It is not uncommon for mothers to have no soiled nappies from nine to ten months onwards.

*The heart*

Most studies find that between 30 and 40 per cent of Down's syndrome babies have some form of heart defect. No specific type of heart defect is characteristic: the whole range of possible problems have been reported. These vary from mild defects, which may disappear with time or which do not seriously affect the child's growth and development, to severe cases which will require major surgery or be inoperable. Present figures suggest that between ten and 15 per cent of babies with Down's syndrome have a severe heart defect. Some are unlikely to survive beyond the first months of life without surgery. There is no evidence to show that the chances of success of such operations are lower for children with Down's syndrome than for any other child. Accurate figures are not available, as recent advances in surgical techniques have meant that many babies are now surviving who, just a few years ago, would have died. For most babies the doctor can detect the heart defect soon after birth, especially in the more severe cases, but sometimes the defect is not detectable for several months.

Usually, a heart murmur first alerts a Doctor to the possibility of a congenital heart defect. Not all children have murmurs, however, and other characteristics are used to make the diagnosis. These include: the colour of the skin, pale, grey or blue; the breathing rate effort required; and oedema (swelling) of eyelids. X-rays can reveal enlarged hearts and congested lungs.

An electro-cardiogram or an echocardiagram can establish if there is an abnormality and the need for a catheterisation. This requires hospitalisation as a small catheter is inserted into the system to give precise details of the extent and location of the problem.

The most common cardiac defect in children with Down's syndrome is a hole in the centre of the heart (Atrial Ventricular Canal Defect). It accounts for about half of all severe heart defects in these children and can be corrected by surgery in infancy. The second most common problem (just under a third of cases) is the Ventricular Septal Defect. This is a hole in the wall of the two ventricles (the two large, lower chambers of the heart). Small holes do not cause any strain and often close by themselves. Larger ones may need surgery. The two most severe types of defect are the Patent Ductus which is found in about two per cent of cases and the Tetralogy of Fallot found in about seven per cent of cases. The latter is a combination of four defects including a large hole between the ventricles and a narrowing in the pulmonary valve. Typically, children with these problems are cyanosed, with blueness of the lips and fingernails, and total correction is difficult in the infant. An operation is sometimes carried out to provide temporary relief. When the child is older there is a better chance to correct the defect. When children with Down's syndrome have major heart defects there is often an added delay in growth and weight gain. Also, they are likely to have less muscle tone and be more floppy (hypotonic). Together this causes an additional delay in gross motor development compared to children with Down's syndrome without a severe heart problem. However, we have not found that their mental development is any slower or that they are less sociable or have more problems of behaviour. Just because a child sits up late or walks late does not predict that he or she will be less able in cognitive areas.

Also, severe heart defects do not necessarily mean the child should not take part in physical activities. Of course, parents should always check this with the physician, but we have found that many of the children in our sample, even those with inoperable defects, happily take part in physical activities, and with ordinary children in ordinary schools.

As with any child who has a major health problem one can expect temporary setbacks, especially when ill or receiving treatment. However, one must remind oneself *that these are temporary*.

I should emphasise, however, that the majority of children with Down's syndrome do not have a heart defect: it is more likely than not that the baby will be fine, and certainly not very likely that a serious defect will be found in the second year of life or later.

*Circulation*

Studies have also suggested that there are differences in the circulatory system, such as slightly narrower and thinner arteries with fewer branches and capillaries. Again one must emphasise that there are many individual differences, and many people with the syndrome will have quite a 'normal' system.

However, if the circulatory system is less efficient than normal one can expect some consequences. Through the blood, the system transports energy and food to the body. If the body does not get these supplies in sufficient quantity, one might expect less activity, even a tendency towards lethargy, and possibly some effect on growth and development. For this reason, many people strongly encourage parents of these babies and young children to give them plenty of handling and stimulation from the first weeks of life, as this encourages better circulation.

*Leukaemia*

About one in 100 children with Down's syndrome develops leukaemia—a condition in which there is an abnormal growth of white blood cells. This usually occurs in the first two to three years and is generally of the acute type. In these cases treatment can extend the child's life. Some types of leukaemia respond to recent treatments, and we have a very happy seven-year-old in our group who has been responding successfully. During treatment he did have bouts of illness, and his development of motor skills—particularly walking—was frequently halted or even reversed. However, by five to six years of age he was well on his feet.

*Vision*

I have already mentioned the possibility of hearing disorders. Disorders of vision are also common. In the baby one often sees the eyes crossing (strabismus), and co-ordinated eye-together-movements are slower to develop than normally. It is thought that this is partly due to the 'floppiness' (hypotonia) of the eye muscles, and as this improves with age and experience, so the crossing disappears. Giving the baby practice in focusing on and tracking slowly moving objects is thought to speed up this co-ordination. Strabismus does not necessarily disrupt the vision, but if a squint is still prominent after 12–18 months you should seek professional advice, as it may be necessary to correct it, even if only to improve the child's appearance. Similarly, rapid movements from side to side (nystagmus) are also quite common, and again will often disappear as the baby matures.

Of more importance is the increased likelihood of these children to be near or far sighted. Because of this it is worthwhile having regular assessments of their vision from about the age of one year, and to use glasses if necessary. Most people find that these children will learn to wear glasses, provided the frames fit comfortably and one is patient but persistent in training. More difficulties appear to be found with hearing aids, but again the majority of the children with the syndrome will learn to use them.

Very rarely, cataracts (a clouding of the lens) are found in babies with Down's syndrome, and surgical treatment is needed. Such cataracts can appear at any age, though they are more common in later life and old age. Whilst they occur more often in people with the syndrome than in the population as a whole, they are not very common.

*Sensitivity and arousal*

There are reports of reduced sensitivity to touch, pain, heat, cold, etc., associated with the syndrome, although no clear picture is available, mainly because of the very great individual differences among people with the syndrome. However there is a fair degree of agreement between the observations of parents and professionals that with many of the children it is necessary to have quite strong stimulation—a good firm tickle rather than a very gentle stroke, or a good robust picking up and swinging game—to get the baby to react.

*Sensory co-ordination*

The brain, like the skull, tends to be smaller in relation to the size of the body than in ordinary people. However, this by itself does not account for the mental handicap. Parts of the brain, particularly the brain stem and cerebellum, have been reported as being smaller relative to the size of the whole brain than in ordinary people. It has been suggested that this would account for the hypotonia, and perhaps for the difficulties found in co-ordinated motor activities such as balanced sitting and walking unaided, as these parts of the brain are concerned with these activities.

In our research we found that the stages between sitting with some support and sitting and balancing on your own; standing with a support and standing alone; and walking with support and taking several steps, all took longer than we or parents expected for a large number of our group. They are like little plateaux when no real progress is seen. But of course progress is taking place internally as the cells in the appropriate part of the brain set up connections. To test if we could speed this up we carried out some studies.

In one we not only did exercises to increase the strength of the babies and overcame the hypotonia (e.g. rolling over, pulling to a sit, weight bearing on legs) we also asked parents to include 'wobblies'—for example, holding the baby firmly around the waist in a sitting position and gently wobbling from side to side and back to front to help balance. Although the babies learned to sit more slowly than ordinary babies, they did sit up six to eight weeks earlier than a group who did not have this very regular wobbly training. Unfortunately, although they sat up earlier, we did not find that they walked earlier, so it did not seem that we had a general effect on the brain area associated with co-ordination, only on the specific activity. Nevertheless, they all had plenty of exercise, enjoyed wobbly games and could sit up and look at their world from a different angle sooner than they would otherwise. In another study we got mothers to encourage the primary walking reflex, by gently holding the baby from behind and touching his or her feet on the floor, moving slowly forward. In the first weeks of life, babies make stepping movements. We found that if we kept these going, then the babies walked about six to eight weeks earlier than babies without the exercise. Of course, babies are all individual and some are not programmed to keep the walking reflex going: it disappears. We found that these babies usually crawled earlier.

The problem of balance and posture control in children with Down's syndrome is quite common and is found in all age groups. Our work shows that well thought out physical activities can help from the early days of life but are specific to the skill. Therefore, it is necessary to provide regular access to experiences which promote muscle tone, balance experience and use of vision in helping to co-ordinate movement. I personally feel that swimming, dancing, gymnastics, trampolining and, if available, climbing frames, balancing beams, etc., are all very important. If these and good diet are provided for, fewer people with Down's syndrome should grow up with that 'mongol' look of old.

Finally, studies have indicated that many children with Down's syndrome experience problems when combining or co-ordinating information from different sensory systems. For example, eye-hand co-ordination. Our own studies show this in the first weeks of learning to reach for objects. Often the baby fails to watch his or her hand as it goes out and so adjust it to contact the objects. Plenty of practice with the objects positioned to maximise the chance of success can help. Similarly, playing games to get the infant to look for sounds (around five to six months) or turn their head to locate a sound (seven to eight months) are helpful. (This area is also discussed in Chapter Seven in relation to mental development and early intervention.)

*Speed of responding*
Studies have also shown that messages appear to take slightly longer to pass along the nerve pathways in people with the syndrome. This is probably due to differences in the structure of the nervous tissue. One practical consequence is that it will take the person longer to receive a message in the brain, and longer to send out a return message in reaction. If we add to this a longer time to process the message—that is, to recognise, understand and decide what to do—then we can begin to understand why many people find that the children and babies with the syndrome are rather slow to respond.

There is a further dimension to this phenomenon. If the person who is talking or playing with the child with Down's syndrome does not expect a reaction to a tickle or question, and does not understand the longer time it takes to get a reaction, then he is likely not to *give the child enough time* to respond. Then, because the child does not appear to respond, he concludes that the child cannot respond, and so proves his own expectations.

In our own research we have found that this misunderstanding can begin to cause problems within the very first weeks of life. When human beings communicate with each other they tend to use a common pattern of pausing, speaking and reacting. For example, if someone is talking and pauses for one or two seconds we do not feel anything is wrong, but if she pauses for a little longer, then we begin to feel that something is strange. The same happens with babies. We 'coo' at or tickle the baby and expect a smile. If the baby does not respond within two or three seconds, we tend to repeat our behaviour. Thus if we meet a baby who is slower to respond, we tend to assume he cannot respond, and so do not give him the extra time he needs to do so. If, in addition, we know the baby has Down's syndrome, and we believe that this means he cannot do things, then we are more likely to expect no response and so fall into this trap.

In our research with mothers and their three-to-four-month-old babies with Down's syndrome, we found that if mothers waited longer for the baby to respond we could count more baby behaviours. Further, if we told mothers to wait for the baby to do something, like smile, coo or sneeze, and then to copy it, we counted even more bits of behaviour from the babies than when mothers just played with them.

In our later work, we found that mothers often begin play with some good physical, boisterous activity to get the baby aroused, then they move into a quieter style. In this they make less demands on the baby, wait longer—often four or five seconds—before a new initiation. They also tend to imitate more. When this happens, the babies, depending on their mood, usually do more. They smile more and vocalise more. This gives the parents more chances to imitate, and the baby more chance to begin to learn the very first stages of social interaction and communication—how to take turns. There is quite a lot of evidence from research which supports what most parents know is commonsense, namely that the way parent and child interact together strongly influences later developments—both cognitive and emotional. When parents are sensitive to the child's way of interacting, understanding and interpreting the infant's actions, they are also more likely to gently direct the infant's attention to new objects and actions *without dominating and taking control*.

This also applies to older children. How often have I heard parents directing the child to perform (show off); programming his or her every move, and answering for the child. Surely this can only add to the child's feeling of low self-esteem, apathy and lethargy.

Again I must emphasise that not all babies with Down's syndrome are slow to respond. Also, as they grow and develop one finds that their speed of response varies at different times, and certainly among different areas of development. Generally babies with Down's syndrome appear to react more quickly to visual than to other forms of stimulation, and it has been suggested that they are 'stronger' or less abnormal in the visual system. However, a good general rule for any child, whether handicapped or not, is to give him time to respond before assuming he is not going to. This can be frustrating, and it does take time for parents to change the well established interaction patterns they have learnt. As one mother once told me, 'When I deal with David I keep putting myself in first gear, but then I have to change up to top when the other children come in! It can get very frustrating at the busy times of the day – like getting them off to school or around 4–6 o'clock – but it is worth it because you can see he does learn to do things and often surprises me with how much he can do.'

Think of how important our interactions with other people are: we are constantly sending out messages for them to react to, and responding to their messages; much of our learning comes from these everyday interactions. Once you appreciate this, you will realise how worthwhile it is to develop a pattern of interaction suitable to your child, and impose a slower, more patient pattern on yourself if it is necessary.

*Ageing, epilepsy and deterioration*

Another, very complex consequence of the difference in the nervous system of a person with Down's syndrome shows up in evidence of slower growth and development in the first years, and signs of ageing sooner in life than are seen in ordinary people.

Many recent studies have reported dementia or senility of the Alzheimer type to be common in people with Down's syndrome, especially over 50 years of age. This, plus other features such as an increase in sensori-neural hearing problems, epilepsy and decreased visual activity, suggests neurological deterioration sooner than in ordinary people. Considerable effort is currently going into studies of Alzheimer's disease, since it is a major problem in society as a whole now that more and more people are living longer. The research with people with Down's syndrome is an important part of this endeavour and it is hoped that various treatments will one day be available. Although it is more common in people with Down's syndrome, current estimates indicate that well over half can be expected to survive into their late fifties or sixties without evidence of dementia or any deterioration. Many in their sixties are active and alert and enjoying life to the full.

Similarly, it has been reported that about 12 per cent of people with Down's syndrome in their late fifties have some epileptic fits, while only one to two per cent of the children show signs of epilepsy. If infantile spasms are seen, it is essential to get medical advice. Often anticonvulsant therapy produces a marked improvement and the children continue to develop well. Unfortunately, where the seizures are severe and persist or require major control, the children tend to have much slower intellectual development than other children with Down's syndrome. Of course there are always exceptions and parents should be hopeful and expectant.

Such findings have been used to argue that there is a gradual deterioration of the nervous system. This issue has been increasingly widely discussed in recent years, and I find more parents asking whether the child will lose his skills, suddenly stop developing, reach a point beyond which he will no longer advance but 'go backwards' instead. I shall discuss these questions in more detail in the chapter on mental development. *In practice, the large majority of children with Down's syndrome mature and learn new skills well into their adolescence and early twenties, and having acquired skills they do not easily lose them.* Thus if there is a deterioration in the nervous system it is usually very slow. There is also evidence that many older people with Down's syndrome readily learn new skills, so it would appear that it is only in exceptional cases that rapid deterioration is found.

*'Biochemical' differences*

There is no biochemical system as such – all parts of the body and all systems are made up of and rely on chemical structures. Like the nervous system, this is a very complex field which requires a great deal of specialist knowledge to understand fully, all the more so because new facts are emerging every year as a result of research into Down's syndrome. A large number of biochemical abnormalities have been noted in people with Down's syndrome, but with some exceptions discussed later, their actual effect on development and mental functioning is not yet fully understood.

Because some of these differences in the body's chemistry concern hormones, or enzymes needed in the breakdown of food, a number of people have advocated medical therapy which provides extra vitamins, hormones or special diets. Whilst many claims have been made for the effectiveness of some of those treatments, none has been substantiated by careful, well controlled scientific studies. However, some treatments are offered to parents and many claims are made for them. Every time a newspaper article headlines 'magical' claims, parents find themselves caught up in questions of 'should we try it?', 'are we bad parents if we don't?' Because of this I shall describe the major treatments that have been or are still being offered.

*Vitamin and mineral therapy*

A number of conditions are known to man where a defect in the genetic code leads to lack of a particular biochemical substance which in turn may lead to mental retardation. These involve inborn errors of metabolism and a special diet can reduce or prevent children becoming intellectually impaired.

The problem in Down's syndrome is that it is not just one biochemical substance in disarray but thousands, and only a few of these are actually known. We shall probably find that some are overactive and some are underactive, with many complicated interactions between each of them. It may be that treating Down's syndrome with high-dose vitamins will improve the function of some of the underactive biochemicals, but equally well, they may make some of the overactive ones even more overactive, which may be harmful. Certainly, it is known that when pyridoxine (vitamin B6) is given in high doses when it is not needed, it can damage nerve cells. Toxic states from too much Vitamin A are also known.

However, because differences have been found in the metabolism of children with Down's syndrome, many people have argued for the need of megavitamins or special additional vitamins. The most widely used megavitamin approach is the 'U' series which Turkel has advised since the 1940s. A mixture of 48 vitamins, minerals, enzymes and other drugs are prescribed and Turkel claims they diminish the 'inborn structural, functional and chemical abnormalities in Down's syndrome'. He has not carried out any controlled studies and, because of the wide range of individual differences found in Down's syndrome, it is quite easy to select the more able individuals and then by comparing these to some extreme stereotype, claim a positive result. A controlled study carried out in the early 1960s found no improvement in treated children compared to non-treated children.

More recently, Harrell and her colleagues reported increased intellectual functioning and improved health and physical appearance after an eight-month treatment of megadoses of 11 vitamins and eight minerals. Some children dropped out of the research and no report is given who they are. They could be the ones whose parents felt that it was not working. Also, 14 of the children were given thyroid supplements (see below). Although this study was criticised for being badly designed, it received wide publicity throughout the world. Many parents demanded treatment. However, several well controlled studies have now all failed to repeat the findings. There is therefore no scientific evidence to support the idea that the additional nutritional supplements are needed or are helpful in Down's syndrome. Although there is no evidence to suggest that any of it helps, thankfully no child seems to have been harmed, either. A number of parents have suffered financial loss, however, and parents must be wary of complicated mixtures at expensive prices.

Like all children, children with Down's syndrome will be most healthy on a balanced diet which should provide all the vitamins they need. If you are in the habit of giving your other children multivitamin tablets from the chemist, they should do your child with Down's syndrome no harm. If you are worried about your child becoming overweight, there is probably a dietician at your local hospital who could advise on what to cut down.

Further research into dietary manipulation is needed and will happen as more biochemical knowledge comes to light.

*5-hydroxytryptophan therapy*

It has been shown that people with Down's syndrome have lower than ordinary levels of a neurotransmitter called serotonin. This is related to the slower response and poor muscle tone. It was argued that treatment with 5-hydroxytryptophan would help because it is a precursor in the metabolic pathway leading to serotonin.

Some early small studies, without comparison with non-treated control children, indicated it could work. However, several later studies, all very well designed, could not find any benefits. Again this points to the need for careful scientific research before believing a cure has been discovered. Often, first studies change the hopes of parents and these change the way they interact with the child. Thus the benefit is not in the drug, facial surgery, etc., but in the changes in the parent.

*Cell therapy*
This approach arises from workers in Germany, notably Dr F. Schmidt. It consists of regular injections of freeze-dried organ cells from foetal lambs, called siccacells. The theory is that the cell material will be absorbed by corresponding organs in the child with Down's syndrome and produce improvement in the function of the organ. But cell therapy is never used alone. Additional vitamins, minerals and enzymes are given as well as advice on diet, educational and therapeutic treatments.

Therefore, it is impossible to work out which area of this holistic treatment is effective. Although Schmidt and others report benefits of the treatment compared to untreated children, there is little information about the background and selection of the groups. This is important because such things as the social and economic background and educational level of parents are related to the level of development found in ordinary and Down's syndrome children. Since this treatment is expensive, it may be that more educated and economically well off parents were selected. As with the other approaches, when carefully controlled, double-blind studies have been conducted, no great benefit has been found for the treatment.

Of course in all such treatments there may be children in the group who have a particular problem, such as thyroid or vitamin deficiency, which is helped. But this does not support the overall treatment; instead it suggests that each child should be carefully examined for additional problems. Thyroid dysfunction is a good example of this.

*Thyroid treatment*
Problems with the thyroid gland are more common in Down's syndrome than in the general population. Less than one in 100 babies with Down's syndrome may have a problem, but this will require treatment with thyroid supplements. Ordinary babies with a thyroid problem who are untreated develop mental handicap; therefore it is well to ensure that all babies with Down's syndrome have been tested. As the children grow older there is increasing risk of thyroid dysfunction. About five to ten per cent of children may have an

underactive thyroid gland and as they advance into adulthood there appears to be an increase in risk.

The most common thyroid problem is when the disordered body defences start to produce antibodies against thyroid tissue. This is rare before the age of six or so. About one third of the children affected this way will have close relatives with related problems.

Important symptoms include: the child becoming quite sluggish, unable to think as quickly as usual, or confused; a loss of appetite despite a noticeable increase in weight, becoming very constipated; the voice becoming huskier, the hair thinner and the skin drier than usual. Treatment with thyroid hormone puts the problem right. It is possible that a lot of the signs of deterioration noted in early studies of Down's syndrome relate to undetected inadequate thyroid function.

This undetection is likely because the clinical signs noted above may not be very obvious in the person with Down's syndrome, due to their other characteristics. Therefore, it is recommended that tests should be carried out at regular intervals.

*Conclusions on medical treatments*

Although it is known that it is extra chromosomal material that leads to the characteristic of Down's syndrome, it is not known in any great detail what exactly goes wrong in the individual cells of the body. The twenty-first chromosome carries the genetic code for hundreds of thousands of biochemicals. Our whole body is just one very big but very ordered biochemical reaction and when extra chromosomal material appears the coding becomes confused and the function of cells becomes disordered. We know but a few of the biochemicals which are coded for on the twenty-first chromosome. Some are related to immunity—the body's defences; others to sugar metabolism; and yet others to the production of neurotransmitters—the chemicals that pass messages from one nerve cell to the next. Years of research lie ahead before the full mystery of the twenty-first chromosome will be revealed. At the end of that research we may find that the problem is too complex ever to be put right—short of rearranging the chromosomes in every cell of the body, and currently this is inconceivable.

Meanwhile, people continue to promote ideas on treatment in the hope that they will at least make the child's problems a little better. This is very good as it is all too easy to be completely negative about handicap, but care is needed to assess individual treatments, remembering that they could just as easily do harm as good.

How do you as a parent decide? You will note from the discussion above that where a *specific treatment has been advised for a specific problem*, e.g. thyroid dysfunction or a specific vitamin deficiency, hearing problem, extra-large tongue, etc., then *there are usually very good arguments to support the treatment*. Also, the same treatments are given to other children—not just to Down's syndrome! However, when a treatment is held up as some general, all-embracing cure with more hope than fact attached to the argument, little evidence can be found to support it.

You will need to consult your own medical advisers on these issues. But many of you will find that your GP will *not* know the answers: Down's syndrome is a relatively rare condition in relation to all the ailments that doctors have to deal with. Hence it may be necessary to search out much of this information yourselves. Again, contact with parent groups and any local specialists can be helpful in keeping abreast of new discoveries.

But please, do not pin your hopes to a sudden discovery of a cure. The condition is so complex that the best we can hope for is treatments for specific aspects of it.

*The lungs and respiratory system*

There are usually no abnormalities of the lungs associated with the syndrome. However, many children, particularly in the first years, will have more infections of the respiratory system than ordinary children. This can lead to pneumonia, which was noted as a major cause of death years ago. Antibiotics have considerably reduced this risk, except when the infant also has a severe heart defect. Even so, the children still catch more colds and are more likely to get chest infections than most children. A number of reasons have been put forward to explain this proneness to infection. First, some of the children with Down's syndrome, especially in the first year of life, have less resistance to infectious diseases than ordinary children. It is also thought that some of these children are more than normally likely to inhale mucus or food: partly because the floppiness in their muscles makes them less efficient in swallowing; partly because the mechanisms which respond to inhalation, and stimulate coughing and expectoration of inhaled materials, are less responsive. Since activity and movement help expectoration, providing the child with plenty of handling and exercising is considered to be important in this respect. Some medical professionals also encourage tipping the infant who has an infection or a lot of mucus slightly head down, and then tapping gently on the back. You can get advice on this from your doctor or health clinic.

Another piece of advice relevant to avoiding respiratory infection concerns feeding in the early months. It is best to hold the infant half-upright or upright when feeding. The head should be well supported and not tilted too far backwards, as this is more likely to cause choking and difficulties in swallowing.

We recently compared the children in our group with matched children with Down's syndrome when parents did not have the type of early support and guidance we offered. One important difference in the two groups was less serious health problems (mainly respiratory ones) at ages five to ten years in our group. It is difficult to be certain, but we think that this was because parents were more knowledgeable about health problems, and were more likely to seek help and advice quickly. We also think that the early physical activities and good diet might have helped.

Whilst on the subject of breathing, some parents may have heard about a supportive jacket to help breathing. A number of claims have been made that supportive waistcoats, some of which inflate and deflate to control breathing, can enhance development in Down's syndrome. One proposed theory is that they increase the amount of oxygen in the blood, which in turn helps the brain. Unless the child has cyanotic heart disease, however, there will already be a normal amount of oxygen in the blood and it would be impossible to increase the amount by this means. Furthermore, the children in our research who had heart problems did not have slower mental development than the rest.

It may be that the jackets could be beneficial through

offering good support to the more floppy children in the same way as good supportive seating or regular physical activities and handling. Whilst the jacket remains so expensive, evaluation through careful, controlled studies is awaited before it could be advocated on a widespread basis.

Again, I would like to end this section by emphasising that many children with Down's syndrome do not suffer more from colds and infections than other children. The limited amount of information available suggests that, up to five years of age, about half the children with Down's syndrome do suffer exceptionally from infectious disease. The rate of severe infection would seem to be about twice as high as among ordinary children. But this still leaves half the Down's syndrome children with no more serious problems than other children.

*The reproductive system*

The sex organs of boys and girls with Down's syndrome are usually not affected.

The penis and testicles are often small in the infants, and it is not unusual to find that the testes have not descended into the scrotum in the early years. Some early reports have noted that even at 15 years of age or over some boys will still have an undescended testicle. This appears to be less common nowadays, as treatment is available.

In the first edition of this book I noted that sexual development was often delayed or never occurred. This finding, taken mainly from old descriptions of institutionalised people with Down's syndrome, is clearly incorrect. With more recent studies of children living in the community a different picture is emerging.

Recent studies comparing the sexual development of boys with Down's syndrome residing in the community with the expected norms, find no major differences in the sequential emergence of primary and secondary sex characteristics, the growth of pubic hair or the size of the genitalia. Increasing levels of sex hormones with age were also similar to the norm. The growth of facial hair was, however, generally delayed.

The girls usually develop secondary sex characteristics, though breast development is often moderate compared to the norm. They also begin to menstruate regularly at about the normal age (12½–13 years) or a little later for some. There have been more than three dozen reports of Down's syndrome females becoming pregnant and giving birth. Present figures indicate that about two thirds of the children born were classified as physically and mentally normal; just under one third had Down's syndrome; and a small number were otherwise mentally handicapped. Thus at least some females with Down's syndrome are capable of producing offspring. However, given the large number of females with Down's syndrome, the number of reports of pregnancies is strikingly low. Some reports note that definite evidence of ovulation was found in less than half their samples and about a third of women with Down's syndrome did not ovulate. These are somewhat dated studies and new ones may indicate changes. However, it does suggest that not all females will be fertile.

The large majority of girls can learn to care for themselves during menstruation, and can also understand that this is part of the process of changing from a girl to a woman. Naturally one has to teach this and explain it, patiently and carefully, depending on their level of mental ability. Many mothers find the best way is to let the girl become aware that older females in the family menstruate and, by openness, show that it is neither frightening nor mysterious. Any questions should be answered specifically and simply and not treated as a prompt for an in-depth lecture. Around the time that menses is expected, occasional comments at appropriate times about the fact the girl will also soon be changing in readiness for womanhood helps her to be prepared. The secret is to provide a gradual and natural, step-by-step preparation over a long time period, rather than a sudden crash course to cope with a crisis.

In contrast to the girls, there are no records of any male with Down's syndrome having fathered a child. Such information is obviously less easily available than for the girls, but the weight of the evidence suggests that the boys are less likely to become fertile. An early study, based on 21 males with Down's syndrome aged 15 or over who lived in a large hospital, found that only nine were able to produce a specimen of semen. Of these, four had a zero sperm count and the rest had counts that were very much below normal expectations. Thus it was generally felt that the males with the condition do not achieve fertility. More recent studies on spermatogenesis (sperm formation) have reported normal spermatogenesis, although there is less than normal sperm production. Therefore, the male with Down's syndrome cannot be considered as sterile.

The changes in findings over the years may be due to the greater maturity of boys with Down's syndrome brought up at home with better diet and care, than earlier samples residing in institutions. However, although the research indicates that the boys show the normally expected sequences of primary and secondary sex characteristics, there is little substantive information on sperm production and fertility and sexual functioning. (Parents will appreciate the research workers' reluctance in exploring this area, since it involves requesting parents' permission to obtain specimens of semen from their sons, which in turn requires masturbation.)

The main information on sexual functioning in people with Down's syndrome comes from parents. It would appear that well over half of the adolescents and young adults are interested in the opposite sex and many have special friends. However, the majority do not appear to develop a sex drive to the same degree as ordinary people. Generally they appear to have far less than normal interest in and desire for sexual intercourse, and their activities are usually limited to self-stimulation. Masturbation has been noted in about half the young people with Down's syndrome.

How we parents react to the developing sexual needs of our children will depend largely on our own attitudes, feelings and ease in dealing with sexual matters. I cannot deal with this subject in any depth in this book, and can only say that young people with Down's syndrome may mature to the extent that they will have sexual needs. If this is mainly self-oriented, then you may not need to do more than teach them to be discreet.

Many children and young people with Down's syndrome are openly affectionate and enjoy physical contact such as hugging and cuddling. This does not necessarily have the same meaning as it might for an ordinary person of the same age. Such behaviour, however, can be socially inappropriate, and parents may need to teach the child how to use more socially acceptable behaviours.

Many mentally handicapped people, including some who

have Down's syndrome, will mature to such a degree that they do have both sexual needs and the need for emotional attachment to another person. In other words, they can fall in love like the rest of us. When this happens they want to share their lives and experiences. In recent years more people have accepted this, and more mentally handicapped people are marrying. Some live in small community hostels and others in their own homes. There are certainly increasing numbers of Down's syndrome people getting married. Whilst these represent a small number of all people with Down's syndrome, it is likely that we shall see an increase as society changes its attitudes, and people with Down's syndrome become more skilled and able as a result of better care and education.

In this context, I would like to make the point that improving the care and treatment of children with Down's syndrome does not necessarily result in fewer problems for parents: it merely changes the problems we face. I suppose this is true for all parents of all children.

What really matters is that the changes improve the quality of life for our children, and so makes us feel more satisfied. Parents are very vulnerable when it comes to new ideas of treatment for their child. Those who may have difficulties getting over the shattered dream of the child they never had, may be particularly likely to jump at any suggestion to 'put it right', to make their child 'normal'. Their depression can lead them on to programmes to 'stimulate' the child eight hours a day; to use unproven forms of treatment or raise money for a trip to a specialist in the hope of a miracle. The true aim of any therapy or advice should be to ensure that our children grow to be happy, content and able to reach their developmental potential and that we as parents, and brothers and sisters, accept them and love them for who they are.

## *Chapter Six*

# PERSONALITY AND TEMPERAMENT

Parental questions about personality, temperament and social development usually concern:

(i) What are people with Down's syndrome like?
(ii) Are there characteristic personality traits or behaviours associated with the condition?
(iii) What is the likelihood of the child developing behavioural difficulties?

I shall begin with the first question.

Many people appear to believe that there is a set of characteristic behaviours associated with Down's syndrome. The man in the street, the professional and many books share the picture of children and adults as 'affectionate, placid or docile, gentle, having a good sense of fun'. People with Down's syndrome are also said to have special talents, such as being 'good mimics' and 'musical'. These ideas can be traced back to Langdon Down, who wrote:

> They have considerable power of imitation, even bordering on being mimics. They are humorous, and a lively sense of the ridiculous often colours their mimicry . . .*

and also:

> Several patients who have been under my care have been wont to convert their pillowslips into surplices and to imitate, in tone and gesture, the clergyman or chaplain they have recently heard.†

*From Down, J. H. L. (1866) 'Observations on an Ethnic Classification of Idiots'. Clinical Lectures and Reports. London: London Hospital. Reprinted in T. E. Jordan (Ed.) Perspectives in Mental Retardation. University of Illinois, Cardondale, Illinois.

†Quoted in Penrose and Smith, G. F. (1966) Down's anomaly. London: J. & A. Churchill.

However, he also noted that they could be very self-willed and stubborn:

> No amount of coercion will induce them to do that which they have made up their minds not to do.*

A problem with any physically recognisable condition, such as Down's syndrome is that stereotypes are easily attached to it. It is also true that we all tend to see what we are looking for. Thus once Down had attached these behavioural characteristics to the condition, everybody began to see them and report them. Consequently there are many descriptions of the stereotype, and these often actually contradict each other. People with Down's syndrome are, for instance, supposed to be both 'pleasant, gentle, outward-going and affectionate' and also 'mischievous, sullen and stubborn'.

I should say now that later attempts to study these behavioural traits more scientifically have not supported the idea of a very strong uniform or dominant set of behaviours. Before trying to summarise what has been found and not found, I would like to take a little time to explain some of the difficulties in this area.

**Influences on personality and temperament**

We can begin by asking what things influence our personality and temperament. At a simple level we would all probably agree on the following propositions:

1 Our environment—our surroundings, the things we can do, the way we are treated by others and so on—will have some influence. We should also note that personality changes and traits have been associated with diet, drug treatments and illnesses.
2 Our mental and physical abilities are important. If, from the first days of play, we are used to tackling problems and being successful, this must influence how we think about ourselves and how we act. A problem with handicapped children is that they often do not have good problem solving skills (mental or physical) and so can become accustomed to failure. This will not help their sense of self-esteem, so it is

*Quoted in Penrose and Smith, G. F. (1966) Down's anomaly. London: J. & A. Churchill.

no wonder they stop trying, become inactive, or turn their frustrations on themselves and others.

3 Our genetic code may well carry information which sets the direction, if not the actual behaviours, of our personality and temperament. Parents will often tell you that one of their children was always impulsive, energetic, tending not to think before acting, whereas another was quiet, observant and cautious even as a baby. It is this belief that part of our personalities and temperament are inherited that leads to the idea that extra genetic information carried by the extra chromosome 21 in Down's syndrome will not only alter the physical and mental development, but also the behaviour and personality. I must say that I find the idea of the extra chromosome material producing people who are cheerful, pleasant and gentle very consoling. Why should the effect of the extra material only be seen in a negative way?

4 Finally, we should not ignore the fact that the behaviour and temperament of many of us changes as we grow—especially around adolescence and when we begin to age. This is not due only to the increase in our knowledge and experience, but also to chemical changes in our bodies—particularly hormonal changes.

Of course these sources of influence will all work together, or sometimes against each other, to produce the personalities and temperaments of each of us. For this reason it is very difficult to be exact about whether there is a strong likelihood that people with Down's syndrome will have a characteristic set of behaviours. The major problem is that most of the early anecdotal reports—and even later studies—were carried out on children and adults who lived in large institutions.

**Information from older studies**

I should point out that up to the 1960s most doctors recommended that parents place their baby with Down's syndrome in an institution. It was genuinely believed that this course of action was best for the family and the child. Much of this belief rested upon the assumption that the problems of the condition were biological, and that environmental aspects had little influence. Hence there was no reason to try to stimulate or teach them. Around the 1960s and 1970s several research studies compared the mental and social development of children who lived and were cared for at home (or fostered with a family) with the development of those who had lived in institutions. As one might expect, those children living at home were usually found to be more developmentally advanced, to have more outward-going behaviour and to have acquired a larger range of interests and social skills. (It is important to understand that it is not the institution *per se* that produces these results—it is the lack of stimulation and activities provided for the child that fails to encourage the development. Smaller community or residential schools, well staffed and providing ample educational, recreational and social opportunities, need not have these deficiencies.)

Another problem is that many mentally handicapped children are placed in institutions because they have become 'too difficult to manage' at home. Therefore the percentage figures of difficulties and behaviour problems of people with Down's syndrome who live in institutions will be biased not just by the lack of opportunity there, but also by selection. Thus we have to treat any observations based on children and adults in institutions with some caution.

Further, if we feel that environmental influences strongly affect our temperament and personality, we will inevitably be sceptical of such reports. If we also accept recent arguments that much of our 'personality' is set in the so-called formative years (up to five), it would seem rather foolish to derive characteristic behaviours from older children and adults—particularly those who have been moulded by years of living in dull and unstimulating surroundings.

Alternatively, if we believe that biological influences are stronger, we will be more willing to accept some of the institutional findings. (We cannot resolve this question of the relative contributions of environment and inheritance, and we shall meet it again in the section on mental ability.)

## Recent studies

Overall, the studies do not support the idea of a dominant set of behaviour characteristics for all people with Down's syndrome. Certainly one cannot predict what type of person a particular baby with Down's syndrome will become, as there is considerable individual variation. However, there is some agreement about *some* behavioural characteristics that seem to be more often associated with the condition. These characteristics vary with age—just as they do with all of us—and so I shall try to summarise them in a developmental sequence.

*The baby*

In the first months, the baby with Down's syndrome tends to be quiet and is unlikely to be difficult. Mothers frequently note what good babies they are and how much easier they are than their other children were.

People have indeed often described them as very placid, inactive babies who sleep a lot, and this is often true of those with severe heart defects or other complications. Mothers in our research kept diaries of how long the baby slept, how often he or she cried and for how long, and what length of time was spent on activities throughout the day. The only conclusion we reached was that the babies with Down's syndrome cried far less than ordinary babies—some never at all in the first weeks. They were also more likely to sleep through the night. Thus the idea of placid, inactive babies may arise partly as a result of the babies being less demanding in that they cry less. However the floppiness in some babies in the first weeks, and the apparent lack of strong arm and leg thrusts, also tends to give the appearance of non-activity. Many parents are also a little afraid to handle the baby as robustly as an ordinary baby, and of course are often still in a state of shock and confusion over the diagnosis. Or they may leave the quiet baby in the cot or pram in the belief that she is sleeping, and that sleep helps.

Therefore whilst it is true that many babies with Down's syndrome are rather quiet and placid in the first weeks, this image may be exaggerated and perpetuated for lack of normal levels of handling and play.

For this reason we advise mothers not to rely on the baby to let them know when she wants feeding or needs attention. Instead, we suggest they establish the feeding routines and ensure the baby has lots of opportunities for stimulation and plenty of handling when awake.

Once parents begin to handle and stimulate the baby they usually find the infant far more active than they thought. By three to four months most parents find the baby is alert, active and responsive. Studies which have required mothers to fill in questionnaires about the babies' temperament from around three months onwards, usually report no differences between the replies of mothers with ordinary babies and those with Down's syndrome.

*The young child*

The very few studies over the age range of the first five years generally find that the behaviour of the child with Down's syndrome is similar to that of other children *at the same level of development*. In our research we compared the temperament of 106 children with Down's syndrome aged between two and nine years with 105 one- to five-year-old children living in the same areas. The mothers of the children with Down's syndrome rated them as less emotional, less aggressive, less bossy, less moody and more likeable and affectionate compared to how the mothers of the ordinary children rated their children. Therefore there was some support for the common idea that these children are more placid, affectionate and outward-going than ordinary children in the first five or so years of life. Although the findings support the idea that these children are more likely to have an even temperament, the range of temperamental differences between the children with Down's syndrome was as large as the ordinary children. There was also a great deal of overlap between the groups. The overriding finding therefore, was of a great variety of temperaments with quiet, thoughtful children and impulsive, active children.

Of interest was an indication that the traits of even temperament, affection and outward-goingness, seemed to be stronger in the older children. Associated with this was the finding that the best match of the patterns with those of ordinary children was found using the children's developmental level rather than their chronological age. Thus, apart from some indication that more children with Down's syndrome are likely to be less arousable and emotional than ordinary children, they were very similar to ordinary children of the same developmental level.

The results also showed that the slower developing children were more likely to be impulsive and energetic, while the more able children tended to be quieter, more moody, anxious and fussy. In a later study of five- to ten-year-olds, we also found this. It appears that as the children develop higher mental abilities they are more able to understand and anticipate and so, just like everyone else, they can worry and get upset over ideas and thoughts rather than just react to immediate events.

One interesting difference between the two groups was the way in which the mothers likened the child's future temperament to a relative. Forty per cent of the mothers of the ordinary children did this, but only 12 per cent of the Down's syndrome group. This appears a little unusual, given the fact that the temperament in the Down's syndrome children was as varied and different as in ordinary children and also, as described in Chapter Four, that the genes that plan the development of the child with Down's syndrome are the same as for any child and come from the mother and father. The only difference is that there are some extra ones.

Therefore, when thinking about the temperament and behaviour of the young child with Down's syndrome, it is best to think about it in the same way as for any child and avoid thinking that it has to be abnormal. But of course it tends to relate to the developmental level of the child and not to the chronological age. For example, there are fewer temper tantrums and self-willed behaviour in one and a half to two-year-old children with Down's syndrome than in ordinary children. By three to four years, however, the children with Down's syndrome are producing only slightly fewer temper tantrums than the ordinary two-year-olds. Once the children with Down's syndrome become mobile, they begin to 'get into trouble' and 'mischief' like any child. Most mothers find that the 'type of trouble' is very similar to that of any other child of the same level of development. However, as the toddler stage progresses, mothers of children with Down's syndrome tend to report more mischief and trouble than with ordinary children. This is mainly due to the fact that the ordinary child by this age has grown out of the worst of the toddler stage. He no longer gets frustrated by knowing what he wants but not how to get it. It is not so much that he grows out of the frustrating period, but that he learns to express his wants and can be reasoned with more easily. By three to four years most children have developed good language and communication skills, and a wide range of interests and activities. They can usually be directed to these; they will also occupy themselves for longer and have the initiative to find something to do.

Clearly, the mental ability of the child and the rate at which this develops is closely associated with the difficulties he experiences. Since children with Down's syndrome do not develop these mental abilities and skills as quickly as ordinary children, they remain in the toddler stage for longer. In particular they often lag more behind in their language skills than in other abilities, and this can add to the frustrations and difficulties. The child's temperament will also influence the behaviours. If the child is energetic and impulsive this can add to the difficulties. As the mother of one of our four-year-old boys remarked:

> I can't keep up with him, he never stops, he won't play with anything for more than a few moments . . . he gets cross because I don't know what he wants . . . I dread the holidays . . . will he ever grow out of it!

If the child is not very energetic and has a rather quiet nature, parents may not experience difficulties.

> I know she isn't as bright or advanced as Alan, but at least I'm not run off my feet like Alan's mum, she's a very peaceful, gentle little soul and no trouble at all . . .

I believe that both of these comments could have been made by any mother, and this is really what 80–90 per cent of families seem to feel: namely, that the behaviour problems and difficulties are not very different from those of the ordinary child in these first years.

Recently we have carried out a series of very detailed studies to find out about the range and nature of behaviour difficulties in children with Down's syndrome aged five to 12 years. We interviewed 120 families about the sort of things the children did and about any problems that arose. We also asked families to complete rating scales of behaviour difficulties similar to those used with ordinary children. We found that the number of families experiencing a lot of problems was about the same as that found for ordinary children (12 to 15 per cent). We also found that the factors associated with high levels of difficulty in the families were similar: they usually had many relationship problems between family members. In addition, many had extra problems causing strain, such as financial difficulties, unemployment, poor housing and poor health. Thus it was not the child's Down's syndrome that appeared to be the main source of the difficulties but the home environment. This was also supported by the fact that we did not find any higher levels of behaviour problems in the brothers and sisters of children with Down's syndrome than found in ordinary children. However, in the families with the above difficulties, the brothers and sisters also had high levels of problems. This strongly suggests social factors are influential.

Although we did not find a higher than normal proportion of families of children with Down's syndrome to be having severe difficulties with the child, we did find that nearly three-quarters of the mothers in our research felt they had some behaviour difficulty with the child and also that the type of problems experienced were different from those more commonly reported for ordinary children.

The children with Down's syndrome were reported as having higher levels of problems in going to bed and settling down to sleep (20 per cent); waking up at night (over 40 per cent); sleeping with parents (24 per cent); poor concentration and attention seeking (20 per cent); and fears (15 per cent), e.g. of loud noises, the dark, lifts, dogs, etc. In contrast, the problems most often noted for ordinary children of the same developmental level are: faddy eating and night wetting (often associated with emotional difficulties); being over-active and restless; showing high dependency and clingingness to mothers, and having more difficult relationships with brothers and sisters.

Toileting difficulties reduced with both groups over time. However, ordinary children are generally toilet trained earlier than children with Down's syndrome. With some exceptions our calculations suggest that toilet training is largely related to the child's mental age and level of maturation. In other words, if you are finding that toileting is difficult, ask yourself if the child's general levels of ability are those at which you would expect most children to be trained. If not, then keep encouraging the child but do not expect rapid progress. In some cases, as with any child, toileting is not 100 per cent for some years. Again these tend to be individual but normal differences and the child will eventually grow out of them.

The sleeping problems are more complicated. They can be very disruptive on families, particularly when everyone loses sleep. With some infants and young children between one to five years of age, many parents experience sleep problems. They tend to try to get the child to sleep in his or her own bed, but if this is not achieved relatively quickly, they give up and hope the child will soon grow out of the problem. With most ordinary children this happens but with many children who have delayed development, refusing to go to bed, getting up and waking at night, getting into the parents' bed or the bed of a brother and sister becomes a habit. When they are little it is easier to put up with such behaviour. Unfortunately, they will learn the routine and will expect it. After all, they learn from their daily routine and it is only when they mature and develop the intellectual abilities to reason and understand explanations, that one can begin to explain why they should change a routine that they have experienced all their lives. Therefore, from an early age it is best to train habits that are likely to be compatible with the family. It is also far easier to establish or change a routine at the beginning, than later when it has become second nature. Of course it is difficult to remember this at three in the morning, after several disturbed nights. The general rules are to establish a routine about going to bed which is as close to the grown-up routine as you can make it. Give some signals that bedtime is approaching, like getting out the pyjamas, finding the Teddy, washing and cleaning teeth, a little cuddle. Try to get the timing right so that the child goes to bed when he is likely to be tired but before he becomes overtired. If he wakes at night, have a programme of small steps worked out, with the first step being the most compatible with the child sleeping, e.g. stroking his head. Do not, for example, put the light on, pick him up and play or take him downstairs to watch TV or have a drink. Most children will soon learn to wake up for this type of entertainment. Finally, from our calculations we believe that problems with sleep are largely related to social factors and the way the child is treated, and not so much to developmental level. We did not find very strong associations between sleep problems and the levels of mental ability in the children. Many very able children had sleep problems and many slower children had none. The difference was usually to do with the attitude of the family and how they treated the issue.

Some of the other problems found more often in the children with Down's syndrome do appear to relate to mental ability. Children with lower levels of development were more likely to be rated by mothers as having poor concentration, as being restless and attention seeking. The problem for parents of these children is to keep up with them and keep them amused: since most things will only hold their attention for a short while, this can be a difficult task. Families who could share the task of amusing and stimulating the child with relatives and friends, and had access to play schemes, clubs and occasional shared care, appeared to cope better and experience less strain. Shared care included the use of a family who would have the child for a few days on a regular basis, and also access to small residential facilities. Such schemes are usually run by local services who will provide information. Generally progress is slow in these children, but it does happen and, with time, many gradually become easier to manage. Patient teaching and encouragement of activities that are within the ability and interest of the child are needed. Parents often find that other parents and teachers can be helpful in suggesting such activities.

Of course one cannot explain all behaviour problems in terms of the lower mental ability of the child. As was noted above, we found evidence of several behaviours which, although they are more common in young children, linger on in the children with Down's syndrome. Among these are things like temper tantrums, throwing, wandering off and running away, failing to amuse himself and play for any length of time, and not being compliant and easy to manage. These sorts of behaviour were often associated with families who were experiencing many problems, where the level of education of the parents was low, the family income was low, and the children tended to have more ear infections and health problems. Many of these families had more problems getting on with each other and experienced more stress. The relationship between the mother and her child was also more strained, although this did not often show itself in a less affectionate relationship than in other families. What was most interesting was that these behaviour difficulties did not associate with mental ability but did relate to poorer levels of language and communication and poorer ability in self-help skills such as washing, dressing, etc. This makes sense. If families are only just coping and if there is not a lot of time or energy left to talk to each other and have positive interactions, then the conditions necessary for helping the development of good communication and appropriate behaviour patterns are far from ideal. Therefore one should be careful not to believe that all the problems of behaviour or low achievement in children with Down's syndrome are the result of the extra chromosome. Like any children, they are susceptible to adverse environmental conditions.

This was even more obvious in a further group of behaviours which were not related to mental ability or communication skills, nor associated with poor housing or adverse social factors. The behaviours included aggressiveness, pestering others and attention seeking, high levels of being miserable and irritable, and poor relationships with siblings. These sorts of behaviour were associated with low affection shown towards the child by the parents, poor relationships between parent and child (revealed by a lot of criticism) and few positive statements about the child by the parents. They were also associated with poorer ratings of marital relationships and poor measures of adjustment to the child's handicap.

Only a small number of children and families fall into this pattern, probably less than one in seven. However, they do show up quite sharply when one is used to families saying how happy and likeable the child with Down's syndrome is; how they have an ability to cheer you up and make you feel better; how they are a social asset by making people come together and be sociable; how they remain cheerful and are not moody.

It is difficult to sort out which particular factors are more or less likely to contribute to families experiencing poor relationships with the child. There are a few who are unhappy families generally and again, the fact that one child has Down's syndrome is not the major problem. However, when the child is very active, attention seeking and has difficult behaviours such as making noises, throwing objects or is difficult to control—often because he has poor language and communication ability—then families can feel very strained. It is often the unpredictability of the child and the constant need for parents to supervise and entertain him, that cause the problem.

This type of child is more likely to have low intellectual ability and severe mental handicap. However they are a minority.

Many children with Down's syndrome will have a period between three and five years when they fail to acquire language and communication skills as quickly as other aspects of their development. This can bring frustrations and a taxing time for parents. Recently schools and support groups have started teaching the child and the family how to use signing with the hands as a way of helping communication at this time, so reducing the frustration experienced by the child and the family. There are many anecdotal statements indicating that where the child and family had learnt a signing system it was a great help. Of course, it should not be a substitute for verbal communication. The idea is to learn the system and teach the child when he or she is around a year old and beginning to communicate more formally. Parents who are thinking about this should get advice from a speech therapist at the local health clinic.

Many parents find that things become easier around the time when the child develops language and communication skills and begins to link more ideas together in longer sequences. At this time he or she is also more likely to make immediate and accurate imitations of sequences of behaviour and enter into more interactive play with others. This corresponds to developmental abilities seen around two to three years in ordinary children. In children with Down's syndrome this is sometime between three and five years for over 50 per cent (see Chapter Seven). It is also around this age that some parents feel the child is getting stubborn and self-willed, and so feel that they themselves should be stricter. My impressions are that many instances of stubbornness are identical to those seen in the ordinary two- to four-year-old who is beginning to develop some independence, initiative and self-will—all vital for healthy development. Other instances of 'stubbornness' in the children with Down's syndrome seem to arise from their slowness in understanding and reacting to what is being requested of them, and the needs of harrassed mothers trying to get through a busy day.

As the children get older, most parents find that the child with Down's syndrome becomes easier to manage as his or her mental ability increases. Communication, and hence management, becomes easier. The child can begin to explain things that happened and that interest him or her. In this way parents find it easier to organise activities which are of interest to the children and so help them to amuse themselves for longer. However, even in early adolescence, and for the more able children, parents still find they often have to work hard to get the children doing things. As one father said of his twelve-year-old son:

> Things are much better in the last year or so. Since his language came on we can have conversations. He is good company at times but before he just sat in the car saying yes or no. Mind you, I still have to be the organiser and entertainment officer, otherwise he would just sit and watch TV all day.

Other parents also comment on the 'what's he up to syndrome'. For example, things are peaceful and they have not seen their thirteen-year-old for over half an hour, they become anxious and usually go to find out what is going on. This supervisory aspect appears to be common to the majority of parents in the childhood years. Again it is related to the child's developmental ability and to the parents' attitude and willingness to take risks. It is closely associated with where the family lives and the dangers that parents perceive. Thus, again, the issues are not just about the child and the handicap but about the sort of support and facilities that are available and about the way the parent views the child, the handicap and the situation.

This last point is important. In Chapter Two I discussed the issues of adjusting to the handicap. Earlier in this chapter it was also noted that problems in some children seem to be associated with how well the parent adjusted to having a child with Down's syndrome. We have also looked at this from a different direction. On several occasions we have asked the parents in our research what they think their children with Down's syndrome will be like when they are older. About half felt very positive. They felt the child would be sociable, easy to manage, happy and relatively independent. Our assessments at later ages show that these predictions have largely been correct. The other half were less sure, but less than ten per cent had very negative predictions about the future. We also found that the fears of the mothers of children with Down's syndrome were much stronger than for ordinary children. This was particularly so when the child was difficult to control. As one mother put it, 'He's difficult enough now . . . I daren't look that far ahead.'

However, in many cases these fears were not really to do with the child but with the confusion and uncertainty of the parents. Another mother expressed it this way: 'I'm dreading the future. He's strong now and might get stronger. I'm worried he might get uncontrollable. But it's other people that put these doubts into your mind, isn't it?' This uncertainty creates anxiety and keeps people on edge.

In our study on behaviour difficulties we found some mothers who appeared to be 'ill at ease' with the child's handicap and who had not quite come to terms with their feelings or adjusted to the problem. These mothers had higher ratings of strain and health worries when compared to the mothers who indicated they were more at ease with the handicap and their feelings about it. We looked to see if other factors like illness in other members of the family or financial worries were different between the two groups but could not find them. We also found that the children of both groups had equal levels of behaviour difficulties and independence skills, and that both groups were equally supported by husbands, relatives and friends. We concluded that a small number of mothers find it difficult to sort out their feelings about having a child with a handicap. They often appear to dwell on their fears about the future and, because of the constant feeling of uncertainty, they are particularly vulnerable to the uninformed comments of other people. As the mother in the above quote said, 'It's other people that put these doubts into your mind'.

I do not think there is an easy solution to the difficulties that parents like this have. To a large extent it relates to the type of people we have grown up to be. Some are always assured and confident and others have to live with constant doubts and uncertainties. But it is possible to reduce these if they are associated with the fact that the child has a handicap. Firstly, in the early months after the birth, parents need to work through how they feel about themselves and the handicap. Sometimes, people only do a little of this, until they feel able just to cope. They then avoid some of their deeper fears and feelings. Unfortunately these do not necessarily go away but can surface at later times, particularly when other sources of strain are around and one's defences are low. In the case of the above mothers, these feelings appear to be under the surface and do effect their everyday lives and the way they interpret the behaviour of the child. It is important, therefore, to get some form of help, either from a professional or from other parents. Discussing one's feelings with people who are trusted and knowledgeable often helps all of us to get a better understanding of ourselves. Secondly, dwelling on such things as 'what might happen' and 'if he does this' can be very tiring and a strain. It is better to get hold of some facts. In the above quoted case, the mother needed to ask, What is the evidence that the boy will grow up very strong and uncontrollable? What is it about his present behaviour that predicts this? Only when one has carefully analysed the problem can one have a chance of making sensible predictions and doing something that is likely to help.

Overall, therefore, we can see many influences on the behaviour of the child with Down's syndrome and it is a mistake to assume that there is a strong, innate and characteristic type of temperament. If anything, the evidence shows a wide range of temperaments and personalities, from outward-going show-offs, to timid and shy children; from active, boisterous and impulsive types to quiet, thoughtful ones. These different types of temperament will interact with different types of environment and, in particular, with the way people close to the child treat them. If they are treated with love and respect then they will be more likely to develop confident and affectionate natures. Clearly, the way the child can express himself and interact with the world will depend to a large extent on his abilities. If these develop more slowly, or there are specific problems, this will influence the child's nature as well as the reactions of others. If the child keeps experiencing high levels of failure or is not expected to do things, he will be different from the child who is encouraged to meet challenges to his abilities in a safe, caring atmosphere, without the risk of ridicule or chastisement. Therefore, when we look at the studies of personality in the older child and adult with Down's syndrome, we must keep such points in mind.

*Older children and adults*

Several studies of older children and adults have identified three types of behaviour pattern in Down's syndrome. These studies each classified the majority of people as being pleasant, outward going, active, affectionate and sociable with a sense of humour. A minority were described as being less able in skills, and dull and listless. Into a third category were placed a few who were found to be aggressive, pugnacious, destructive and sometimes very difficult to control.

This is similar to our results in which a minority were lethargic and inactive, with very low levels of energy output,* and a few were extremely irritable and restless and difficult to manage.

As I have noted, the less attractive behaviours appear to be associated with lack of mental ability, skills and interests. In particular, there seems to be an increase in negative behaviours if language and communication skills fail to develop reasonably well, and if the child does not move from early concrete mental activity to increased reasoning and conceptualisation (see Chapter Seven). The ability to understand and communicate about the things that happen to one is important for the growth of personality and for the maintenance of an appropriate temperament.

Therefore many people now take the view that the chances of anti-social behaviours appearing will be reduced if children grow up in caring, loving homes and are given every aid to ensure good, healthy, physical growth, and if parents are given good early counselling, advice and support on the best management, stimulation and teaching methods. Improvements in schooling and community services are also likely to improve the prospects for later life and reduce the incidence of behavioural difficulties.

Even so, some of these children will have disorders of personality—as will a number of children who are thought to

*Some doctors think that some of this listlessness may be due to hypothyroidism and could be treated (see p. 134).

be quite normal at birth—which are not just the result of poor management and environmental conditions. Some will have biological disorders which cause difficulties, and these often set off a chain reaction with the way we treat and react to the child, which can increase the problem. This is why special advice and treatment is often required, and parents who face these difficulties will need to seek help. In some cases the severity of the behaviour disorder, particularly for the very restless, irritable child with poor skills and reasoning ability, will be too great for the family to cope with and the available treatments and management techniques may not be successful. In such cases some parents find that they have to consider residential care for their child.

Fortunately the available information indicates that such difficulties are not common in Down's syndrome. There is general agreement that behaviour disorders are found less often in children and adults with Down's syndrome than in other conditions associated with mental handicap. This is true particularly for aggressive and hyperactive behaviours. Current estimates indicate that between eight and 15 per cent of children and adults with Down's syndrome will have a behaviour or personality disorder severe enough to cause concern and require treatment.

Older people with Down's syndrome can, like any other person, suffer from depression and mental illness. Sometimes there is a gradual withdrawing and an apparent lack of interest in things generally. In the past this has often been overlooked and thought to be part of a general deterioration in mental functioning. This is a mistake and, before it is decided that the person is simply deteriorating, the advice of a specialist in mental handicap and mental illness should be sought. Sometimes the young adult becomes unhappy and morose. Although there is not a lot written about such changes, I believe that in some cases it coincides with new levels of maturation and advances in mental ability. The young person suddenly gains new insights into his or her way of life which can be unsettling. For example, one young lady was adamant that she would grow up and marry Prince Charles. About the time of his wedding she suddenly realised that this would not happen and indeed that it was unlikely she would ever get married. This insight proved to be very upsetting and she needed quite a lot of supportive counselling to develop new ideas for her future. In other cases the young people developed sudden phobias. One refused to sleep in his bedroom, believing someone was hiding there. This was resolved by psychiatric treatment, but it was interesting that, before seeking treatment, the parent had thought it must be part of the Down's syndrome and that there was not much that could be done.

Some changes in personality are related to ageing and deterioration. People with Down's syndrome are more likely than the rest of us to age quicker and may suffer from early senility. However, it is a mistake to assume that this will explain all later changes and, in fact, there are many mistaken ideas about deterioration of mental functioning in Down's syndrome, as will be discussed in the next chapter.

**Management**

The above account of temperament and behaviour in children with Down's syndrome strongly indicates that the temperament of the large majority of these children is very similar to that expected in a range of ordinary children. When difficulties arise they are often similar to those of the ordinary child at the same developmental stage, but of course the child with Down's syndrome is older. Temper tantrums or running away in a two-year-old poses a different management problem from that of a larger child. There is also the added complication of the child's learning difficulty. This is really an inability to take in large amounts of information quickly and process it so that it is understood and acted upon. It is also a problem with communication. Often the children do not have the language skills to listen and understand quickly and, more importantly, to express their needs. Not only can this cause frustration which is likely to lead to behaviour difficulties, but it is likely that the type of management that parents use with ordinary children of the same age, in this case will not work.

The research on how parents manage children with Down's syndrome is not very clear. It varies enormously between parents and it is often difficult to work out if the child's problem is a result of the way the parent has treated the child, or whether parents have run out of energy and patience. But do remember that over half the parents do not have many problems and certainly find that they soon adapt to their child's special differences and just modify the approaches they would use with any child. In the case of very slow and severely handicapped children, they have to use increasingly special techniques.

Before describing these, I would like to comment on the importance of the attitude of parents. The research we have suggests that, in the first year or so, the child with Down's syndrome is fairly easy to deal with. Also, just under half of the parents state that they are less strict with them than with their other children, and less than one in ten of the other half felt that they were more strict. Around about three to four years, the 'terrible twos' stage when children are into everything and demand variety and attention, most parents find that their child with Down's syndrome becomes more difficult. Many parents find they become stricter at this time, but some continue to indulge the child. They are less consistent in demanding that the child behaves reasonably compared to their other children. Sometimes parents' feelings about the handicap and the child prevent them from being firm.

There are ways which can help to reduce and modify major behaviour difficulties. Firstly, it is necessary really to analyse the problem. It is of little use saying the child has a sleeping or eating problem or continually runs away. You need to ask, and make notes or records of, exactly what he or she does. When does he wake up? How often? Every night or only at weekends? What happened before going to bed? Did he drink a lot, or was he excited or late or early or had a busy day? What happens when he wakes up—does he get rewarded with lots of attention? When does she refuse to feed or throw the food? At every meal, or not at breakfast when she is very hungry? Does she really refuse to eat or is it a case of eating a bit to satisfy her appetite and then playing a game? What foods will she always eat? What happens when she refuses or throws—do you keep coaxing and therefore reward her with your attention? In your concern that she is not eating enough, do you keep changing foods to find one she likes? If so, is it the variety of experience and the chance of something favourite that rewards her and therefore keeps the behaviour going? When he runs away in the street, do you always give chase? Does he run away in the park? Do you chase him? How far will he run before waiting to see if you will chase? Have you tested this in a safe place?

You need to find out, 1) what happens before the behaviour that may trigger it? This could be a particular event or a place. 2) What exactly is the problem? Count it; describe in detail precisely what happens. 3) What happens immediately after the behaviour that could be acting as a reward? And do not think that because you tell the child off this could not be a reward. Your attention might be far more stimulating than sitting quietly. Only when you know the problem can you begin to plan and try out experiments to get rid of it. If you do try a plan of action, please be positive and do not give up after a few days. In my experience, if the behaviour is learnt it can be changed. It is all a matter of good planning and then getting through to the child (communicating) what you want and do not want. Things usually fail because the problem was not fully understood and analysed and/or everyone gave up before the child had time to learn what was expected. If he has established a real habit over many months or years, it is hardly likely to be re-learnt in days. Finally, if it really is difficult, try to get some help from a psychologist or other professional. They can often give you moral support and be more objective, especially when you feel it just is not worth the effort.

> This psychologist came about the sleeping problem. We worked out a step-by-step programme of what to do to get him to bed—a routine, really. We also worked out how I had to send him back to bed every time he got up. On his wall we made a chart and if he stayed in bed we stuck a star on it in the morning. A big ceremony with lots of fuss.
>
> I thought it was a waste of time at first. I had tried to reward him for not getting up before. If the psychologist hadn't been coming every week to check up on me I would have given up.
>
> I kept at it. Sending him back. It was only a few weeks but it seemed like months. It made me consistent. And it worked. Looking back it made me feel more confident about sorting out problems. I won't give up or believe you can't do something to help.

**Facts in this chapter**

1 There is no consistent support for the idea of a uniform personality type in Down's syndrome. Instead, there is considerable variation in both normal and abnormal behaviours.

2 But there is some consensus and a strong impression that very young babies are rather placid and quiet at first, but soon turn into outward-going, lively, exploratory children with few management problems.

The majority grow up to be cheerful and pleasant with an affectionate nature. This temperamental pattern is more likely to be associated with those who:

(a) have been well cared for emotionally and physically from birth;

(b) have received good management, stimulation and education, especially during the critical stages of the early years and middle childhood, but also at the later stage around 15–20 years; and

(c) are more mentally able and develop the communication skills and reasoning and conceptualising abilities associated with the normal developmental stages of three years onwards.

3 Those who are less able and appear to have less energy output can become rather sullen and stubborn in the adolescent years. Consequently parents can find management an increasingly difficult and tiring problem. Such problems are often associated with lack of development in communication and reasoning abilities.

4 However, few appear to develop severe behaviour disorders such as aggressiveness, irritability, hyperactivity and impulsivity. The risk of severe behaviour disorders appearing is lower in Down's syndrome than in other mentally handicapping conditions.

5 Methods for managing the behaviour and modifying difficulties can work, and help from psychologists is worth seeking.

6 We will need to wait for a more accurate picture of behaviour and personality until those children who are receiving good early stimulation, care and medical treatment grow up and are studied in sufficient numbers to allow a general pattern to be seen. Meanwhile the changes

in early care and treatment, schooling and community care services must make us all more hopeful for the future.

*Chapter Seven*

# MENTAL, MOTOR AND SOCIAL DEVELOPMENT

This chapter is in four parts:

1 The first part is an outline of changes that have taken place in our thinking and treatment of mentally handicapped people. I hope this will show you that *it is very difficult to predict the future attainments of children with Down's syndrome from our knowledge of older people with the condition.*
2 The second section describes some of the technicalities of testing and measuring mental and social ability. I have included this because you will certainly meet the terms mental age or IQ in the future. I hope to explain how such terms are used and also how they are misused and can become misleading. I have also drawn out some of the implications of these issues.
3 In this part I have briefly discussed mental and social development in Down's syndrome and tried to explain how I think about mental handicap and learning difficulties. I have tried to pay special attention to the question of whether people with Down's syndrome stop developing at certain ages.
4 This last section briefly describes the range of ability and progress that can be expected of children and young people with Down's syndrome.

**NB** If you have only recently learnt about the baby having Down's syndrome and want to get an idea of what to expect by way of early development, look at Section 4 first.

**1 Changes in thinking and treatment**

As we found in the previous chapter on personality, much of the early information about the mental ability and development of persons with Down's syndrome was obtained from children and adults who grew up in the dull environments of large institutions. Many were placed in these institutions because of the belief, held by most people in the early half of this century, that mental ability was largely something one was born with and was little affected by the environment. Hence mental 'disability' was something which could not be influenced by training or education.

The danger in such thinking is that it becomes a self-fulfilling prophecy. If you say there is nothing that can be done, then you are likely to do nothing. If you have low expectations, this influences how you react to children and people. For example, instead of expecting (even only hoping) that the child will learn to dress himself, you assume he never will and so you always dress him and do not try to teach the child to help himself. In the case of many children with Down's syndrome, who may have low levels of arousal and initiative, this can lead to the child learning to be helpless and always relying on others for direction and action. The likelihood of the child learning is therefore very low. If one then argues that this proves he cannot learn, one is in the vicious circle of the self-fulfilling prophecy.

Up to recent years, this type of thinking had a very great influence on our treatment of children with mental handicap. The majority of children with Down's syndrome were classified as ineducable, and teachers and educators largely ignored the field of mental handicap. Thus, most of the early work and writing about Down's syndrome was left to the medical profession. Understandably this writing reflected their beliefs and their interests: it emphasised the physical characteristics and medical aspects which were important for diagnosis and health, and was rather limited and pessimistic about mental and social development. Rarely did it suggest that one might be able to help through training. Parents were also told that there was little that could be done to alleviate the effects of the mental disability. Many accepted this and often provided the child with less stimulation and activity than ordinary children. They generally did not look for ways of helping the child to learn and develop, and so it is not surprising that many did not achieve their potential. *This is why you should check carefully when books on this subject were written, and try to assess the main interests of the author.*

Langdon Down, however, recognised the importance of teaching and training from the beginning. He wrote that people with Down's syndrome:

> . . . are usually able to speak; the speech is thick and indistinct, but may be improved very greatly by a well-directed scheme of tongue gymnastics. The co-ordinating faculty is abnormal, but not so defective that it cannot be greatly strengthened. By systematic training, considerable manipulation power may be obtained.
>
> (J. Langdon Down, 1866)

The years have certainly proved his observations to be correct, and it is rather sad that this part of his work was largely neglected until around the middle of this century. The change started when people began to recognise that the environment had a large part to play in the development of mental and social abilities. This led to a number of people questioning whether some of the limitations seen in older children living in institutions was due to a lack of stimulation and training. Several studies compared the level of mental and social development of children with Down's syndrome who had been cared for at home, with those cared for in the large institutions. All found clear differences. The children cared for at home were generally more advanced than those cared for in institutions. Further work showed that this was largely due to the institution being unable to provide the same level and quality of individual attention that a baby and child can get from his natural or foster parents.

Another very interesting finding from such studies concerned children with Down's syndrome who were cared for in their own homes for the first three to four years of life and then, for whatever reason, were cared for in an institution. These children were not only developmentally more advanced than those in the institutions but apparently maintained the advanced level for many years. Thus it became clear that the longer the children were cared for at home, the greater were their chances of achieving their potential mental and social development. There were also reports that children cared for at home were more emotionally mature and had a wider range of interests and activities. Even so, depending on the institution, once they were placed in these large hospitals the children were generally found to progress less quickly than those who remained at home during middle and late childhood. (This may be a biased finding, as parents who experience difficulties with their child may be more inclined to seek a residential placement than those who do not.)

These studies went hand in hand with the change in attitude to babies and the first years of childhood. It was recognised that in the first five or so years of life children learn and develop very quickly indeed, and possibly at a relatively faster rate than in later years. This observation was linked to the knowledge that the brain also develops and matures very rapidly in these first years of life.

Thus many people began to feel that the first years of life were of special importance to all children, but particularly to those who are disadvantaged by environment or by physical or mental disability. Because of this change in thinking, many studies were undertaken to provide well planned activities which would stimulate the physical and mental development of children in these early years. Several such studies were conducted in different parts of the world in the late 1960s and 1970s with families who had a baby with Down's syndrome. Without exception all the studies showed much higher levels of mental, social and physical development in the children taking part than would have been predicted from past records of development of children with Down's syndrome. Studies have also reported more rapid development for children with Down's syndrome given early systematic stimulation, compared with those without such help. Since the 1950s many studies have also shown that older children and adults with Down's syndrome can be helped to learn new and often complex skills previously thought to be beyond their abilities.

An important question here is whether or not there are long-term effects of such early stimulation. There is evidence from a very small number of studies which suggests that there may be long-term benefits. At the ages of eight to ten years the children who have been involved in early stimulation programmes are generally more advanced than those who have not been involved. Unfortunately many such studies are difficult to interpret because the way they were carried out was not scientifically correct. Therefore one has to be very cautious about believing the results. This is particularly the case for the early studies and those which compare their results to the findings of older studies.

Before 1971, for example, most children with Down's syndrome in this country attended Junior Training Centres, because they were considered to be ineducable and unable to benefit from education. These centres may not have provided the same quality of systematic teaching as is presently available in schools. They were controlled by the Department of Health and had very few qualified teachers. When the law was changed and all children attended schools, these centres came under the Department of Education. Since then, there have been rapid changes in the schools, with, for example, more specially trained teachers and an emphasis on structured teaching with appropriate educational material. Many of these special schools also take children from the age of two years if required. Furthermore, most families of young children with Down's syndrome now receive support and advice on early stimulation from soon after birth. They also attend special health and development clinics and, later, pre-school play-groups and nurseries. Therefore few will be like the children in older studies who were considered ineducable and probably received very little stimulation. If we accept that without such stimulation any child is likely to develop more slowly, then this will explain some of the big differences found between the children who were helped compared to those who were not helped in the older studies.

All the present indications, then, are that these changes in thinking and treatment have led to a much higher level of attainment and functional ability of people with Down's syndrome. *This means we cannot, with any real confidence, use the descriptions of the attainment of past groups to predict the attainments of future groups.* Prediction will become possible only when we have done all we can to provide the best opportunities for learning and development for the *life-time* of large numbers of persons with Down's syndrome. What we do know is that there is always a degree of slow development and learning difficulties associated with Down's syndrome. Before I can discuss this in more detail it is necessary to explain the terminology and some of the technicalities of testing mental ability.

## 2 Terminology and testing

There has been, and still is, much heated discussion about the terminology in this area. At present the terms 'mental retardation' and 'mental handicap' are accepted, and there is an increasing use of the phrase 'children with learning disabilities'. Retardation implies slow development. It relates to the fact that one usually becomes aware of the child's problem because the milestones of development such as smiling, reaching, sitting up, walking, talking, and so on appear later than in most children. This then, is a delay or retardation in the development. The term 'mental handicap' refers to the notion that a child has difficulties in learning and understanding —because of some impairment, the child will not be able to do many of the things in life that most people can expect to do. Thus the handicap is not the impairment itself, but the difficulties experienced as a result of the impairment. For example, a man with one leg has the impairment of having a leg missing, but how much of a handicap this produces depends on how much he can compensate through using an artificial leg and what he is prevented from doing that he wants to do. We try to reduce the mental retardation by using special teaching to speed up development. Similarly, we try to reduce the handicap by teaching or by finding ways to compensate for it—e.g. we may use a hearing aid for a child who has a hearing impairment; or we may use a sign language with a child with speech difficulties. For children who have difficulties in sorting out the complex information that their senses receive from the outside world, we try to present the information in a simpler form: we break tasks down into small steps and provide plenty of encouragement and repetition to help the child learn one step at a time.

Both slow development and learning difficulties are associated with Down's syndrome. Whichever term is used, it is important to note that it does not describe a specific, single entity. Instead it refers to a wide range of ability and development. At one end there are children who do not learn as quickly as the normal range of children but nevertheless make steady progress. At the other end there are multiply

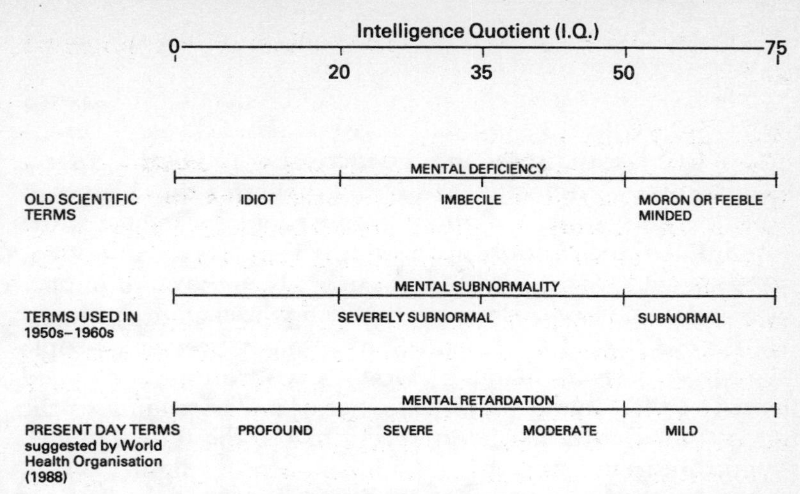


Fig 12. Intelligence quotients, terminology and categorisation in mental handicap.
Adapted from Clarke, A. D. B., and Clarke, A. M., 1974, *British Medical Bulletin*, Vol. 30, p. 179.

handicapped children who make very little developmental progress. Over the years this range has been classified into different categories which try to reflect the degree of mental ability. The basis of this classification is the measurement of mental ability or intelligence. You will probably know of the IQ (intelligence quotient) which attempts to measure intelligence. The average is 100 (see page 175). Anyone obtaining an IQ of around 75 or less is likely to be classified as mentally handicapped or retarded. Therefore in Figure 12 the top line represents the IQs from 0 to 75, which cover the range of mental handicap.

When you look at the terms used to describe the categories, you may be rather shocked to realise that the terms 'idiot', 'imbecile' and 'moron' were once respectable scientific labels. The popular use of these terms to abuse others largely reflected society's view of the mentally handicapped. They certainly carried with them the stigma of this label. The reaction to this, and the effort to find a more accurate description, led to changes. One hopes that this is not just a change in labels but also reflects real changes in the way society thinks about mental handicap. If people learn to understand mental handicap, they may become more tolerant and less fearful of persons who are mentally handicapped.

We have also seen changes in terminology with Down's syndrome. The rapid fall into disuse of the nick-name 'mongol' in the last ten years and the increasing use of the correct term 'Down's syndrome' has, I think, reflected the changes in our thinking. It has definitely produced a new image of the condition, which is more in tune with the higher capabilities of persons with Down's syndrome currently in the community.

Mind you, it took a long time to bring the change about. As far back as 1949, Dr C. Benda, one of many very able people who have been fascinated by Down's syndrome and devoted much of their lives to arrive at a better understanding of the condition, wrote that he preferred to use the term Down's syndrome as it: 'gives the condition a scientific dignity which it has deserved for a long time'. I like to think that the changes in terminology in mental handicap have also brought respect and dignity to those members of our society who are mentally handicapped. After all, it could be any one of us. Disease, old age or accident can all produce disabilities in learning and communication. It will be interesting to see if the new 'labels' Down's baby, Down's child and DS child are also considered to be disreputable in future years. However, I have wandered from the main point.

You can see from Figure 12 that whilst the names have changed, the 'cut-off' points at an IQ of around 20 and an IQ around 50, have remained. Why? Partly it is because many people think that the categories do reflect real differences between groups. It is also argued that these categories require different provisions. For example, the IQ of 20 or less is almost meaningless. It is not really possible, and serves no practical purpose, to give an IQ test to children with such limited ability. In the past the IQ of around 50 has tended to separate children with a major organic condition like Down's syndrome from those who are just rather dull or slow learning and those who are retarded because they come from deprived backgrounds with limited opportunities for learning. However, it was the IQ of 50 which separated the children considered to be educable from those who were not so considered. Therefore if you read, in old books, about children falling into the educable range, it means they are those who were considered subnormal rather than severely subnormal, or in recent terms, 'mildly mentally retarded'. Another confusion you may meet is between the present use of 'severe mental retardation', which approximately covers IQs 20–35, and the past use of 'severely subnormal' which covers IQs lower than 50. Today, in Britain, we use the term 'learning difficulties'. There are two categories of schools which cater for children with either severe learning difficulties (SLD) or mild learning difficulties (MLD). These correspond to the old terms of educationally subnormal severe or mild. (ESN(S) or ESN(M)).

But perhaps the main reason why this system of classification has survived is that it is used for administrative purposes. It is argued that when children are assessed they can be classified according to need, and then given the necessary provision. Unfortunately, it is a relatively simple framework which, whilst being manageable from an administrative viewpoint, can often fail at the individual level—particularly when children are assessed at borderline. It also produces labels, e.g. 'severe' or 'mild' handicap, and labels can prevent us from seeing the individual person. Unfortunately, people too often equate the label 'Down's syndrome' with the labels 'severely subnormal', 'ineducable', 'low IQ'. This can then prejudice their expectations and their observations. They see what they expect. They may not endeavour to assess the individual's strengths but make hasty conclusions in view of their expectations. This is totally unacceptable in a condition like Down's syndrome which encompasses such a wide range of ability.

Even an IQ can act as a label. Often people think if you have a 'low' IQ you are 'low' in everything. This is not true, and one needs to have some idea about how these tests are constructed and how IQs are arrived at in order to get a better understanding.

*Mental ability tests*

Most tests begin with the construction of a large number of items, such as spotting the odd one out of a series, matching similar pictures, naming pictures, defining the meaning of words, identifying missing parts of a picture, solving a logical problem and so on. These items are selected because it is thought they will indicate various aspects of mental ability such as memory, attention, language, conceptual thinking, problem solving. They usually cover a range from what one expects young children to do, to items for older children. These items are then tested on a large number of children who vary in age and ability. The results are then put in order according to the items passed or failed at different ages. Where items are passed by about half of the children in a specific age range, say five to five-and-a-half years, these are felt to represent the sort of ability expected of the average child at this age.

If the test is then given to an individual child in the same way as it was administered to the large group (this is called the standard procedure), one can compare the result with the average results. It is important to remember that the way one gives the test can influence the score. Parents often object to the form in which such tests are administered, especially when the child does not do as well as expected. But if one is going to compare the child's score with the range of scores of other children, it must be given in as identical a way as possible. If the child is five years old and he passes more items than the original group of five-year-olds, we can say he is above average *at this time in his life*. If he passes fewer, we can say he is not as advanced *at this time in his life*. This comparison is with the performance of the original group of children used to develop the test. If this group comes from a cultural background different from that of the child being tested, this can affect the results. Thus tests developed for children in one country are of little use with children in other countries who do not have similar experiences. For example, a test using pictures of double-decker buses, ice-cream cones and seasides are unlikely to be applicable to children living in isolated inland areas. In the same way a test developed for ordinary five-year-olds who can see, hear, are mobile and have access to a wide variety of stimulation may be inappropriate for children with a disability who do not have the necessary skills to perform on the test or the assumed background of familiar experiences. We shall return to this issue later.

Assuming the test is appropriate, we can also say that any child, of no matter what age, who passes the five-year-old items *or* who obtains scores that are equal to the five-year-olds, is equivalent to the average five-year-old on the test. This is called the *mental age*. If he or she obtains a score equal to the three-year level or seven-year level, we can note that the child has a *mental age* of three years or seven years. Once one has a mental age it is then possible to compare this with the child's real age (the chronological age). To do this we divide the mental age (MA) by the chronological age (CA). If we multiply the answer by 100 we have a quotient. Hence the intelligence quotient (the IQ) is the MA ÷ CA × 100. (Some tests use more sophisticated formulas, but the basic equation is the same.)

I hope you can see from this that the IQ is really a way of trying to show how quickly or slowly a child has developed compared with other children of a similar age. If the child's mental age is the same as his chronological age he will have an IQ of 100, i.e. $5 \div 5 \times 100 = 100$. Therefore the *average* IQ is 100. (In practical terms, of course, one cannot be that exact, because the test can be influenced by how the children feel on the day they are tested, whether they are keen to get as many right as possible, their experience with tests and so on.)

When one obtains IQs one usually finds the majority of children fall into the range 90 to 110. This is the normal range, and when we say a child has normal mental ability we mean he or she has a score similar to the majority of children. Some children will score above this range and some below. Thus they are not normal—they are abnormal. You can see that the use of the words normal and abnormal here are really just statistical descriptions. The further away from the normal range that the IQ falls, the more abnormal or different it is from the average. Thus IQs lower than 75 are significantly far away from the normal range and children in this range will usually have made such slow development that they are thought to have learning difficulties and need special teaching.

It is an assumption of these tests that they reflect a child's mental ability or intelligence. Quite what intelligence is, is a matter of considerable debate and argument. A rather simplified definition is the ability to learn and to solve problems. But as we have seen, mental ability tests carried out in childhood actually indicate the rate of development. The assumption, then, is that the faster one develops, the more intelligent one is. Put this way it is clear that something is not quite right. We all know that children develop at different speeds; there are times when they develop quickly and other times when they do not appear to make very much progress at all. We know that many are 'late developers' and suddenly come on in their school work around the time of puberty or late adolescence. We also know that development proceeds much more quickly in some areas, like walking, than others, such as talking, at different times. We know that development depends to some extent on the opportunities given to learn and on the quality of teaching and education. In recent years some research studies are finding that young children are tending to score higher than the expected averages on many of the mental ability tests. It is believed that this is the result of early experiences. Nowadays, most babies will be sat up in baby chairs and have special baby toys which previous generations never had. Most young children watch special 'education/play' programmes on television and have picture books, games and activity toys, and attend playgroups or nursery classes. Thus the early experiences for such activities will have some influence on the tests. The children will appear to develop more quickly and will perform better on tests. Thus they may get higher mental ages and IQs compared to previous groups of children. But this does not necessarily mean they will be more intelligent later on.

This picks up the point made earlier about the need to be aware of the characteristics of the group of children used to develop the test. If, through experiences, today's children are more likely to score higher on the tests than children of twenty years ago, then one must be careful to take this into account when interpreting the results. For example, the mean IQs given in Table 3 on page 186 are generally based on the test norms for children born in the early 1960s or before. This is fine for the purpose of comparison of groups. But if one then uses the Table to argue that today's children with Down's syndrome have average IQs of, say, 60, this is not correct. Compared with ordinary children of today who have also become 'more advanced' as a result of changes in their early experiences, the average IQ on the tests used would be 6 to 8 points less. This is because the average ordinary child is passing the four- or five-year test items some months earlier (compared to the earlier generation of children). Therefore when you do the computation of the IQ the average IQ is not

SOME LEISURE AND SCHOOL ACTIVITIES

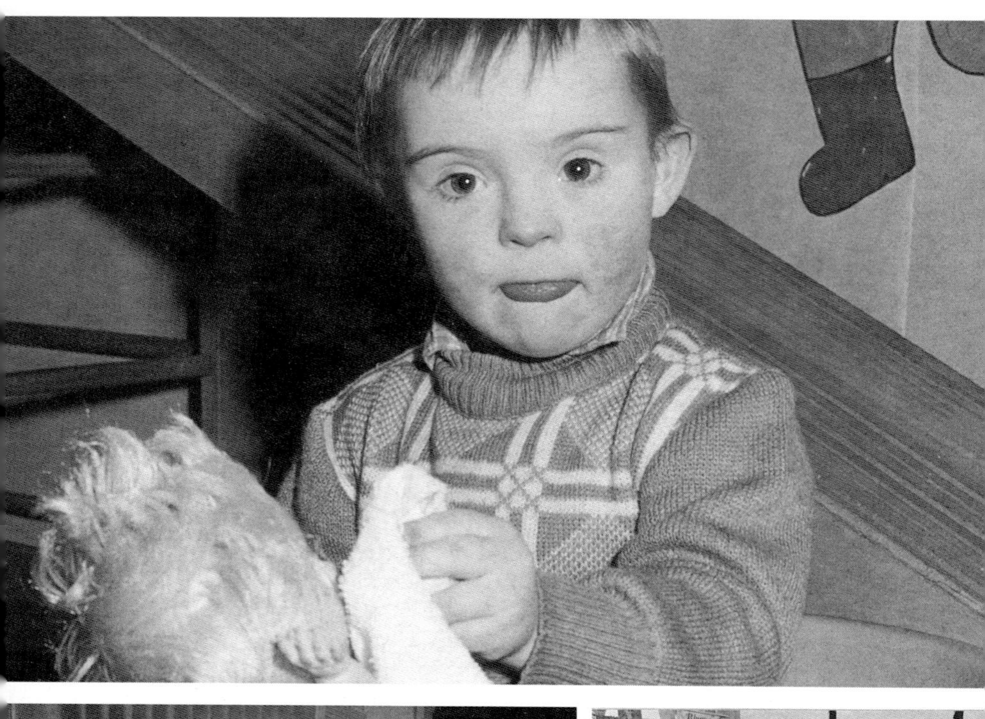

CHRISTMAS
Class 8

Busy Wheels

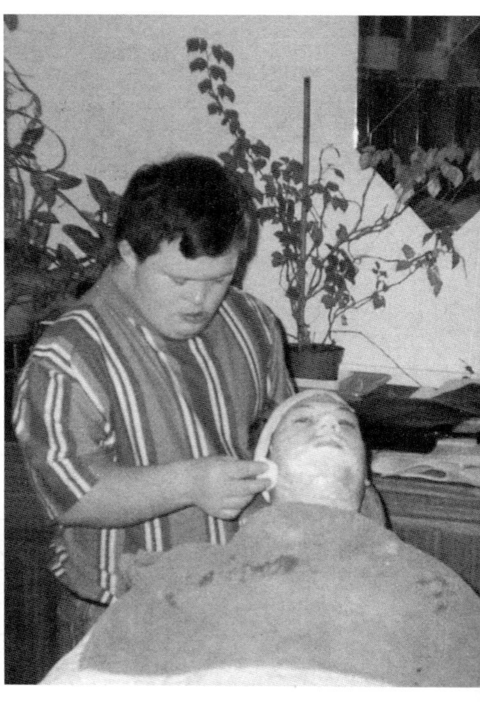

Linda and Gordon, picknicking just after their engagement.

Photo courtesy of Stephen Leighton.

Mr and Mrs Rothwell – November 1981.

100 but 106 or so. Since the idea is to keep the average at 100, then the test is re-standardised.

We can expect children with Down's syndrome also to benefit from these changes in early 'education'. We also know that we can 'improve' the IQ scores of children by giving them practice on tests, and experience and teaching in the sort of things the test measures. Thus if one compares the test performance of today's children with Down's syndrome to earlier groups of children with Down's syndrome, one gets higher scores if one uses the same tests and norms. (The norms are the tables of figures showing how the score corresponds to mental age and to IQ.) This certainly indicates that they perform on the tests better than previous generations. However, if one then argues that this higher score than the old test norms shows that they are more advanced compared to ordinary children, or put another way, they are comparatively less retarded, this is not necessarily true. The only way to find this out is to compare them with ordinary children of the same generation. As I shall discuss in section 4, this aspect is very important when asking what we should do to help the development of children with Down's syndrome.

For children with Down's syndrome the effects of early experience and use of IQ tests can have some important implications. If the child has been given a lot of practice in tasks similar to those used by the mental ability test, this can make the score higher than if no practice is given. For the child this can only be for the good, as we want him or her as skilled as possible. But the tester may feel the child is more able compared to other children.

I shall spell out an example. Many children attending classes for the mildly handicapped in Great Britain will have been assessed as having an IQ in the 50–75 range. But many of these children will have had little special help before being assessed and so will not score well on the test. We then find a child with Down's syndrome with the same score and place him or her in the class. If the child has been given special help, he or she will be functioning at, one hopes, the top level of his or her abilities, whilst the other children will be underfunctioning. Once the other children start to be given help they may come on very quickly. The teachers or parents then compare the children, and may misinterpret their observations. They feel the child with Down's syndrome is not working hard enough, has stopped developing or that the test result was faulty.

Six points must be emphasised:

1 The person who constructs the test will choose activities that he or she thinks will show up different types of mental ability *and* be within the children's range of experience: but since children's experiences will vary according to their backgrounds, children from different cultures do not score as highly as those from the background the test-maker had in mind.
2 The test-maker usually assumes that the child has certain skills. Thus he may wish to measure memory at the six-year level and will assume the child has language abilities at this level. This is fine for normal children, but what of those who may have a language problem? The test will show low mental ability where there is perhaps only a language disorder.
3 These tests measure only the activities and abilities that are selected to be put into the test. Thus most intelligence tests or mental ability tests do not measure practical aptitudes, emotional maturity or social ability. Therefore, as I said before, just because someone has a 'low' IQ does not mean she is 'low' in other qualities. And there are many people with 'low' IQs who live very fulfilled, happy and independent lives. They may have many other special abilities which the test has not measured.
4 As noted earlier, the IQ gives a global idea of the rate of development up to the age when the child is tested. But for individual children, especially if tested in the early childhood years, the score has been found to be not very accurate at predicting later IQ scores. This is mainly because the sort of abilities tested in the early years are very different from those tested in later years. In fact tests of development for the first two to three years of life are no longer called Infant Intelligence Tests but Developmental Tests. This is because no accurate correlation can be found between the scores of the rate of development (DQs) in these early years and IQs in later years *for the normal range*.

However, this prediction *is* much more reliable for children who develop slowly—that is for those in the moderate, severe and profound retardation range. The more severe the mental retardation, the more accurate are the predictions. (We get a mental age from these Developmental Tests, and produce a quotient, in the same way as with the IQ—but it is called DQ [developmental quotient], and some authors refer to a DA [developmental age] instead of an MA [mental age] when discussing the results of the tests.)

Children with Down's syndrome can have IQs ranging from less than 20 to over 100. For children falling in the moderate to profound range, the rate of development over the first 12 to 18 months can give a reasonable idea (with some exceptions) of the rate of development up to five or six years. In other words, if the child falls in the slower rates of development compared with most children with Down's syndrome, he or she is very likely to be in the same slower group at age five or six. The children in the faster groups at 18 months are also likely, but with less certainty, to be in the faster developing group at five to six years. There is at present insufficient information on children with the condition who have had a high quality of education from the first years to predict similar correlations in adolescence, but they are likely to be fairly accurate in terms of groups, if not necessarily so for individuals.

We must be very careful not to allow these predictions to make us less expectant of development in the child, as this can influence how we behave with the child. However, some parents find it useful to have some indications so that they can begin to plan for schooling. But do remember that these are predictions about achievements on developmental tests, and they do not include any assessment of emotional development. They do give some indication of the rate at which independent skills, language and reasoning will be attained.

Two children may have obtained the same IQ on the same test, but have scored on quite different items. One child may, for instance, have got most of the word and language items correct, the other may have solved the visual problems or the logical reasoning items.

This is because intelligence or mental ability is not a single, given entity. It is made up of many skills and abilities. So most modern ability tests produce a profile of the different areas, rather than just an overall IQ. Also, the IQ has little usefulness for planning day-to-day teaching, or in diagnosing learning difficulties. More and more teachers and psychologists are now using specific diagnostic tests for separate areas—e.g. language, reading, visual discrimination, sequencing of sounds and so on. And even within these areas we need to break down the abilities still further: in language, for example, we look at the ability to comprehend words as separate from the ability to express oneself.

6 Many factors can influence the test results, and so one must be very careful in interpreting the results and not make hasty conclusions. For most handicapped children one should have assessments at regular intervals.

*Behavioural assessments*

Because of increasing awareness that many mental ability tests, (i) fail to provide an overall picture of a child's strengths and weaknesses; (ii) often do not provide diagnostic information sufficient to plan teaching programmes; and (iii) may be inappropriate for children with special learning problems, many teachers and psychologists are beginning to use direct observation methods as well as a range of tests to assess children. The child attends a class and the teacher and psychologist try to build up a picture of his or her strengths and weaknesses by watching and recording *how the child goes about his everyday learning activities*—including play. Thus instead of concentrating on some global and rather vague notion called intelligence, they are trying to find out about the skills and abilities the child has, and what she will need to learn, to *function as an independent person*.

We are thus interested in what we call *functional behaviours*—what the child can do and cannot do, rather than measures which compare him or her with average scores, which often only serve to emphasise disability, or to lower our expectations. I shall try to explain this with an example that I use in teaching. I have a slide of a boy who is being held with slight support in a sitting position. He is holding a feeding cup to his lips as though to drink. For several years I have asked audiences of parents, nurses, doctors and teachers, 'How old do you think this boy is?' Most confidently shout out answers between six and twelve months. I then tell them he has Down's syndrome (which he has, but it is not so obvious on the slide) and repeat my question. Very few shout out answers. Even those who do are less confident. The answers have ranged from six months to three years and most are around one or two years. This highlights the great degree of variation that exists among children with the syndrome, and the inappropriateness of using 'normal' expectations as a basis for prediction. It also illustrates how we all use age to judge early development. Most people know that children with Down's syndrome are slower to develop. Therefore they add to the 'normal' age a period according to *their expectations*. The boy in the slide is in fact 24 weeks old. True, he was one of the children who learnt to drink from a cup quite early and I photographed him a few days after he started. But if his mother had been using ages and averages to decide when he was ready to learn to use his cup, he would not have begun at that age. I had read all the books and I 'knew' he could not learn to drink from his cup so early, so I had not thought of trying to teach him! To drink from a cup you need to be able, (i) to sit with some support and hold your head reasonably firm; (ii) to hold the cup; (iii) to raise the cup to your lips; (iv) either to (a) tip your head and arms backwards or (b) rotate your wrists and lift your arms, so that the liquid goes into the mouth. Of course you also need to be able to suck and swallow and to know that the cup holds liquid which you want. The point is that we need to ask *what can the child do* and *what must he be able to do to learn the next task*. If the answers match, we can teach him or her the task. Hence, like the IQ or mental age, the child's chronological age is not very useful in indicating what we need to teach. When parents stop comparing their handicapped child with the 'normal' child, or with his or her age, they often find that life is much easier.

Thinking in terms of functional behaviour means we ask what the child needs to be able to do to be as independent as possible at this moment. By 'independent' I mean to be able to do things for him or herself. This will include such skills as getting around, dressing, feeding and toileting as well as being able to play and explore, think up interests, entertain him or herself, and, last but not least, make decisions.

*Parental and professional collaboration*

Many professionals are well aware of the important contribution that parents can make in these assessments. After all, the parent knows the child, and is with the child far more than the professionals. *Parents have the right and the need to be involved in the decision making about their child.* But this co-operation between parent and professional is a relatively new idea. At present very few people know what are the best ways that we professionals and parents can work together. We are all bound to make mistakes during this period of learning, and tolerance and respect from all parties will be needed. I think you as parents will need to learn about the jargon and methods that professionals use, in order to feel on reasonably equal terms with them. That is why I have tried to explain some basic concepts in some detail in this chapter. We professionals have an unfortunate habit of lapsing into jargon which parents do not understand, and parents have an unfortunate habit of letting us get away with it. You will have to learn not to be overpowered by us. Be patient with us, and ask us to explain things again. Make a list of all your questions before you go to see the doctor, teacher, therapist or psychologist. Make notes of the answers you are given or, better still, ask to be given a written explanation if you need it. This can help enormously when trying to explain things to relatives or other professionals.

You may feel embarrassed when you do this at first, but more and more parents are insisting on proper briefing, and more and more professionals are getting used to it. If you meet a professional or expert who explains something in jargon and, when asked to re-explain it, repeats the same jargon, give up. He is probably as confused as you, and you will be better off seeking advice elsewhere. If he says 'I don't know, but will try to find out', respect his honesty and try not to be too quick to criticise his ignorance. It is far better that someone should admit to lack of knowledge, than try to give an answer which is incomprehensible or incorrect.

*Mental age: expectations and protectiveness*

I would like to make a last point in this section. One often hears parents and professionals talk about a child's mental age. 'He has a mental age of six.' Many then seem to assume he is like a six-year-old. As you will have gathered from the above, this is really a false assumption. His mental age of six refers to his performance on a mental ability test. If he is sixteen, he may have a measured mental age of six but he is *not* a six-year-old. He will be socially and emotionally very different from a six-year-old, because he will have had the mental abilities of a six-year-old for many years and will have used them in many different ways.

In the first years of life, some parents find it useful to think of the child as a typical two-year-old even though she is three or four. This does not appear to do any harm—though it may alter one's expectations of what she should do. But too often one sees older children and adults treated as young children, or given the toys and books meant for a four- or six-year-old, because their mental age is between four and six. Who of us can be expected to develop a sense of self-esteem, self-dignity and take pride in ourselves if we are treated in such an inappropriate manner? Yet this is one of the main problems we face. Many parents are inclined to be highly protective towards their child with Down's syndrome—as are many professionals. We have all to find the courage to take risks.

How much freedom and scope for initiative can we give our children without placing them in danger, or in situations which are so beyond their capabilities that we make them feel inadequate? Children who find learning difficult have a much greater chance of failing than those who do not. If they continually meet failure, they are likely to stop trying to learn new things: they are likely to seek out safe, familiar experiences. However, if they are protected from challenges because of the risk of failure, they will also not learn to try out new experiences. If they are aware that parents feel they will be unable to cope, they may begin to believe it, and so learn to be dependent rather than independent. The art is to find the balance. The more one knows about the child's abilities and the more one plans challenges and experiences that are likely to meet with success, the higher the likelihood that one will find the balance. But it is easier said than done.

### 3 Development in Down's syndrome

Our growth and development is influenced by:

(i) our genetic endowment—the plan carried in the genetic code of the chromosomes (see Chapter Four);
(ii) our environment—diet, health, opportunities for experiences; and
(iii) our specific strengths and weaknesses—such as physical, sensory, personality and learning.

We cannot change the genetic make-up of the child, and the additional chromosome in Down's syndrome must set certain limits to the child's growth and development. In Chapter Five I described how the children usually have slower physical growth. Similarly, mental and motor development are slower, and the child will usually take longer to reach the developmental 'milestones' such as sitting, walking, talking and so on. Also in Chapter Five I noted that many children with the syndrome have additional sensory and learning difficulties. These difficulties can all slow down the child's development.

But we can do something to counteract them.

For example, I noted that babies with Down's syndrome tend to be floppy, may have poor circulation and may be prone to chest infections. By exercising the baby, with plenty of handling and tickling, and helping to pull the baby into a sitting position (see book list at the back for further advice), one can help strengthen muscles, stimulate circulation and reduce the risk of chest infections, since the 'active' baby is less prone to collect mucus in the lungs. The baby who is sitting up also has more to look at, and is more likely to communicate with people walking past. (If you don't believe me, lie on your back with your head in one position and see how difficult it is to attract or respond to people walking by.) Once she can sit and control her arms she can reach and play with toys, feed herself, etc. Therefore early activities aimed at stimulating the baby will have a whole range of beneficial effects: they will in general prevent additional handicap developing as a result of lack of treatment of remedy or compensate for difficulties.

The question I am trying to answer in this section is: '*How much can we influence the degree of retardation or handicap by providing good quality care, early stimulation and education?*'

I shall begin the answer by describing briefly the many studies that have reported on the classification and average IQs of groups of children and adults with Down's syndrome. I am assuming that you have read the two earlier sections of this chapter, and are aware of the dangers of applying survey results to a particular child.

Most reports up to the early 1900s classified the large majority of people with Down's syndrome in the idiot range which, in current terms, would be the profound mental retardation category. In the first half of this century there were numerous surveys of children and adults living in large hospitals. Most reported that between half to three-quarters of the groups had an IQ in the 20–50 range—the average scores for groups falling between 20–35. Thus they would be classified in the severe mental retardation category. Hence most textbooks describe Down's syndrome as being associated with severe subnormality. However, these early reports always noted that a few people also fell in the mild range.

Studies of children and adults in the community have generally reported higher IQs, with the majority falling between 30 to 50 and group average between 40 and 50. Thus the majority would be classified as moderately retarded. Whilst many technical criticisms can be made of the way these studies were carried out, they tend to be in agreement. They indicate that average IQs appear to increase the more recent the study, and the more the people studied lived in the community. This is very clear in studies carried out in the 1960s and 1970s. For example, many reports in the early 1960s suggested that about five to ten per cent of older children and adults could be classified as 'educable', or in current terms, mildly mentally retarded. By the mid 1970s more reports were suggesting that perhaps as many as a third to a half would be in the mild range in mid-childhood and early adulthood. They were also noting that some children fell within the dull normal range (IQs 75–90) and occasionally into the normal range. Most of these reports were based on the progress of children whose parents had access to early support and advice on stimulating the child, and/or where the child was included in an educational programme in the pre-school years. We can get an idea of the effect of such early intervention by looking at the results of a small number of studies which measured the mental abilities of groups of children with Down's syndrome at regular intervals from their first months of life to five or more years of age.

I have taken studies that report mental ages or DQs or IQs, and have calculated the average scores at yearly intervals. In Table 3 I have separated them into two categories – those which provided limited or no educational advice, and those which included the family in an early education and support programme.

I must strongly emphasise that this Table is meant only to give a global picture, and does not tell you what the IQ of an individual child with the syndrome should be or how it will change. There are also, again, numerous technical criticisms that can be made of these studies. But what I find striking about the results is that they were carried out by different people, at different times, in different countries and often using different developmental and intelligence tests, yet the yearly averages are so consistent. There are many more studies which suggest similar findings, but have not published their results in a form that I could fit into the Table.

Many of the reports describe the progress of children whose parents received counselling from soon after birth, and who were given plenty of appropriate stimulation. Often they have been included in pre-school placements and given a high quality of education aimed at meeting individual needs. The results from such studies suggest that the averages reported in Table 3 are conservative. But I must point out that we are still trying to create a more accurate picture. For example, some

*TABLE 3*

| Age in years | 1 | 2 | 3 | 4 | 5 | No. of children |
|---|---|---|---|---|---|---|
| *Children living at home but with limited help* | | | | | | |
| Share et al. (1964) | 68 | 58 | 51 | 46 | 49 | 45 |
| Loeffler & Smith (1964) | 65 | 51 | 46 | 43 | 43 | 47–34 |
| Carr (1970) | 67 | 56 | 48 | 48 | — | 45 |
| de Coriat et al. (1967) | 66 | 54 | 48 | 44 | 43 | 9–189 |
| Ludlow & Allen (1979) | 69 | 61 | 53 | 49 | 44 | 23–71 |
| *Children living at home and enrolled in an early education programme* | | | | | | |
| de Coriat et al. (1967) | 83 | 70 | 66 | 61 | 61 | 9–189 |
| Ludlow & Allen (1979) | 80 | 70 | 63 | 58 | 56 | 9–63 |
| Cunningham | 75 | 67 | 59 | 60 | 59 | 59–90 |

studies may have biased samples. If the researchers rely on parents to come to clinics or education centres, a number of parents and babies may be excluded, and those who stop coming may be the very ones whose children make little progress. Some reports also do not explain what they do about children who are untestable at certain times: if they ignore these, since they are likely to be the more severely affected children the group averages will be too high.

The educational programmes also include training on activities that are very similar to the mental ability tests, such as drawing circles, naming pictures and simple puzzle and shape games—particularly at the two- to five-year level. Practice must exert some influence on the scores.

In some studies the scores are actually collected by the people responsible for the education programme. Since these are obviously highly motivated, they will normally persevere with the child to ensure they get the best out of her.

Against this we should balance the fact that the tests can be inappropriate for children with learning difficulties, and may not therefore allow them to show their strengths while highlighting their weaknesses.

After all these problems are taken into account, however, most people working in this field still agree that children with Down's syndrome who receive help from early in life are more advanced than those without such help. Up to the middle years of childhood at least, they are more likely to fall in the mild to moderate categories of mental retardation than the severe or profound.

*'What are the benefits of early intervention and stimulation?'*

Although there is agreement that early experiences are important influences on the development of all young children, there is some controversy about what type of experiences are most beneficial. There is also debate on how soon one needs to start such activity and whether the benefits are long-lasting.

Our research has been particularly concerned with these questions and is based on following the development of more than 180 children with Down's syndrome from the first weeks of life. Some of the children received very intensive stimulation, with mothers carrying out training activities and games five times a day and repeating each activity several times.

Needless to say, some mothers and fathers found this too much and stopped; many, however, carried on for several months. In one group they carried out intensive programmes like this for over 18 months. We also had groups who received regular visits and carried out plenty of stimulating activities but not in a very intensive way. They would try to spend time each day playing with and stimulating the baby, and planning the play to fit in with the baby's current level of development. However, this was all fitted into a fairly natural routine much as one would do with any baby.

When we compared the progress in the different groups we found:

(a) Babies who had very intensive schedules were a little more advanced than those on the more natural ones but only *during the period of the intensive training and only on the behaviours that were being trained.* Therefore in the first year or two of life, very intensive and highly structured training programmes do not appear to be any more beneficial than less intensive and more natural approaches. However, if the baby has a specific difficulty, like being very floppy or not feeding, or having a specific motor problem, then specific and intensive programmes are needed whilst the problem is being treated.

(b) Babies whose parents joined the research and began the stimulating exercises in the first month or so, were more advanced on the developmental test assessments than babies who started later in the first year of life. However, all the later starters caught up to the early ones within a few months. We think this shows that babies with Down's syndrome, even in the first weeks of life, are influenced by their experiences and that parents need to handle the baby and play all the normal games with him or her. On top of this, parents need to understand the special difficulties the baby may have and then match the type of play and handling to the baby. However, we all have to remind ourselves that the main needs of a baby with Down's syndrome are the same as any baby.

(c) When the children were over five years of age we compared them to children with Down's syndrome whose families did not receive early help, such as regular home or clinic visits aimed at giving parents advice on stimulating the baby's development more systematically. We did not find any major differences between the two groups on mental ability or language tests, or on checklists of functional development and attainments. We think that if these children were slower than our group then they soon caught up when they started to go to pre-school. We also think that many of the mothers and fathers in this comparison group had positive attitudes to the children and were actually stimulating them in a natural way.

*Therefore we did not find that there was any major benefit in carrying out very intensive training except for specific behaviours which required attention. Nor did we find any evidence to show that the babies would be permanently affected if they did not receive plenty of stimulation in the first months or year.*

These findings do not mean that the early stimulation and exercises are a waste of time.

(d) The babies in our research group tended to be healthier and more had had help for hearing and visual problems. We feel that the parents were more aware of the likely health difficulties and had been more willing to have these checked. It could also be that the physical exercises to help improve the floppiness and physical development of the children had also kept them healthier.

(e) The parents receiving the help felt more confident about the child and felt better when they were doing things, like the exercises and games. I am quite certain the babies felt better when the parents did stimulate and play with them, and had a more enjoyable day.

(f) When applied at the right time in the child's development, specific training which focuses on specific activities does work. Thus the intensive groups did sit up a month earlier and walk a month or two earlier. Similarly, when children were taught to eat or drink, to wash, use the toilet, etc., they learnt these more quickly if taught in a consistent and structured way, than if not taught but left to find out for themselves. What the training does not do is make the child more intelligent, nor does it give the child some permanent advancement. Of course, if one does not help and encourage the child then he or she will be *deprived* of the necessary experiences to foster development. Although this can often be overcome by later help, children deprived of the necessary experiences to challenge and excite them cannot be very happy. If the lack of experience lasts for several years it may be very difficult to remedy. In particular it may be that the child's style of learning and enthusiasm and initiative is most strongly affected.

Overall we feel that our research has shown that, from the earliest weeks of life, children with Down's syndrome are responsive to environmental influences and prosper best in homes that provide love, care and plenty of stimulation and a variety of experiences. Planning and carrying out special games and activities can be beneficial both to parents and the babies. It helps them to get to know each other, makes the days more satisfying and enjoyable and prevents any possibility of the child developing more slowly because of the lack of the necessary encouragement and stimulation. However, there does not appear to be any particular benefit to carrying out intensive training regimes which may be unpleasant to the child and the parent, and in some cases can interfere with a balanced family life.

*'What about the drop-off in the IQ scores? Is there a deterioration in the children's mental abilities?'*

You will see in Table 3 that the IQs drop from the first year to the fifth year. Many studies have reported this IQ decline. One explanation is to be found in the use of the formula $MA \div CA \times 100 = IQ$, discussed in the last section. To keep an IQ stable the mental age (MA) must increase at the same rate as the chronological age (CA). If the rise in the mental age is slower than the chronological age, then the IQ has to get smaller each time it is worked out. Therefore the fact that IQs get smaller does not mean that the child has necessarily stopped developing or has 'gone backwards'. If you are developing more slowly than the average, then the older you get the greater will be the difference.

Secondly, the drop in IQs is based on averages of children, and so does not show the huge individual differences. The individual children in the groups show some who do not slow down, some who do and some who slow down and then speed up. Often these periods of 'slow down' and 'speed up' relate to the types of activites and abilities being tested. I shall discuss this a little later. Others have a stable IQ for many years, and in fact you can see from the Table that the main decline occurs in the first two to three years. After this the scores seem to be more stable. If one looks at the scores taken at very frequent intervals, i.e. six- to 12 months, one finds the most rapid decline in the DQ comes in the first year—usually between six and 12 months. This is for two reasons.

First, the types of behaviours tested by developmental tests in the first months are largely to do with

(a) the baby developing good control of the visual system —the eyes become co-ordinated and work together, the child looks at and responds to things it can see;
(b) the baby responding to social events, like calming down when picked up, vocalising, smiling and so on;
(c) the baby responding to sounds—looking and listening to you when you talk;
(d) the baby waving its arms and legs and wriggling.

When you check these types of 'early responsive' activities on the tests, you usually just tick them off if they are present. You do not try to check their quality by, for example, counting how often the baby smiles, how easy it is to get a smile. But if you do carry out detailed studies on the quality, you can often find differences between ordinary babies and those with Down's syndrome. Therefore (i) the tests are not sensitive enough to highlight such differences, and (ii) the behaviours being checked are not particularly abnormal in these infants—compared to some later behaviours, which are.

In the first months, then, one will usually find quite high scores on the tests. These scores do not predict later ability, and you cannot use them to tell the degree of handicap at later ages. These are, in fact, artificially high scores and do not reflect the true nature of the child's handicap. Because of this they exaggerate the decline in DQs.

Secondly, if you look at Figure 13, you can see the periods of fast and slow mental development. To get this graph we have computed the average rate of development between each time we tested the babies, and then matched this up to the developmental level. Since in the first 18 months we assessed the babies every six weeks, then every twelve weeks until two years and every six months after that, the graph is based on very sensitive measures. If the babies progressed one month developmentally for every chronological month, then one would get a straight line at the developmental rate of one month. This is what one would theoretically expect for 'normal development'. But as described in section 2, the rate in Figure 13 is based on the children in our research and using one developmental test which was standardised in the 1960s. The rate of normal development worked out in the same way would probably be higher. It is also important to note that Figure 13 represents averages across children. Since all do not exactly coincide in their rate of development the figure hides individual patterns. In fact these are often much more dramatic and step-like.

From Figure 13, you will see that the rate of development drops off around four to six months developmental level. At this time one also finds a slowing in the rate of motor development as the child begins to learn to sit up without help. The slowing in rate appears to be due to co-ordination difficulties for infants with Down's syndrome. This stage in development requires that they develop co-ordination between eye and hand in order to reach and pick up objects with ease. It also requires that they co-ordinate balance and muscle control to sit by themselves. Therefore this drop in rate of development, which is like a plateau, is probably due to a specific problem with sensory-motor co-ordination. It can be helped with plenty of exercises in sitting up to strengthen the muscles and improve the muscle tone, and when sitting 'wobbling' the baby gently to and fro to practise the balancing. However, this does not appear to cure the co-ordination difficulty. In one study we found that infants given very intensive daily exercises for improving sitting and reaching did achieve these skills quicker than a comparison group. But, they did not walk any quicker or use pencils, etc., any quicker. Like all the children, they had another slowing in the rate of development at the time they needed to move from walking with help to walking alone. Again, it appears to be a difficulty in co-ordinating balance and motor activity. Studies of older children show that muscle tone and co-ordination remains a problem for many. *However, it can be helped and overcome with exercise and physical activities. Many of the children become good swimmers, gymnasts and dancers. But they do need constant encouragement and training in activities to foster good muscle tone and*

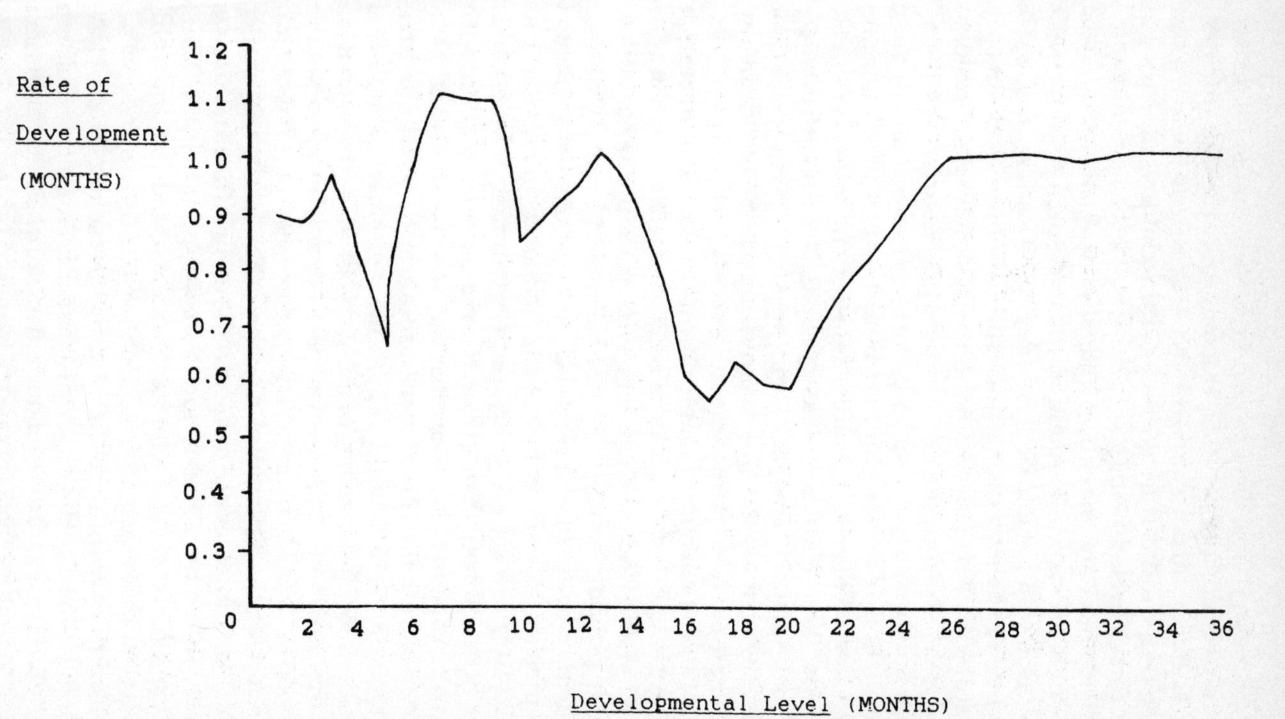


Fig 13. Changes in mean developmental rates: mental age.

*co-ordination*. Similar help is required to encourage good fine motor co-ordination such as reaching out, picking up small objects like a currant, threading, using a pencil, etc., all of which prove difficult behaviours for the children to master in their early development.

The point I am making is that this problem of sensory-motor co-ordination is found in most children with Down's syndrome to a greater or lesser degree. Training in specific activities can help them to acquire the skills but it does not cure the problem. Therefore, although we can help them to learn the specific skill quicker, they need this same sort of help for all future skills that depend on co-ordination. Since many of these skills make up the items on developmental tests, then training and practice will partly reduce the slower rate of development. But since these skills are unlikely to be associated with intellectual activities like reasoning and problem solving, it is not surprising that we do not make them more 'intelligent' by training them to acquire these skills sooner.

It is also worth noting that for most children in our research the age at which they sat up gave a good idea of when they would walk. Thus the children who sat earlier also walked earlier, providing they were not hampered by any illness or accident in between and received plenty of encouragement. I interpret this as indicating that the children inherit a lot of individual differences. Some are programmed to be faster in their development than others. Some have been born with greater problems in co-ordination and muscle tone than others. These two aspects may also differ between children, the slowest child being programmed in slow growth and development and having major difficulty in co-ordination and/or muscle tone. We can expect slow growth to predict later slow development in associated areas but it will not predict specific difficulties. On the other hand, we cannot predict later intelligence from specific early difficulties (unless they are directly related to intellectual-type activities). What we *can* predict is that children with these difficulties will require continual help in these areas.

To some extent, therefore, the dips in the rate of development in Figure 13 reflect specific difficulties for many children with Down's syndrome. This can make their development appear very uneven. You can see from the figure that the first dip is followed by a rapid increase. This is because the next stage of playing with and exploring objects by sucking, banging, throwing, holding them up and looking at them, and passing them from hand to hand, depends on the baby being able to reach and grasp and sit up fairly well. Once the infant gets over this barrier these behaviours are ready and waiting to blossom. At around nine to twelve months of age, most of the children with Down's syndrome are at this stage. Of course, there are many individual differences: some prefer to explore objects by banging and throwing, others prefer to turn them over and over, looking and poking, and others are great explorers with their mouths.

It is about this time that we find another slowing in the rate of development. As can be seen from Figure 13, it coincides with mental ages between ten and thirteen months. The next step forward is to learn that objects are different—some roll, some can have things put into them or taken out, some make a noise, some make a mark. Thus the next stage is to learn about the special qualities of the objects and to learn to relate two objects together—i.e. putting in and taking out, banging drums, etc. Part of this slow period or plateau might be due to the difficulties the children have in processing the information that arises from their play—e.g. learning that you can put things into cups. But part of it will also be their extra need to practise and consolidate the 'new' skills they have learnt, i.e. sucking, banging, throwing, etc. When you learn a new skill you probably find that at first you identify each part, e.g. changing the gear on the car, pushing in the clutch, releasing the brake, etc. Gradually you blend these together. Then one day it seems to click and you drive well. You think you have made it. But the next day your co-ordination has fallen apart and you have to practise again—*you have to have a period of consolidation* before the skill is so much a part of you that you 'do it without thinking'. It would seem that consolidation can take longer in children with Down's syndrome. Since none of our tests measure consolidation and few of us can actually see it taking place, the impression we get is that the child is not making much progress.

But plateaux are not just confined to mental handicap, and do not necessarily mean there is a learning difficulty. Ordinary children also have times when they develop in some areas quicker than others, and times when they consolidate. But because they develop so quickly we miss this. I often feel that looking at children with Down's syndrome is like looking at learning and development in slow motion.

Between the ages of two to four years approximately, the majority of children have a period of slower development. This is seen in Figure 13 between the developmental levels of around 14 to 26 months, and particularly the 16 to 20 month stage. I shall discuss this in some detail because I think it is quite important.

Most ordinary children acquire three or four single words around the beginning of the second year of life. They also begin to solve simple problems like pulling strings to get objects and using sticks to reach an object. They experiment in their play to discover new ways of getting some desired goal. They imitate simple single actions like kissing a doll, banging a drum and repeating a sound or word. To do all this they need to expand their memory and their span of attention. This means they can keep several things in mind at once and also have some sort of plan to direct their actions. They will, for example, put several objects into a box rather than one, and then do something different. This stage in development appears to present a barrier to many children with Down's syndrome. We did try to train many of the behaviours intensively with daily programmes. These were no more successful than plenty of play and a variety of organised experience aimed at the children's current level of development.

My interpretation at the moment is that, for many children, the growth and maturation of memory and attention span was a major problem. Trying to push the child's development forward was a waste of time. In fact we found that many of the children would not be pushed. They would refuse to co-operate in the training, turning away or sweeping away all objects in front of them.

As well as this slow maturation, there was also the problem that many of the infants did not appear to sort out what was wanted and then link a sequence of actions together. They would put one object in the box and look up for approval, and would need to have their attention redirected to the game. This was not just a problem of limited attention but more that they did not analyse the task and make an internal plan of what to do. If they needed to link a sequence of actions together, this was especially difficult. Yet when a parent or brother or sister prompted at the key points in a sequence, the child would often complete the task. It seemed that all the skills were available but the actual analysis of the task and putting together a plan was a problem. This same difficulty has been described by many researchers, especially when studying the development of play in children with Down's syndrome. The children progress through the same stages of play as ordinary children but within each stage they do not sequence the play or devise new variations as quickly. They are more likely to repeat the same action many, many times. This difficulty, then, is something that is not easily remedied and is a continual problem at all ages. It requires others to understand it, and to plan and organise accordingly the way they interact with the person with Down's syndrome. One has to present information at a slower rate and in small, well signposted chunks. This helps to show the sequence and direct attention to the key parts. When this happens the child can learn and will remember what is learnt.

*In other words, there is a problem with slow growth and maturation and, when we face a barrier due to this, we need to expand the child's experiences sideways rather than pushing up the developmental tree. There are also problems with the child's learning abilities. We need to compensate for these in the way we present information to the child in our everyday communications and in the organisation of the learning experiences. It means a lot of repetition and practice and a lot of thought about how tasks can be broken down and presented in a 'fun' way.*

Returning to the figure, and period between 18 and 24 months is one of marked changes for ordinary children and a major plateau for children with Down's syndrome. From 12 to 18 months most children acquire some single words and use these and gestures to communicate. From the latter half of the second year there is a rapid expansion in vocabulary, and words begin to be linked together. The play of the child is far more goal-directed and there is a lot of exploring to find new ways of achieving a desired end. The child becomes much more fluent in imitation and systematically imitates actions and sequences. This is moving towards the lively 'toddler' period and as the child's communication ability and play develop, so too does their social interaction. Their play often imitates the actions of those around them, they play alongside other children and then more and more with other children for longer periods.

The long period of rather slow development seen in Figure 13 corresponds to the difficulties that many children with Down's syndrome experience at this time. Because the figure represents averages across all the children in our research it hides the patterns of individual children. Some show hardly any slowing down at this time. Others do not show any progress on the developmental test (in other words, their mental age remains the same) for two years or more. Therefore their IQ falls rapidly. The slower the children are to move through this stage the more likely they are to be more handicapped in later years. However, there are some notable exceptions. Although we have not yet fully analysed all the data, there are some children who appear to be quite slow at this time. In particular, they take a longer time to develop language. The boys are more likely to be slow at language at this time than the girls. However, if one looks at the broader aspects of the child's development, such as how he or she copes with self-help skills and social occasions, then even though the language is delayed, a lot of development is taking place. For these children use of a signing system (i.e. using the hands to sign words in a systematic way) can help to reduce the frustration they experience at this time by not being able to communicate the thoughts in their head. By around four and a half to six years the children have the same relatively rapid move forward in language that ordinary children have at an earlier age. In fact on Figure 13 the rate of development gradually increases from the 20-month level as more and more children move into this stage. This is then followed by a period of relatively rapid progress as indicated by the one month per month rate from around the mental age of two years. For the reasons noted in sections 1 and 2, this does not mean that the children develop at a rate equivalent to ordinary children. It is rate based on the progress of our children in the research on the test we used. Even so, the rate is faster and one also finds that for over half the children the IQ now goes up a little.

The reason I have gone into this in some detail is that many parents get upset and worried when the child is not making progress. I believe this is because they feel that development is a regular incremental process. It is not. It is a series of stops and starts. Rapid progress is seen in one area, then another. Also there are many individual differences. Some children appear to concentrate on walking and getting mobile, while others want to concentrate on talk, or on more and more precise use of their hands in play. Some do all together. When one plays with a child one needs to appreciate these differences. Try getting a child who wants to get on his feet and learn to walk, to sit on your lap and look at a book! The child's unique genetic code has a great influence on how he or she will develop. *It is not just a matter of experience and teaching.*

*Developmental stages*

If you think about mental growth not as an increase in quantity, but as a sequence of changes in the type of 'thinking', you will have a different viewpoint about mental retardation. This way of looking at mental growth was put forward by the eminent French psychologist Jean Piaget. I cannot go into the details here, but by briefly noting the major stages you may gain some insight.

From birth to two years the child is mainly concerned with exploring the immediate world. He or she is discovering how to act upon the world, what things are and what can be done with them. It is aptly called the sensori-motor period. The child learns to co-ordinate senses and actions, and to organise his or her perceptions of the world around. The child will also learn to set up goals and try various ways of achieving them. It is interesting to note that the periods of decline in Figure 13, to a large extent, coincide with the stages that Piaget described as making up the sensori-motor period.

Most children in the profound mentally retarded category tend to function within this stage of development.

Around the two-year level children begin to use symbols to help them classify and organise their perceptions. They can also use one thing to represent another, e.g. a stick for a gun. Words are the most useful symbols to use to organise the world, and language develops quite quickly.

At around four the child is very efficient at using symbols and at ordering and classifying. But when it comes to reasoning out causal explanations the child will normally use intuition. For example, if asked what makes it rain the child may answer, because it is thundering. Often such explanations are based on the fact that things happen at the same time. Coincidences are often used to seek explanations.

Because it is mainly intuition which guides the explanations of cause and effect, this stage is known as the intuitive stage. It lasts up to about seven years of age. Thus it covers mental ages two to seven, which are similar to the categories of severe and moderate retardation.

Between seven and 11 years, children begin to move from intuitive explanations to those which are based on the reality of the world. They learn that things have a constancy about them: Monday is always followed by Tuesday; a piece of clay can be made into many shapes but it is still the same size and weight; $5 + 2 = 7 = 2 + 5 = 8 - 1 = 7$, and so on. Thus their reasoning is increasingly based on knowledge about the laws and physical properties of events. This is called the concrete-operational stage. It is very much concerned with finding out and knowing about what is in the world.

Around 11 years children move on to the next stage, which is characterised by the ability to reason in formal and abstract terms. They begin to think in terms of propositions. They can evaluate a range of information, set up possible explanations and reason out which ones may be appropriate.

This stage is seldom reached by people who are mentally retarded. It would seem to represent a cut-off in reasoning and conceptualising ability. Thus the concrete-operational stage of seven to 11 years would approximate to the mild retardation category. (It is interesting to note that at the turn of the century, the first mental ability tests gave only mental ages. Mental ages zero to two were classified as idiot, mental age two to seven as imbecile and mental age seven to 11 as moron.)

Of course the cut-off points between stages are not precise. And the ages given are very approximate and vary enormously, especially as the child gets older. One can also find examples of more advanced formal reasoning, in children who mainly function in the concrete-operational stage.

But, from this way of looking at mental growth, it is possible to understand how some people may not move into the next 'level of thinking' or will do so only with great difficulty.

The fact that a child may not develop formal or abstract reasoning ability, however, does not mean he or she will stop acquiring new skills and knowledge. We do know that if education begins early and is continuous, then the 'fall-off' in IQ is less likely to occur. Several studies have even suggested that it does not happen. Certainly the IQ appears to remain fairly stable from around the first years of life to late adolescence for many children with Down's syndrome in educational programmes. Part of this is due to the fact that most mental ability tests do not directly measure 'intelligence'. Instead they measure what a child can do and what a child knows. Therefore educational methods which increase what the child can do and what she knows will influence the IQ.

Consequently one cannot conclude from the evidence available that the mental growth of most children and adults with Down's syndrome deteriorates or stops. There will be plateaux, and these will differ among individual children and different aspects of development, such as walking and talking, and also among different levels of mental ability.

One cannot, on the other hand, rule out the possibility of deterioration due to organic difficulties. As I noted in Chapter Five, there is sufficient evidence to indicate that some persons with Down's syndrome will suffer from disorders which result in neurological deterioration. However, they are likely to be only a small percentage. Temporary plateaux can also be found, as in any child, as a consequence of illness, or social/emotional upset.

But we can conclude with much confidence that the majority of children with Down's syndrome can be expected to progress, to acquire new skills and abilities, albeit at a slower pace than ordinary children. This raises the next question.

*'If they do develop more slowly, does their mental growth continue for longer?'*

Only a few researchers have looked at this question, and the evidence for or against is limited. But there are studies which suggest that mental growth in the more able people with Down's syndrome continues well into the twenties and possibly up to their late thirties. The less able seem to flatten off much earlier and remain in the severe mental retardation category. However, even those in this category can be taught new skills. Instead of pushing forward to more advanced ways of thinking, one can extend sideways and help them to use the abilities they have to acquire new interests and skills at that level. One must not assume that just because a child has Down's syndrome his or her development will suddenly stop. Instead one must continue to provide education well into their later years. In the past, and in some places still, many mentally retarded children reach the age of 16 and leave school. Their mental ability at this time is often around the four to seven-year level, i.e. it is equivalent to the stage when most children are just beginning school. It can also coincide with an increase in concrete-operational types of thinking. Thus it is very possible that the continuation of educational programmes beyond 16 will result in much higher levels of achievement for mentally retarded people. There are many reports of adults with Down's syndrome making much progress in their later years. If they are provided with educational opportunities and skilled and systematic methods of teaching to compensate for learning difficulties, many continue to learn new educational, social, leisure and occupational skills.

*'Is there a difference between their social and mental abilities?'*

Some of the books you read will say that the social development, such as self-help skills and interpersonal skills required to interact with people, are more advanced than mental ability skills in people with Down's syndrome. You may see social quotients (SQs) quoted. These are worked out just the same as DQs and IQs, but the items in the test are judged to measure different areas of ability. One usually finds that the social quotients (SQs) are higher than the IQs. In early and middle childhood they often average three years in advance. This may be due to the fact that the items tested, particularly self-help skills, can be taught to, and acquired by, children with Down's syndrome more easily than mental ability items and language items, which may depend more on a range of experiences and maturation.

I think there is some truth in this, but I must add that the items in the social ability tests are less rigorous than in mental ability tests. There is a great deal of discretion left to the examiner in the tests, and many rely upon parent recollections and observations rather than on objective 'on-the-spot' testing of mental ability. This must account for a degree of the difference. Even so, many people remark on the bright and positive social impression that children with Down's syndrome give, often adding that they 'appear more intelligent than they are!'. Usually this means that the child is eager to do things, has good personal and social habits, is reasonably well controlled and can be directed to do things. This is an opposite picture to the expected 'dullness' that people incorrectly associate with low IQs.

Finally, we found that mental ability, language ability and social ability test results were all highly correlated; the child who has a high mental age is also likely to have a high social age and language age. In most cases, however, the social age is highest, the mental age next and the language age lowest. It would appear that the development of language is more difficult for children with Down's syndrome than learning self-help skills. Even so, all areas appear to be associated with a general mental ability or 'intelligence', and the slower the child's developmental rate from around two years of age when these areas of development appear, the more handicapped he or she is likely to be in the future, when compared to the faster children.

*Some conclusions*

I am sorry if you have found this section rather complex, and confusing. But it does show how difficult it is to answer what appear to be simple questions: 'What do you mean, she will be retarded?' 'Is retarded the same as handicapped?' 'What can we expect by way of mental attainments?' It also gives some indication of the difficulties encountered when we try to understand the nature of mental retardation and handicap. In my experience, many parents find they are quite happy to get on with the day-to-day management and education of the child and leave all the difficulties noted above to the 'experts'. They are happy to be guided by professionals and act upon their advice. But there are also many parents who find the need to explore the area in much more detail. They need to feel they have some understanding of the wider issues and aspects. This is what I have attempted to offer. I do not feel it is merely an academic exercise, either. *If you ask whether early and continuous education makes the child less retarded, the answer is 'Yes: because he or she will attain the developmental milestones more quickly.' If you ask whether early and continuous education will make the child less handicapped, the answer is 'Yes: because he or she will acquire more skills and knowledge and so will be able to do more things in life.' But if you ask whether early and continuous education will make the child more 'intelligent', or more able to reason and conceptualise for him or herself, the answer must be 'It depends upon what we mean'. We certainly cannot give them 'normal' mental abilities, and it is unlikely that many will achieve the more complex intellectual activities involved in formal and abstract reasoning.*

So let us now take a more functional approach. Let us ask 'What can we expect them to be able to do?'.

## 4 Early developmental attainments

In Table 4 I have listed the major developmental milestones used in developmental tests, and the average age range when children with Down's syndrome achieve these. Much of this information is based on our group of children, but I have incorporated results from other studies. All results are based on children whose parents have received some help and guidance on how to stimulate the babies. I have not included the very small number of children who have added severe complications and may thus achieve the milestones very late indeed. For example, out of over 150 babies in our study who survived to five years of age, only two did not learn to walk. One had very severe motor difficulties and the other developed leukaemia at two years, and the recurring bouts of weakness set his walking back considerably. However, his treatment was successful and he did walk by six years of age.

It is important to realise that the Table is a description of averages and does not indicate the individuality of the children. Some who achieve one milestone later than average may achieve another earlier. Therefore it provides only a general guide. Also many reports find that the girls develop more quickly than boys. This is also found in normal children and, of course, some girls will be slower than some boys.

The Table will give some indication of overall rates of progress, but it may be helpful if I give an overview at each year. Very broadly I shall describe what we can expect for *50 to 75 per cent of the children* at each age in the main areas of development. This means about one half will be slower than the descriptions and another quarter will be well in advance.

By the end of the *first year* the babies will be able to sit with reasonably good balance, and to pick up and play with toys. Most will be able to roll over and can be pulled to a standing position and support their own weight.

They will be able to take solids from a spoon, feed themselves with a biscuit and will have begun to hold a cup and to drink from it—with some mess, of course!

*TABLE 4* Developmental milestones for children with Down's syndrome

*1 GROSS MOTOR ACTIVITIES*

| ACTIVITY | Children with Down's syndrome Average Age | Range | 'Normal' children Average Age | Range |
|---|---|---|---|---|
| Holds head steady and balanced | 5m | 3m to 9m | 3m | 1m to 4m |
| Rolls over | 8m | 4m to 12m | 5m | 2m to 10m |
| Sits without support for one minute or more | 9m | 6m to 16m | 7m | 5m to 9m |
| Pulls to stand using furniture | 15m | 8m to 26m | 8m | 7m to 12m |
| Walks with support | 16m | 6m to 30m | 10m | 7m to 12m |
| Stands alone | 18m | 12m to 38m | 11m | 9m to 16m |
| Walks alone | 23m | 13m to 48m | 12m | 9m to 17m |
| Walks up stairs with help | 30m | 20m to 48m | 17m | 12m to 24m |
| Walks down stairs with help | 36m | 24m to 60m+ | 17m | 13m to 24m |
| Runs | around 4 years | | — | |
| Jumps on the spot | 4 to 5 years | | — | |

*2 PERSONAL/SOCIAL/SELF HELP ACTIVITIES*

| ACTIVITY | Children with Down's syndrome Average Age | Range | 'Normal' children Average Age | Range |
|---|---|---|---|---|
| Smiles when touched and talked to | 2m | 1½m to 4m | 1m | 1m to 2m |
| Smiles spontaneously | 3m | 2m to 6m | 2m | 1½m to 5m |
| Recognises mother/father | 3½m | 3m to 6m | 2m | 1m to 5m |
| Takes solids well | 8m | 5m to 18m | 7m | 4m to 12m |
| Feeds self with biscuit | 10m | 6m to 14m | 5m | 4m to 10m |
| Plays pat-a-cake, peep-bo games | 11m | 9m to 16m | 8m | 5m to 13m |
| Drinks from cup | 20m | 12m to 30m | 12m | 9m to 17m |
| Uses spoon or fork | 20m | 12m to 36m | 13m | 8m to 20m |
| Undresses | 38m | 24m to 60m+ | 30m | 20m to 40m |
| Feeds self fully | 30m | 20m to 48m | 24m | 18m to 36m |
| Urine control during day | 36m | 18m to 50m+ | 24m | 14m to 36m |
| Plays social/interacting games | 3½ to 4½ years | | — | |
| Bowel control | 36m | 20m to 60m+ | 24m | 16m to 48m |
| Dresses self partially (not buttons/laces) | 4 to 5 years | | | |
| Uses toilet or potty without help | 4 to 5 years | | | |

(often too small to get up onto a toilet, unless a special step is available)

Table 4 *Continued*

*3 FINE MOTOR AND ADAPTIVE ACTIVITIES*

| ACTIVITY | Children with Down's syndrome Average Age | Range | 'Normal' children Average Age | Range |
|---|---|---|---|---|
| Follows objects with eyes, in circle | 3m | 1½m to 6m | 1½m | 1m to 3m |
| Grasps dangling ring | 6m | 4m to 11m | 4m | 2m to 6m |
| Passes objects from hand to hand | 8m | 6m to 12m | 5½m | 4m to 8m |
| Pulls string to attain toy | 11½m | 7m to 17m | 7m | 5m to 10m |
| Finds objects hidden under cloth | 13m | 9m to 21m | 8m | 6m to 12m |
| Puts 3 or more objects into cup or box | 19m | 12m to 34m | 12m | 9m to 18m |
| Builds a tower of two 1″ cubes | 20m | 14m to 32m | 14m | 10m to 19m |
| Completes a simple three shape jigsaw | 33m | 20m to 48m | 22m | 16m to 30m+ |
| Copies a circle | 48m | 36m to 60m+ | 30m | 24m to 40m |
| Matching shapes/colours | 4 to 5 years | | | |
| Plays games with simple rules | 4 to 5 years | | | |

*4 COMMUNICATION ACTIVITIES*

| ACTIVITY | Children with Down's syndrome Average Age | Range | 'Normal' children Average Age | Range |
|---|---|---|---|---|
| Reacts to sounds | 1m | ½m to 1½m | | 0 to 1m |
| Turns to sound of voice | 7m | 4m to 8m | 4m | 2m to 6m |
| Say da-da, ma-ma | 11m | 7m to 18m | 8m | 5m to 14m |
| Responds to familiar words | 13m | 10m to 18m | 8m | 5m to 14m |
| Responds to simple verbal instructions | 16m | 12m to 24m | 10m | 6m to 14m |
| Jabbers expressively | 18m | 12m to 30m | 12m | 9m to 18m |
| Says first word(s) | 18m | 13m to 36m | 14m | 10m to 23m |
| Shows needs by gestures | 22m | 14m to 30m | 14½m | 11m to 19m |
| A few two word sentences | 30m | 18m to 60m+ | | |
| Uses words spontaneously and to communicate | 1½ to 6 years | | | |

They will be able to reach and pick up objects, even grasp at small objects such as raisins, though not with a neat finger-thumb pincer movement. They will hold an object in each hand, bang them together, bang one object on another (like a drum), suck things and shake them. They will transfer objects from one hand to the other and spend much time visually examining them. If they make a noise they will enjoy trying to make the noise again and again, and listening to it. They will try to get toys out of their reach and many will pull a string to get them.

They will enjoy rough and tumble games and will laugh and giggle spontaneously. They will be beginning to laugh at 'tug-of-war', 'peek-a-boo' and 'teasing' games, but not as often or with the same gusto as ordinary babies. They will listen to voices and will recognise familiar voices and people, some being shy of strangers. Around their first birthday many will enjoy peek-a-boo and clapping-hands games, and will be saying 'da-da', 'ga-ga' and 'ma-ma'.

By the end of their *second year* they will be able to get up on their feet, stand alone and take several steps—if a little unsteadily in some cases. Many will be able to crawl—but do note we find quite a number of children with Down's syndrome who do not crawl but learn to walk first.

They will use 'da-da'/'ma-ma' with meaning, and will have a few other words. They will also be jabbering with expression and using gestures to tell you what they want. They will be beginning to follow simple instructions and to imitate words. They will enjoy 'conversations' with people, listening and jabbering.

They will be able to use a cup by themselves, and will be trying to use a spoon to feed themselves—with varying success! They will try to help in undressing and dressing—i.e. pulling vests or sweaters off once they are over their head; stepping into pants—if holding on to something for support.

They will be putting objects in and taking out of cups, boxes, etc.; they will scribble with a pencil or crayon and look at pictures in books, turning the pages for themselves. They will usually be able to push or roll a ball and play rolling games. They will play with simple post-boxes and pegboards; use jack-in-box type toys with a switch or catch to release the toy, and know how to make them work. They will be interested in boxes with lids, opening cupboards and emptying handbags! They will also be imitating the things they see you and other children do.

As the children get older, so the range of achievements gets wider, and it is difficult to be as precise and confident in describing what they can do. However, at *three years* they will start to trot, pull a toy behind them, walk backwards, and climb up and often down stairs with support (i.e. hand-held or rail). They will be able to climb up and sit on any chair. They will throw a ball and make varying attempts at kicking. They usually manage to feed themselves, with varying degrees of mess. The majority will have bowel control and be clean. Over half will be dry during the day. They will be able to put on and take off simple clothing with varying degrees of help.

They will do simple jig-saws; will draw lines rather than scribble; match simple pictures and enjoy simple picture dominoes or snap games, even if not very concerned with the rules. They will have favourite books and recognise pictures in stories. They will be beginning to name a few familiar pictures, and will understand instructions such as 'go and get your teddy'. They will engage in simple play sequences, which will include much make-believe, e.g. putting dolls to bed, feeding teddy bears, etc. Their play sequences are noticeably short when compared with those of the ordinary child, and they do not develop unless another child or adult is present who can extend the activities.

The greatest variations from the norm will be found in language. Whilst most will understand many words and instructions, only a small number will use language extensively. This is more likely in the girls than the boys.

*By four years of age* they will be able to ask or indicate to use the toilet, and manage it by themselves or with little help. Over half will be clean and dry by day and night, but odd accidents will occur and some individuals may have bouts of wetting when ill, over-excited, or far too busy with doing things to 'go'.

The majority will be able to feed themselves without difficulty but not necessarily without some mess.

They will be able to clean their teeth, wipe their bottoms, wash their hands and face, dry themselves and dress and undress (except for difficult buttons, zips, etc.)—all with varying degrees of success. This does not mean they will do it, only that they can do it.

Many will have a strong sense of independence and demand to do their own thing, so temper tantrums are likely—as with normal children. They will enjoy games with people and other children and often seek out company—getting cross when it is not available. There is quite a lot of imaginative play, but it does not compare in range of spontaneity with that of ordinary children. They will be exploratory and want new and varied experiences—they will want to be doing things like any toddler. But because they will often be unable to develop their play without the help of an adult or child, they appear to give up quickly and demand frequent changes of activities. This can be very demanding for parents and teachers, so one does need a high level of resources to cope, including additional 'hands'—grandparents, brothers and sisters, playmates and play-groups, schools, etc. However, they can imitate well and if in the company of other children will be able to engage in quite complex play games by imitating.

*Choosing a pre-school facility*

I shall digress here to discuss the selection of pre-school facilities. Apart from the feelings of concern felt by most mothers when any child 'goes off to playgroup or school for the first time', the main issue is choosing the best facility for your child. There are usually two aspects which can pull in different directions. Do you choose a facility with special staff who are expert with children with major learning difficulties, or do you choose a 'normal' placement with ordinary children?

If one chooses special facilities it is likely that the child with Down's syndrome will not get access to ordinary children but will get specialist help. The question is, which is more important to the child at this stage in his or her development? Our research found that the slower children were more likely to be placed in special school nursery classes. However, we also found that more of the children in our early intervention programme went to mainstream playgroups and nursery schools than similar children in our area who did not take part in the programme. When we compared the children at five years old and later we could not find any differences in terms of mental age, language age, behaviour difficulties, or self-help skills. Nor did we find more went to ordinary than special schools. Therefore this suggests that special provision in the pre-school years may not be of any greater benefit to the majority of children with Down's syndrome than local playgroups and nursery schools. My interpretation is that where there are no problems preventing the parent and family from giving the child plenty of individual help which understands his or her learning difficulties (see section 3), there is no major benefit in the early attendance at a special provision. *Ideally the mainstream provision should have some specialist input, like advice and support for the staff so that they can interact with the child and organise experiences in a more effective way*. This does not need to be very extensive or highpowered because the main needs of the majority of pre-school children with Down's syndrome are like any child of the same developmental level.

This raises the second important point. In section 3, I described patterns of development in the first few years (Figure 13). There was a long plateau around the developmental level of 18 to 28 months, followed by quite rapid development. This corresponds to chronological ages of two to four years. Thus round about the age of four to five we expect to see the child with Down's syndrome rapidly begin to develop better communication, more socially orientated behaviour, complex means-end play, imaginative play and a much improved ability to learn by imitating the actions of others. If you think about it, this is exactly the type of abilities that we expect of ordinary children at about three when we send them to playgroups. From around two-and-a-half years, interacting with other children of a similar level becomes important to children. Peer interaction is very different from interacting with adults. This is well known. Parents often have great concern about how their child is learning 'bad habits' from other children. The reason many parents give for their child with special needs to go to ordinary schools is because they will have a chance to learn about ordinary ways of getting on with others. This is why many parents send their child with Down's syndrome to ordinary pre-school facilities. However, although we did not find that attending a special provision advanced the child's development and skills any more than a playgroup, we also did not find that attending the ordinary provision was any more advantageous on these measures. We think one reason is that the children are moved out of the ordinary nursery and playgroup too soon. The selection for school takes place in the fourth year. This is in the plateau period and often just before the child has reached the stage to interact more fully with his or her peers. We often found the staff saying that the child was not getting involved and tended to be by-passed by the other children and not included in many activities. Thus it was agreed that he or she would be better off in special provision. At this age this usually meant special school. It is our impression that had the decision been delayed just a few months, the staff and parents would have seen some dramatic changes for many of the children. These changes would be predicted from the understanding of the developmental sequences. Indeed, in many individual cases we saw such changes. In some provisions who were willing to keep the child on for an extra year, they noted that the benefits were large enough to make this part of their general recommendations. *Therefore it would appear that it is better to match the children on developmental level and provide them with as normal a set of experiences as possible.*

Another assumption about special provisions is that it provides more individual adult attention. This may be true in large classes but it is not automatically the case. Often a playgroup will have more adults around than a special school. The school is likely to have one teacher and an assistant for eight to ten children. Since all have special needs the amount of sustained individual attention is limited. Further, to give this attention at the most productive time in the learning activity requires a great deal of flexibility of resources. If one works it out, a child with special needs will probably get more help of this type in the mainstream situation with an assistant assigned to the child or where there are more people. In fact the point is that the other children are also likely to provide the key experience and so act as models or teachers.

The point for me is that since I cannot find any substantial evidence that specialist help in a segregated setting is more beneficial than ordinary provisions for the large majority of young children with Down's syndrome, then the child should attend ordinary pre-school provision. There is no reason to segregate the child at this time and there are disadvantages. Attendance at special school generally means more distant travel, the child is more likely to become cut off from the local children and the parent, especially of the first-born children, is often denied the opportunities to meet other local parents at the school gate and at meetings and so can become isolated. This can be serious when you think of the help and support we all give each other—those unplanned daily contacts and chats about things generally. It can also prevent the neighbours learning about the child's handicap and offering to baby-sit, etc.

As the children grow older, so their learning difficulties become more obvious compared to ordinary children. Their special needs increase and they do require more and more specialist help. There is such a range of ability between children with Down's syndrome that it is not possible to make any general points about what special help may be needed and when it may be needed. Each case has to be assessed according to the individual child's special needs. Some will require physiotherapy, others speech therapy. Some will need constant supervision and help to control difficult behaviours. Others will require access to different amounts of individual tuition to keep up with the other children. Whether this can be provided in mainstream schools depends upon resources and local policies. *What is clear is that the case for segregating the child should not be made just because he or she has Down's syndrome. It has to be based firmly on a detailed assessment of special needs.*

*Around four to five* language will be developing. The vocabulary will increase and two or three words will begin to be linked together. The articulation is likely to be poor, so the child can experience frustration in making him or herself understood. Access to speech therapy is very useful at this time. However, many children with Down's syndrome, even given a high quality of teaching, appear to have great difficulty with the comprehension of language and with expressing themselves. Therefore 'open' questions such as: 'What is a car for?', 'What do you do if you cut your finger?' can be difficult for them to answer. Many can make simple wants known with single words and gestures, but will not be able to re-tell a simple story or describe what is happening in a picture.

When language does begin to blossom, many children will appear to come out of the 'plateau' and become easier to cope with. They can be reasoned with and become therefore 'more reasonable' (see section 2 and Figure 13). However, well before this stage, they can say 'No!' 'I want it,' 'Iwill do it'. This growing independence is not seen in all, and needs to be encouraged. In some it is so dominant it needs to be handled firmly to prevent the child from controlling the household, but not harshly so that it prevents the child from learning to be independent.

They will begin to copy circles and make simple drawings. They can learn rules and turn-taking and so join in more complex group games. Tricycles, pedal cars and so forth are likely to be mastered, and if they have the opportunity some will be beginning to swim.

By the age of *five to six* the differences among the children are so great that I feel it impossible to give an overview. Instead I shall try to indicate the range of ability at this age—it is very important to realise the vast individual differences found in children with Down's syndrome. Again, I shall only use results where children have had good care and education from the first year or so of life.

In our own study, we have two or three children who at five years of age have IQs lower than 20. This means that we have been unable to assess them. From observations and developmental checklists we 'feel' rather than 'know' that the child is around the nine- to 18-month level of development. But in the two children in our sample like this, both walk, will respond to simple commands, and use some gestures to communicate. Thus in them the variability of development, so often seen in the slower children, is very marked. At the other end of the scale we have a child with an IQ consistently measured at around 110 since he was three. Other studies report similar ranges of IQs from 20 to nearly 100, with averages around the 55–60 level. In terms of percentage in groups, the approximate consensus emerging from recent studies calculates about ten to 15 per cent who have IQs above 75, and so fall into the dull normal range and therefore would not be classified as mentally retarded according to current criteria. However, I should say that many of these children have profited enormously from the use of teaching methods aimed to compensate for learning difficulties and so, in my opinion, will only maintain their progress with the continual use of special education but in mainstream schools. Also, as I noted in the last section, the average IQ of the present generation of young children may be higher than that of those born several years ago. Thus we may need to re-think what is meant by IQs and categories of mental handicap. A small number are coping in ordinary schools and mainstream education, especially those with some special resources. Certainly far more could cope if mainstream schools had more specialist resources.

Within this group one can find children with Down's syndrome who can read at, or in some cases above, the normal age standards. But this can be misleading. Their comprehension of spoken and written language, when measured, is often at a less advanced level. Thus it may be that they can learn basic skills like reading quite efficiently, but are not as able as normal children to conceptualise, to abstract relevant bits of information, to search out relationships between bits of information, or to re-formulate or synthesise this into new ideas and concepts. It is in these areas that they seem to need the assistance of a teacher, adult or child who can draw their attention to the relevant information and its meaning.

The majority of children fall into the mild category at age five to six on mental test scores. Estimates vary enormously between 45 per cent and 60 per cent in this category. I am quite confident that at least 50 per cent will fall into this category, given suitable early education, though many will be in the lower end of the category and not the upper end. But let me remind you again that they will be competent in self-help, social and self-entertainment skills. For most the hurdle at this time will be the development of language, particularly being able to talk in a reasonably complex manner.

Fewer than half will fall into the moderate and severe range. Rather rough estimates indicate that about 20–25 per cent will be moderate, about 15–20 per cent will be severe and fewer than five per cent will be profoundly mentally retarded.

Instead of working in IQs, one can simply stick to mental ages (see page 174). In Figure 14 we have plotted the mental ages of all the children in our research from six weeks to five years. The bottom (1%) and top (100%) lines plot the pattern of the slowest and fastest child. We have plotted the average mental age for the rest of the children at seven levels of accumulated percentage. At the bottom is the mean mental age achieved at each chronological age for three per cent of the group. The next is for ten per cent, in other words one in ten of the children had a mental age of 11 months when 25 months old and 24 months when five years old. The line marked 50 per cent is the mean or average. If you have a mental age for a child with Down's syndrome it is possible to see how he or she compares to our group. Simply work out the age of the child in months and find this along the bottom axis of the graph. Then draw a straight line up until you reach the mental age level of the child on the vertical axis. Where they cross will show the percentage level of the child compared to our group. If, for example, the cross falls between the 25 and 50 per cent lines, then the child has developed more quickly than 25 per cent of our group but is developing slower than the average.

From the figure you can see the range of scores and ability in this large sample of children with Down's syndrome and get some idea of the distribution as described earlier.

Again, you must remember that these are average results based on the scores of many children. Often an individual child will be at one percentage point at one age and at a different point at another. We found that if we divided the percentage range into five groups, (0 to 20, 21 to 40, 41 to 60, 61 to 80, 81 to 100) and computed how often a child would stay or change groups, we could get some idea of the stability of their development. We could begin to predict the progress we expected them to make from their previous groupings. From 12 months of age about half the children were in the same group three months later. By four years over 80 per cent were in the same group. From the first year no child moved more than three groups. Therefore by the second year of life the children are fairly stable in their progress. We also asked what the chance was of the child being in the same group at five years of age as he or she was in between 24 to 30 months of age.

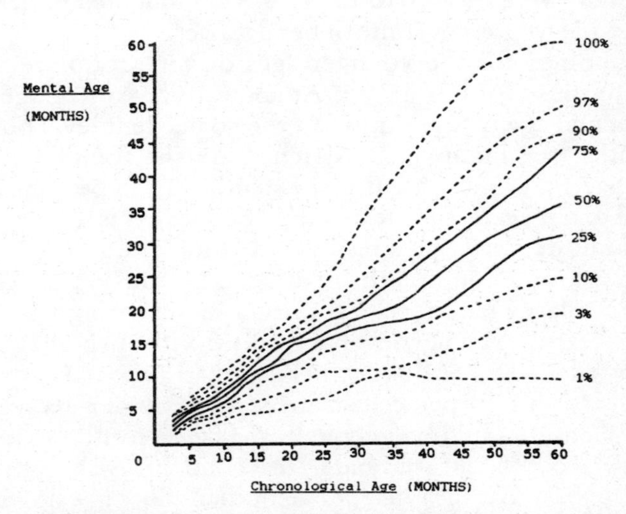


**Fig 14. Down's syndrome: centile distribution of mental ages.**

Eight out of ten children were in the same percentage group. Therefore if the child is developing above the 50 per cent level fairly consistently at two to three years of age, you can be reasonably sure that he or she will not suddenly drop into the 20 per cent level unless he has a serious accident or becomes very ill.

We do not have all the figures computed for the ages up to ten years, but so far the pattern seems to be the same and the children are developing in the same order. The slower ones are getting into long plateaux at an earlier age, the middle group are plateauing at later ages and at different stages and the fastest developing ones are just beginning to show some plateauing.

*Later developmental attainments*

Much of the information on the attainments of the adolescent and young adult with Down's syndrome is dated and one is not sure of the quality. To give some idea of later attainments I describe the results from one study, that of Dr Joyce Ludlow. Dr Ludlow began studying the development of infants with Down's syndrome in the early 1960s in Kent, in south-east England. Her main interest was to help the families and the children. In 1983 she went back to more than 100 of the families and assessed the young people with Down's syndrome who were aged 16 to 22 years. I am indebted to her for allowing me to present some of her data here.

Her findings for the younger ages of her group are very similar to those for our group. At about five years of age her mean mental age is 32 months. At the 50 per cent level ours is 36 months (see Figure 14). At ten years she found a mean mental age of 54 months. If one extends our 50 per cent line forward to ten years, the mean would be about this level which would indicate steady progress. At 18 years Dr Ludlow found a mean of around 66 months or five and a half years. Again there was a large range, with some children scoring less than the two-year mental age level and some with mental ages of eight and nine years. About 17 per cent had a mental age over seven years and 40 per cent a mental age under six years. Therefore, as the children get older, the range continues to get bigger between the slowest and fastest children. Also from this data, it appears that the rate of development does get slower in these later years as has been found in many of the earlier studies. But it does not stop for many of the children, indeed there is still a lot of progress being made in early adulthood. The curve at eighteen years is still climbing and has not levelled off, which would indicate the end of mental growth. Again, this progress into early adulthood confirms other studies and shows quite clearly that the young adult with Down's syndrome is still developing mentally and so should receive the help to continue his or her education and to stimulate development. Like any of us, the end of mental growth does not stop us from continuing to learn new skills.

Dr Ludlow also obtained information from parents and professionals about the attainments of the young people. Table 5 presents the percentage of the group who were considered by the parents to be independent and competent in the skill areas noted. As can be seen, with the exception of handling money, over half the group were competent in the other areas. In basic self-care and self-help skills the percentage was generally over three-quarters. Money, and indeed all arithmetical computation, is a weak area for most children with Down's syndrome. Other activities such as freedom of movement, eating out and cleaning basic household equipment are as much to do with opportunity as with ability.

The picture that emerges from this group is that well over half can be confidently expected to achieve basic competence in living skills and be relatively independent. Given the right support, they can certainly be expected to lead full and interesting lives.

*Comments*

I must make an important point here: this range of achievement and the many different abilities in the children, is found even when *all* are given access to good care and education from birth. Thus we may have two children from the same type of home, with the same level of help, one of whom will have an IQ in the 80s, the other in the 30s. This clearly shows that the environment—care and education—is only one of the sources of influence on development. Children are born with different potentials to develop. We can only try to ensure that nothing is done to hinder this, and everything (within reason) is done to encourage the development. The idea that we can prevent these children from being as handicapped as previous studies

*TABLE 5* Attainments of independent living skills. (Data from Dr Joyce Ludlow's Study)

| *PERSONAL* | % competent |
|---|---|
| Using knife, fork, spoon | 98 |
| Drinking | 98 |
| Table manners | 97 |
| Eating out, ordering/conduct | 50 |
| Washing hands/face | 81 |
| Cleaning teeth | 83 |
| Bathing/drying | 82 |
| Washing and caring for hair | 75 |
| Keeping nose clean | 85 |
| Fully toilet trained/any toilet | 96 |
| Menstruation/shaving | 65 |
| Tends to basic health needs | 55 |
| Dresses and undresses | 92 |
| Care and selection of clothes | 66 |
| *DOMESTIC* | |
| Sets table | 94 |
| Clears/washes dishes | 85 |
| Prepares basic meals | 61 |
| Copes in kitchen | 62 |
| Makes bed | 78 |
| Cleans room/uses domestic appliances | 71 |
| Cleans household equipment | 37 |
| *OUT AND ABOUT* | |
| Copes with spoken instructions | 84 |
| Copes with written instructions | 67 |
| Communicates verbally | 84 |
| Can write simple messages | 64 |
| Handles money | 44 |
| Uses a saving account/budgets own money | 34 |
| Uses public amenities | 66 |
| Uses telephone | 58 |
| Has working knowledge of time. Hours, days, weeks, months | 69 |
| Can generally get out and about and travel without difficulty | 46 |

suggested has tipped the see-saw from undue pessimism to, perhaps, unjustified optimism. I have seen so many parents become quite distressed when their child does not progress as well as another or appears to stop and plateau. They frequently blame themselves for not doing enough or blame the schools and teachers for apparent failure in learning. It may be true, but it is not necessarily true. One must blame some of this distress on the way we—that is, professionals who are engaged in early education for children with Down's syndrome—argue our case for early education. We often quote the exceptions, the successes, without giving the whole picture. We often get so enthusiastic about education that we give the impression that if we teach the children they will all be 'nearly' normal, and if we do not teach them they will all be severely handicapped.

I hope that after reading this chapter you can see that this is not the case. I hope that as you learn more about development and watch your baby grow, you will become skilled at weighing up whether progress or apparent lack of progress is due to slow development and maturation, learning difficulties or the environment. But none of us can ever hope to do more than make informed guesses at this, because the process of development is as yet barely understood and is extremely complex. So do the best you can, but do not be afraid to use your intuitions to guide your judgements. On many occasions your intuitions about your child are likely to be as good as, if not better than, all the generalised expertise available, in guiding you as to what is best.

This brings us to the next question: *'What if there are no early intervention programmes available to us?'*

There are many reports by parents to show clearly that, even without being involved in a programme from birth, there is no reason to feel that a particular child is underfunctioning. In our own research and some of the other similar studies there is evidence that the children of parents not involved in an early education programme can achieve the same levels of attainments as those who are. It is only the *overall* group averages that show differences between those with and those without help.

We have a number of parents who live too far away for regular home visits. They have used the available books and local resources (e.g. playgroups, nurseries, schools), and in some cases formed their own small self-support groups with other mothers. We have assessed these children at six- to twelve-monthly intervals, and as a group they compare with those we have visited. The main difference is not in the children, but in the parents. Those without access to a programme can feel more isolated and find it more difficult to feel confident in what they do.

Here are some quotes from parents we visit:

> Nobody ever mentioned to me before, why I needed to stimulate the baby.
>
> I had little idea what to do with a Down's child, but even when I had that information, more important was why I was doing things.
>
> People visiting explained the reasons for doing things—it helps you to persevere with things.
>
> I look forward to someone coming. Sometimes I feel like I'm wasting my time, and if someone came, they could tell me what to do.
>
> I needed things written down and needed to know what I was looking for.
>
> It's helpful to have a discipline given to you, it's like going out to work, it's nice to know what you've got to achieve in the next few weeks.

Most parents, whether in a programme or using books with instructions about early stimulation, find this can be very beneficial.

> With my other children I didn't realise how much was going on. I have had to learn so much with her but it is a real eye-opener.
>
> Once I started to see things in more detail—to take notice of tiny steps of development like the charts show—I suddenly saw how much he could do. We struggled for a while to get him to pick up his rattle. When he did I was over the moon . . . I couldn't wait for his Dad to come in to tell him.
>
> We've got more joy out of him than a normal baby because everything he does is an added bonus. With a normal child everybody takes it for granted.

Also, many fathers find that having a set of activities —particularly physical exercises for helping sitting and walking—is of great benefit.

> I come home at night and see what she's done . . . we have a set of things to do and we tick off those we've tried during the day. I can then do some and tick off what I've done. It helps keep us more organised . . . I think without them I wouldn't have bothered to try anything . . . doing the things written down on the charts made it easier and I got to know the baby much better than with the other children.

But *'How much do parents need to do?'*

I discussed the benefits of early stimulation in the section on pages 187–90, and concluded that intensive training was of limited benefit. Even so, this final question in this section, is difficult to answer. Babies get tired and need their rest. So do parents. Therefore it is not a case of doing stimulating games and exercises at every opportunity. It is more a case of ensuring that the opportunities for stimulation are taken. At first many parents find it difficult to stop thinking that the baby is handicapped. This can prevent them from providing the normal handling, playing, cuddling, etc., that all babies need. Therefore much of the 'improvement' in babies with Down's syndrome will come from not missing out on everyday activities. If you go into the kitchen, take the baby in with you and sit him in a chair where you can talk to him, and be seen. The activities for developing head control, sitting, walking, should be done for short periods at frequent intervals. When feeding, changing and playing with the baby, include some of the activities. This is no more than you will probably do with any baby, but what you are ensuring is that the activities are the ones most likely to benefit the baby. Of course, as the child gets older, what one can and cannot do will change. For example, babies up to nine to 12 months are often easy to 'teach' but then they move into a stage where you can no longer teach them directly. They will not be taught, instead you have to work indirectly, through play and games.

Some parents who have other young children under five find it difficult to find all the time they need to help the baby. Others who have only the baby, and no other children, complain that they are at a disadvantage because other children would 'bring on' the baby. All make progress. One can find instances where a first-born appears more advanced in skills such as doing puzzles, but less sociable than those with brothers and sisters, yet once they start playschool, they soon blossom socially, too.

The main disadvantages if the first-born has Down's syndrome are that *parents* are more likely to feel 'reproductive inadequacy'; and also that they have no experience of a normal baby to compare with the baby with Down's syndrome. Hence they are less confident in knowing 'what is normal and what is due to the Down's syndrome'.

So bringing up the young child with Down's syndrome, and providing appropriate early stimulation, does not necessarily demand more time from the parents; rather, it demands more thought and organisation. *In fact most parents do not find the child is more demanding than any other child; the difficulties arise from their constant concern about the child and his or her handicap.*

*To Conclude*

Nearly all children with Down's syndrome can be expected to continue to develop until late adolescence or early adulthood, and will continue to learn new skills and knowledge for most of their lives. The development is marked by periods of little apparent progress and periods of rapid progress. As a group, their IQ is fairly stable by two to three years of age, at least to late adolescence. If they are provided with good health care, emotional security and early education, the majority will fall into moderate or mild categories of retardation. They can be expected to respond to educational experiences and make steady progress well into the twenties and possibly beyond.

Thus we can expect that the majority will attain self-help skills, sufficient language to communicate and converse, a range of interests, hobbies and activities. The majority will be able to live in the community, either at home, in sheltered or hostel accommodation, sheltered communities or, in some cases, in their own accommodation.

There have always been some people with Down's syndrome who show exceptional abilities and qualities. There are instances of people with the condition who have written books, acted in television plays, won art competitions, and achieved high levels in dance, scouting and music. Though rare, there are those who live and work independently in the community. Some are married and many have mature and caring relationships with others. Recently there have been more persons with Down's syndrome forming and joining in groups to discuss the needs of the disabled, and demanding the right to make decisions about their own lives. These may be the exceptions, but if so, we can expect far more of these in the future. But whether or not they amaze us by their achievements—and this will depend upon what we expect—far more will be able to lead happy, fulfilled and more independent lives than Langdon Down could ever possibly have imagined when he first recognised and described the condition in 1866.

# CONCLUDING REMARKS

I find it difficult to end this book, because it is really only a beginning. As I said in the introduction, it is an attempt to provide some answers to the immediate questions parents ask. It covers the first period of adjustment to the diagnosis of Down's syndrome, and I hope prepares parents for the day-to-day business of living with and learning about their baby. But I am acutely aware of future areas of concern, which are common to most parents and which I have not discussed in detail. For example, parents need to learn about development and appropriate stimulation and educational activities which they can carry out. Most parents find it difficult to decide where and when the child should start pre-school or school. The next most common 'crisis' is when the child is about to leave school. Where should they go? Should they try for further education courses in colleges of technology; attend the Adult Training Centre (or as it is now being called, Social Education Centre); go to a sheltered workshop; or a residential farm trust?

All these questions will depend on:

1. The individual child; how he develops, what learning strengths and weakness he may have; her personality and behaviour. Thus it is often not worth worrying about such questions until the child is older, and one can get a better idea of his or her mental and social abilities.
2. Local resources and policies. Some areas have a range of pre-school, school and post-school facilities, others do not. At present there is considerable re-thinking being done, and a move towards special facilities in ordinary schools, sheltered accommodation similar to that for old people, small residential hostels, etc. You will have to find out about facilities just before the need arises. Certainly what is available for the adult person with Down's syndrome may have changed considerably in ten years' time.

3 Family circumstances—which can change, and alter future plans.

Therefore try to decide which are the immediate needs, and avoid worrying about future problems which may never arise.

I have listed some books and sources of useful information in the next section.

I would like to say, however, that many parents find their concern and apprehension about the future—going to school or living in a residential establishment—turns out to be quite unwarranted. Most find that their children enjoy pre-school or school and settle in well and that they, the parents, feel it an enormous benefit. Some at first feel guilty that they are glad to 'get away' from the child for a period, but they soon realise that this is a normal reaction experienced by many parents of ordinary children. Most parents find it a great relief to know that someone else is helping the child, and that the responsibility is not solely left to them.

When older children move away from home to a residential hostel or sheltered community, parents may again be full of apprehension. Many are hurt and surprised to find the young adult or teenager actually enjoying living away from home, and in some cases preferring it.

I am particularly aware that I have not discussed the question which is a constant worry to many older parents: 'What will happen when I die?'. I have not tried to answer this because I can't. Again, we hope that improvements in care and education will lead to far more people with Down's syndrome having good social and independent skills. Equally, we hope for an increase in the provision of accommodation in small community homes, hostels, sheltered communities, so that we no longer need to shut anyone away in large hospitals and institutions. Present thinking proposes that those who are more severely handicapped should be cared for in small residential homes with good quality care. And by 'small', most authorities mean no more than 25–30 residents, and in some cases only six or eight.

With all the above problems, contacting your local services should bring you much information. But do not neglect to contact the parent groups and voluntary associations, too. These often have much more information, and are especially concerned to help you, the parent. I do know that many parents, as many as 50 per cent, are reluctant to contact other parents or groups in the first months after the birth. However, by the end of the first year most parents—especially mothers—do find parent groups can be helpful. This is especially true if they are self-help groups, with children of a similar age, so that they can discuss practical problems and solutions. Other parents do not like to join an association at all, but this need not stop them from getting information on local resources, holiday schemes, care schemes, insurance, legal rights, etc., from the associations.

I shall end this book by returning to the main theme. The birth of a child with Down's syndrome is a great shock for all parents. No matter what happens after the birth, it is an event in your life which will always be with you and must produce changes. It is a challenge.

Bringing up any child is a challenge. Whether bringing up a child with a handicap is a greater challenge, or just a different challenge from bringing up an ordinary child, is a matter of opinion. But bringing up a child with Down's syndrome is not only a challenge to cope, and provide the child with the best available opportunities to grow and develop—it is a challenge to the set of values by which we judge others, and decide what we want from life.

I look forward to the day when a mother and father can be given assurances that they will not have a baby with a severe disability. But I am not sure whether such a day will be to the benefit of society as a whole. Those members of our society who are severely disabled are a constant challenge to society; they cause us to question our values, they test our compassion, they remind us that 'ability' is not all.

## *Appendix*

# PRENATAL TESTS FOR SOME HANDICAPPING CONDITIONS

The purpose of prenatal tests is to discover whether the foetus is likely to have any abnormalities. The most common test at the present is called *amniocentesis*. More recently a new test is beginning to be used and is called the *chorionic villus biopsy* or chorionic villus sampling (CVS).

The amniocentesis test relies upon the fact that cells are in the amniotic fluid which surrounds and protects the baby, and have come from the foetus which is shedding skin cells just as you and I shed cells as new ones generate.

An ultrascan must be carried out first, to establish the position of the foetus and the placenta. A syringe is then inserted through the lower part of mother's abdominal wall and womb into the amniotic fluid space. The extracted fluid then has to be cultured for *two to three weeks*, at which time the chromosomes can be stained and counted.

This test is not usually carried out before 14–15 weeks of pregnancy, because it is too difficult to culture and grow the foetal cells before this. Generally it is done at about 16 weeks of pregnancy.

Like all tests, things can go wrong. Sometimes the amniotic fluid sample has no cells that will grow—the procedure of culturing cells is not simple, though problems like this were more common in the early years when the test was still new and few people were practised in the techniques. Nowadays the majority of tests are successful and straightforward.

One important question is whether or not the foetus is at risk as a result of the test. Present figures show that, provided the test is carried out by skilled, practised people and an ultrascan is used, the maximum risk of losing a foetus through miscarriage is about one in 200. For many mothers it will be lower than this.

CVB consists of taking a small sample of the placenta which will contain cells of the foetus. These can be checked for chromosomal abnormalities. Usually the sample is collected via the vagina but recently a method similar to amniocentesis has been developed. This requires a needle to be passed through the wall of the abdomen and is less likely to risk possible infection. CVB is still a relatively new technique and is not fully available everywhere.

The advantage of CVS over amniocentesis is that it can be carried out eight to ten weeks after conception and the results obtained in a matter of days. Therefore should termination of the pregnancy be decided it can take place very soon and certainly before the mother is physically aware of the foetus.

The main disadvantage of CVS is that it has, at present, a higher risk of losing the foetus. Current figures are not especially accurate but fall in the region of four in one hundred.

The use of ultrascan has increasingly improved and reduced the risks of tests as well as being able to give indications about any structural problems in the foetus at later ages.

At present, however, for most mothers under 35–40 there is a greater risk of losing the foetus as a result of a test than of having a baby with a chromosomal fault. Therefore many doctors recommend the tests only for mothers over 35, or for those who have already had a child with a chromosomal disorder and who are at risk.

# CHILDREN LEARN WHAT THEY LIVE

If a child lives with criticism, she learns to criticise

If a child lives with hostility, he learns to fight

If a child lives with ridicule, she learns to be shy

If a child lives with shame, he learns to feel guilt

If a child lives with tolerance, she learns to be patient

If a child lives with encouragement, he learns confidence

If a child lives with praise, she learns to appreciate

If a child lives with fairness, he learns justice

If a child lives with security, she learns to have faith

If a child lives with approval, he learns to like himself

If a child lives with acceptance and friendship, he or she learns to find love in the world.

*(From a poster issued by the Scottish Health Education Unit and redesigned by kind permission of Parents Anonymous Inc. USA)*

# RESOURCES

## Books by and for Parents

1 *Ida: Life with my Handicapped Child*. Ulla Bondo, Faber and Faber 1980.
This is one of my favourite books by a parent. It gives yearly reports of progress of a girl with Down's syndrome up to the mid-childhood years. It is honest, insightful and very practical. Unlike many books, it is about a child given stimulation from birth and reflects new expectations. Very readable and well recommended.

2 *Will, My Son: The Life and Death of a Mongol Child*. Boston, S., Pluto Press 1981.
A very readable book about the life and death of a little Down's syndrome baby.

3 *Helping Your Handicapped Baby*. Cunningham, C. C. & Sloper, P. Souvenir Press 1978.
This describes many practical ways of stimulating the baby in the first years of life, plus discussion on methods and concepts in special education.

4 *Down's Syndrome: Growing and Learning*. Pueschel, S. M. (editor) Kansas City; Sheed Andrews and McNeel Inc. 1978.
Written by parents and professionals for parents. Good introduction covering characteristics, reactions and feelings, resources, development and practical chapters on early activities. This book is for parents in the USA and so some parts are not applicable to the UK. Very readable.

5 *Judith: Teaching Our Mongol Baby. Teaching a Down's child*. Smith, W. W.—pamphlets.
Royal Society for Mentally Handicapped Children (MENCAP). Also obtainable from the Down's Children's Association.

6 *Teaching Your Down's Syndrome Infant: A Guide for Parents*. Marci J. Hanson, Baltimore: University Park Press 1977.

7 *Show Me No Mercy: A compelling story of remarkable courage*. Perske, R. Abingdon Press: Nashville, Tennessee 1984.
A very readable book about a 17-year-old boy with Down's syndrome.

8 *My Friend David*. Edwards, J. & Dawson, D. Ednick Communications, Inc., Portland, Oregon 1984.
This is another recent American book which is difficult to obtain but worthwhile. It is co-authored by a specialist teacher and a man with Down's syndrome and gives a unique insight into growing up and becoming an adult with Down's syndrome.

**Technical books about Down's syndrome**

1 *Down's Syndrome: Mongolism and its Management*. Benda, C. C. (revised edition) London, New York: Grune & Stratton 1969.
This is one of the early books on Down's syndrome and describes much of the early medical information and attempts at management. Parents will find it largely of historical interest and somewhat technical.

2 *The Adolescent with Down's Syndrome*. Buckley, S. & Sacks, B. 1987. Available from the Portsmouth Down's Syndrome Trust, Psychology Department, Portsmouth Polytechnic, King Charles Street, Portsmouth PO1 2ER.
This is a research report of a survey of 90 families who had a teenager with Down's syndrome. It describes what life is like for teenagers and their families. Although a research monograph, it is easily read and many parents should find it interesting.

3 *Families and their Children with Down's Syndrome: One Feature in Common*. Byrne, E. A., Cunningham, C. C. & Sloper, P. London: Routledge 1988.
This is another research monograph about interviews with

mothers of 124 children with Down's syndrome aged three to ten years, living in Manchester. It describes the impact of the child on family life and how families cope. Although the style is formal, many parents will find they can obtain much useful information and insights from the mothers' views which might help them with their own situation.

4 *Young Children with Down's Syndrome. Their Development, Upbringing and Effect on Their Families*. Carr, J. IRMMH Monograph No. 4, London & Boston: Butterworths 1975. This is a report of a survey of 54 babies with Down's syndrome and their families from six weeks to four years of age born in 1963–1964. It reports their developmental progress and the answers of parents to a detailed questionnaire. It is very readable and one of the few detailed studies in this area. But some of the findings have been outdated by advances in recent years.

5 *Children with Down Syndrome*. Cicchetti, D. & Beeghly, M. (editors) Cambridge University Press 1990.
A series of theoretical and review papers about the early development of Down's syndrome. Very comprehensive and thought-provoking. It is aimed at academics and researchers and most parents will find it difficult unless they are also psychologists.

6 *Down's Syndrome and the Family: The Early Years*. Gath, A. London, New York: Academic Press 1978.
This is a report of 30 babies born between 1970–1971 with Down's syndrome, and their families. It was carried out over the first two years of life and looks at effects on the family in detail. It is a scientific account and technical in parts, but many parents will find it useful.

7 *Down's Syndrome: The Psychology of Mongolism*. Gibson, D. Cambridge, London, New York: Cambridge University Press 1978.
This is a most thorough and detailed text covering the psychological aspects of Down's syndrome. It is a very technical book and parents may find some chapters difficult to understand.

8 *Current Approaches to Down's Syndrome*. Lane, D. & Stratford, B. (editors) London: Cassell 1985.
This is an extensive collection of papers from international sources and, although varying in quality and ease of reading, provides a comprehensive overview.

9 *The Young Child with Down Syndrome*. Pueschel, S. M. (editor) New York: Human Sciences Press Inc. 1984.
This is the detailed report of a longitudinal research study of 114 children with Down's syndrome from the earliest years. It is expensive and difficult to obtain but is very useful for the serious student of the condition.

10 *New Perspectives on Down Syndrome*. Pueschel, S., Tingley, C., Rynders, J., Crocker, A. & Crutcher, D. (editors) Baltimore: Paul Brookes Publishing Co. 1987.
The book contains the proceedings of a state-of-the-art conference and includes papers on biomedicine, education, living in the community and psychosocial development. It is a very useful reference as it covers so many aspects of Down's syndrome. It is technical in parts, but not difficult.

11 *Growing Up with Down's Syndrome*. Shepperdson, B. London: Cassell 1988.
This book reports a follow-up of 54 teenagers with Down's syndrome from South Wales. It describes their attainments and how the families cope. It is one of the few studies available which report the progress and changes of a group of children with Down's syndrome from their early childhood. It is a technical report but parents may find it useful to browse through, picking out points of interest.

12 *Down's Anomaly*. Smith, G. F. & Berg, J. M. New York, London: Longmans 1976. (This is the revised edition of Penrose and Smith's book, *Down's Anomaly*, 1966).
This is a comprehensive textbook on the history and medical aspects of Down's syndrome. It is meant for professionals, particular medical staff, and parents may find some sections difficult to understand.

## Some useful books and pamphlets

1 *Play Activities for the Retarded Child.* Carlson, B. W. & Gingeland, D. R. Bailliere-Tindall.
2 *The Story of Nigel Hunt.* Hunt, N. Darwen Finlayson. (Written by a boy with Down's syndrome.)
3 *Play Helps. Toys and activities for handicapped children.* Lear, R. Heinemann Health Books.
4 *Exercises for Your Baby.* Levy, J. Collins.
5 *Choosing Toys and Activities for Handicapped Children.* Morris, G. Toy Libraries Association.
6 *New Life in the Neighbourhood. How persons with retardation or other disabilities can help make a good community better.* Perske, R. & Perske, M. Abingdon. (This is a really interesting and very well presented book.)
7 *Feeding Can be Fun.* Ryan, M. Spastics Society.

## Services and useful addresses

1 *A Handbook for Parents with a Handicapped Child,* Judith Stone and Felicity Taylor, Arrow Books. This is a comprehensive guide to the facilities available.
2 *Voluntary Council for Handicapped Children*
National Children's Bureau, 8 Wakley Street, London EC1V 7QE
The Voluntary Council was set up to provide a forum for multi-disciplinary discussion for professionals and parents in the care and education of handicapped children. *Help Starts Here* by Philippa Russell, herself a parent, is available free of charge.
3 *Down's Syndrome Association*
155 Mitcham Road, London SW17 9PG
Tel: 0181-682-4001
Specifically set up by parents of children with Down's syndrome, it publishes many useful articles and provides advice on care, education and management as well as services. It supports research and promotes the needs of people with Down's syndrome in England and Wales.
4 *Royal Society for Mentally Handicapped Children and Adults* (MENCAP)
123 Golden Lane, London EC1 0RT
Tel: 0171-253-9433
This society can provide many forms of help for you and

your child. Many branches have regular meetings for parents, some run special playgroups, social clubs, residential hostels, holidays, etc. They also have facilities for short-term care. You can obtain the address of your local branch from the telephone book, or contact the headquarters at the above address.

5 *Pre-School Playgroups Association*
61 Kings Cross Road, London WC1X 9LL
Tel: 0171-833-0991
The association gives advice on the setting up and running of playgroups, and information on playgroups in your area. It encourages groups to make provisions for handicapped children, and has a register of Opportunity Groups —playgroups where handicapped and normal children can play together and mothers of handicapped children can meet each other. These groups are open to babies from birth, so that handicapped babies can benefit from play situations as soon as possible. The association also publishes some leaflets on handicapped children and playgroups.

6 *National Association of Toy and Leisure Libraries*
68 Churchway, London NW1 1LT
Tel: 0171-387-9592
Toy Libraries are now operating in many areas, often linked with groups of the RSMHC (MENCAP). The libraries are centres where you can borrow toys for your handicapped child, and also meet other parents and obtain advice and support. The libraries are usually run on a sessional basis once a week, and children can visit the library with their parents and play together during the sessions.

7 *The Family Fund*
This is a voluntary fund to help families caring for a severely mentally or physically handicapped child under 16. It does not replace the statutory provisions made by the services, and is intended to help with particular problems which are not covered by the services.

The help can be in the form of goods, services or a grant of money for some definite purpose related to the care of the child. This fund usually applies only to children over the age of two, but it may consider younger children in

exceptional circumstances.
The address to write to is:
The Family Fund, P.O. Box 50, York YO1 1UY
Tel: 01904-21115

8 *Disabled Living Foundation*
380 Harrow Road, London W9 2HU
Tel: 0171-289-6111
Provides information on special aids, particularly if there are any physical difficulties.

9 *British Institute of Learning Disabilities*
Wolverhampton Road, Kidderminster, Worcestershire DY10 3PP
Tel: 01562-850251
The BILD has an Information and Research Centre. They produce up-to-date lists of books, pamphlets and articles on all aspects of handicap which they will supply for a small fee to cover costs of postage.

10 *Scope*
12 Park Crescent, London W1N 4EQ
Tel: 0171-636-5020

11 *The International League of Societies for Persons with Mental Handicap*
248 Avenue Louise, Box 17, B-1050 Brussels, Belgium
This association of societies works worldwide promoting the needs of people with mental handicap. Very useful contact point for people living abroad or moving abroad.

12 *The Scottish Down's Syndrome Association*
158–160 Balgreen Road, Edinburgh EH11 3AU
Tel: 0131-313-4225
This association is for families in Scotland. It is very lively and provides information and support to parents, organises conferences and supports research.

13 *Contact a Family*
170 Tottenham Court Road, London W1P 9LG
Tel: 0171-383-3555
This voluntary association links over 700 self-help and support groups of parents with children with special needs. They provide a nationwide information service and publish regular newsletters.

**References from Table 3**

Carr, J. (1970) Mental and motor development in young mongol children. *Journal of Mental Deficiency Research, 14*, 205.

de Coriat, L. F., Theslenco, Z. & Waxsman, J. (1967) The effects of psycho-motor stimulation on the IQ of young children with Trisomy 21. In Richards, B. W. (ed.) *Proceedings of the 1st Congress of the International Association for the Scientific Study of Mental Deficiency*. Jackson Publishing Co. Ltd. Reigate, England.

Loeffler & Smith (1966) In Penrose, L. and Smith, G. F. —*Down's Anomaly*.

Ludlow, J. R. & Allen, L. M. (1979) The effect of early intervention and pre-school stimulus on the development of the Down's syndrome child. *Journal of Mental Deficiency Research, 23*, 29–45.

# INDEX

adenoids 109
ageing 96, 130
assessment 180

baby-sitting 62
balance 126–7
brain size 126
breast feeding 121
Brushfield spots 103

cardinal signs 103
cataracts 125
cell 71
cerebellum 126
chest 116
  infections 136–8
chewing 113
chromosomes:
  definition 71
  number of 72–3
circulation 117–8, 124
classification 171–3
clinodactyly 104
communication skills 148
consolidation, of skills 195
constipation 122
cosmetic care 118
cry 104
cytoplasm 71

dancing 115
deterioration 190
digestion 120–1
dress 118
duodenal atresia 121

ear 103
  chambers, canals 110

early intervention 189–90
epicanthal fold 103
epilepsy 130
enzymes 131
expectations 166, 173, 181, 183
eye defects 125

feeding 112–3, 146
  and early weight gain 112, 113
  breast 121
  solids 121–2
  position for 137
fertility 138–40
fingertips (dermatoglyphs) 117
5-hydroxytryptophan 133–4
fontanels 103
functional behaviours 180–2

genes:
  genetic 72
  code 72, 74
  counselling 85
glasses 125
gums 114

hair 118
  pubic 138
hearing:
  loss 110–11
  aids 125
heart 122–4
height 112
hip-dislocation 116
Hirschsprung's disease 121
home care v. institution care 145, 167
hormones 131

hospitalisation 123
hypotonia 104

immunodeficiency 114
intelligence 175, 176, 204
  tests 170–3
  computation of IQ 175

karyotype 76

leukæmia 125
life-expectancy 95–6
lungs 136–8

marmoration 118
masturbation 140
medical treatments 131, 135–6
menstruation 138–9
mental ability:
  tests of 173–8
  range of 213–7
mental age (definition) 175
milk, allergy 121
mischief 141
mortality 95
mosaic 82
mouth 103
  breathing 108
muscles 110, 113
  tone 104, 106
myths 16

nasal bone 108
  drops 108
nondisjunction 78
nucleus 71
nystagmus 125

obesity 112, 114
oblique palpebral fissure 103
occiput 103

palate 104
  cleft 116
palmer crease (simian line) 104, 105
pelvis 115
personality 142–64
placid 146
plastic surgery 119–20
plateaux 195
posture 114–15, 127
prediction, future attainments 169, 179, 191
prenatal tests 227–8
professional-parents 182

reflexes 104
  sucking 121
  swallowing 121
reproduction 138–40
respiratory system 136–8
response, slowness of 128–30
rib 115

saliva 114
school:
  placement 199
  special 169
sex organs 138
sexual development 138–40
siccacell treatment 134
sinuses 108
skeleton 115–6
skin 117–9
skull 108
sleeping 146, 150
social interactions 128–9
stereotyping 143
stigma 171
stimulation:
  and training 166, 167, 184
  early programmes 168, 204, 219–21
  strength of 127
strabismus 125
swimming 114–5

teeth 113–4
  decay 114
terminology 170
temperament 142–64
temperature, sensitivity to 118
temper tantrums 141
thyroid function 134–5
toileting 150
tongue 104
  protruding 107

tonsils 110
translocation 84
Turkel 'U' series 132

umbilical hernia 107
upper airway obstruction
109–10

vision 125–6
visual responding 128–9
vitamins 132–3
vomiting 121

weight 112
birth weight 104